Shakespeare: *Julius Caesar* PETER URE
Shakespeare: *King Lear* FRANK KERMODE
Shakespeare: *Macbeth* JOHN WAIN
Shakespeare: *Measure for Measure* G. K. STEAD
Shakespeare: *The Merchant of Venice* JOHN WILDERS
Shakespeare: *'Much Ado About Nothing' & 'As You Like It'* JOHN RUSSELL BROWN
Shakespeare: *Othello* JOHN WAIN
Shakespeare: *Richard II* NICHOLAS BROOKE
Shakespeare: *The Sonnets* PETER JONES
Shakespeare: *The Tempest* D. J. PALMER
Shakespeare: *Troilus and Cressida* PRISCILLA MARTIN
Shakespeare: *Twelfth Night* D. J. PALMER
Shakespeare: *The Winter's Tale* KENNETH MUIR
Shelley: *Shorter Poems & Lyrics* PATRICK SWINDEN
Spenser: *The Faerie Queene* PETER BAYLEY
Swift: *Gulliver's Travels* RICHARD GRAVIL
Tennyson: *In Memoriam* JOHN DIXON HUNT
Thackeray: *Vanity Fair* ARTHUR POLLARD
Trollope: *The Barsetshire Novels* T. BAREHAM
Webster: *'The White Devil' & 'The Duchess of Malfi'* R. V. HOLDSWORTH
Wilde: *Comedies* WILLIAM TYDEMAN
Woolf: *To the Lighthouse* MORRIS BEJA
Wordsworth: *Lyrical Ballads* ALUN R. JONES & WILLIAM TYDEMAN
Wordsworth: *The Prelude* W. J. HARVEY & RICHARD GRAVIL
Yeats: *Poems, 1919–35* ELIZABETH CULLINGFORD
Yeats: *Last Poems* JON STALLWORTHY

The Metaphysical Poets GERALD HAMMOND
Poetry of the First World War DOMINIC HIBBERD
Thirties Poets: 'The Auden Group' RONALD CARTER
Comedy: Developments in Criticism D. J. PALMER
Drama Criticism: Developments since Ibsen ARNOLD P. HINCHLIFFE
The Pastoral Mode BRYAN LOUGHREY
Tragedy: Developments in Criticism R. P. DRAPER
The English Novel: Developments in Criticism since Henry James STEPHEN HAZELL
The Language of Literature NORMAN PAGE
The Romantic Imagination JOHN SPENCER HILL

CASEBOOKS IN PREPARATION
Beckett: *'Waiting for Godot' & Other Plays* JOHN RUSSELL BROWN
Defoe: *'Robinson Crusoe' & 'Moll Flanders'* PATRICK LYONS
Dickens: *'Dombey and Son' & 'Little Dorrit'* ALAN SHELSTON
T. S. Eliot: *Plays* ARNOLD P. HINCHLIFFE
O'Casey: *'Juno and the Paycock', 'The Plough and the Stars' & 'The Shadow of a Gunman'* RONALD AYLING
Pinter: *'The Caretaker' & Other Plays* MICHAEL SCOTT
Sheridan: *Comedies* PETER DAVISON

Elizabethan Lyric & Narrative Poetry GERALD HAMMOND
Medieval English Drama PETER HAPPÉ
Poetry Criticism: Developments since the Symbolists A. E. DYSON
Post-Fifties Poets: Gunn, Hughes, Larkin & R. S. Thomas A. E. DYSON
Shakespeare: Approaches in Criticism JOHN RUSSELL BROWN
The Gothick Novel VICTOR SAGE

The Pastoral Mode

A CASEBOOK

EDITED BY

BRYAN LOUGHREY

M
MACMILLAN

First published 1984 by
Higher and Further Education Division
MACMILLAN PUBLISHERS LTD
London and Basingstoke
Companies and representatives
throughout the world

Typeset by
Wessex Typesetters Ltd
Frome, Somerset

Printed in Hong Kong

British Library Cataloguing in Publication Data
The Pastoral mode.—(Casebook series)
1. Pastoral literature, European—History and criticism
I. Loughrey, Brian   II. Series
809'.91   PN56.P3
ISBN 0–333–33536–8
ISBN 0–333–33537–6 Pbk

CONTENTS

2 Interpretations of Individual Works

GENERAL EDITOR'S PREFACE

The Casebook series, launched in 1968, has become a well-regarded library of critical studies. The central concern of the series remains the 'single-author' volume, but suggestions from the academic community have led to an extension of the original plan, to include occasional volumes on such general themes as literary 'schools' and genres.

Each volume in the central category deals either with one well-known and influential work by an individual author, or with closely related works by one writer. The main section consists of critical readings, mostly modern, collected from books and journals. A selection of reviews and comments by the author's contemporaries is also included, and sometimes comment from the author himself. The Editor's Introduction charts the reputation of the work or works from the first appearance to the present time.

Volumes in the 'general themes' category are variable in structure but follow the basic purpose of the series in presenting an integrated selection of readings, with an Introduction which explores the theme and discusses the literary and critical issues involved.

A single volume can represent no more than a small selection of critical opinions. Some critics are excluded for reasons of space, and it is hoped that readers will pursue the suggestions for further reading in the Select Bibliography. Other contributions are severed from their original context, to which some readers may wish to turn. Indeed, if they take a hint from the critics represented here, they certainly will.

A. E. DYSON

INTRODUCTION

Pastoral is a contested term which modern critics have applied to an almost bewildering variety of works. In earlier critical discourse, however, it had a fairly limited and stable sense, describing literature which portrayed, often in an idealised manner, 'the life of shepherds, or of the country'.[1] The genre originated with the Greek poet Theocritus (c. 316–260 BC), who entertained the sophisticated Alexandrian court of Ptolemy with a series of vignettes depicting the countryside and peasantry of his native Sicily. His *Idylls* are not entirely typical of the later tradition, since they contain considerable elements of realism and sometimes dwell on the harsher aspects of the lives led by an entire rural community, consisting not just of shepherds, but of farmers, serfs, goatherds, fishermen, neatherds and housewives. Nevertheless, Theocritus's successors found in the *Idylls* almost all the motifs which later crystallised into the conventions of formal pastoral: herdsmen find leisure to indulge in impromptu song contests or debates; extravagantly praise the beauty of their coy mistresses, or the charms of country life; recount tales derived from classical mythology or regional folklore; and bewail the death or absence of lovers. In many cases, Theocritus provided a model for the form as well as the content of subsequent pastoral verse. Idyll I, for example, in which Thyrsis sings of the death of Daphnis, employs all the machinery of pastoral elegy (invocation to the muse, expression of grief, inquiry into the causes of death, pathetic fallacy, description of the bier and procession, lament, concluding note of consolation) which Milton made use of in 'Lycidas' and an anonymous eighteenth-century critic parodied in 'Recipe for a Pastoral Elegy'. [*]

Vergil† based his earliest known works, the *Eclogues*, on Theocritus's *Idylls*. He introduced, however, a number of innovations which decisively influenced almost all later writers of pastoral. In particular, he transferred his herdsmen from Sicily to Arcadia, the now traditional home of the shepherd of literary convention. Arcadia, as Bruno Snell [*] has convincingly argued, represented for Vergil not a humdrum province of Greece, but a poetic landscape whose woods

[*] Indicates reference to critical material included in the relevant section of this Casebook.

† The forms of the Roman poet's name – Vergil, Virgil – are not systematised to one usage in the selection, but retained as in the different writers' original publication.

and mountains were haunted by the Olympian Immortals. It was an imaginary topography where 'the currents of myth and empirical reality flow one into another', and gods mingled freely with men. The shepherd inhabitants of this world were similarly etherealised. Despite the topical and political themes introduced into the *Eclogues*, Vergil's herdsmen are consistently portrayed as refined, serious-minded individuals, ruled by tender passions which they express through poetry. It comes as no surprise when Vergil, in Eclogue x, inserts his own friend, the contemporary poet Gallus, into this setting, for shepherd and artist have become virtually indistinguishable. From Vergil onwards, pastoral poetry has been pre-occupied with such tensions between reality and the world of the imagination, so that the form is often peculiarly self-conscious of its own aesthetic nature, and concerned far more with exploring the meaning of its conventions than in depicting any actual countryside.

The involvement of pastoral with classical mythology helped forge its association with the myth of the Golden Age, an elegiac lament for a lost age of innocence which shares many of the characteristics of the Christian idea of Eden. It was conceived of as a time at the dawn of history when Saturn and Astraea, the virgin goddess of Justice, ruled in the Garden of the Hesperides, and mankind lived unalienated from either its environment or itself. The season was perpetual spring, which rendered clothing superfluous, and allowed a fecund nature to provide sustenance without toil. Unhindered by the divisive influence of ambition, greed, aggression, or jealousy, men and women lived together in a fellowship based on leisure and love. The most familiar rendering of this myth is contained in Ovid's *Metamorphoses*, translated by Arthur Golding in 1567:

Then sprang up first the golden age, which of its selfe maintainde,
The truth and right of every thing unforst and unconstrainde.
There was no feare of punishment, there was no threatning lawe
In brazen tables nayled up, to keepe the folke in awe.
There was no man would crouch or creepe to Judge with cap in hand,
They lived safe without a Judge in every Realme and lande.
The loftie Pynetree was not hewen from mountaines where it stood,
In seeking straunge and forren landes to rove upon the flood.
Men knew none other countries yet, than were themselves did keepe:
There was no towne enclosed yet, with walles and ditches deepe.
No horne nor trumpet was in use, no sword nor helmet worne.
The worlde was suche, that souldiers helpe might easly be forborne.
The fertile earth as yet was free, untoucht of spade or plough,
And yet it yeelded of its selfe of every things inough.
And men themselves contented well with plaine and simple foode,
That on earth by natures gift without their travell stoode,

Did live by Raspis, heppes and hawes, by cornelles, plummes and cherries,
By sloes and apples, nuttes and peares, and lothsome bramble berries,
And by the acornes dropt on ground from *Joves* brode tree in fielde.
The Springtime lasted all the yeare, and *Zephyr* with his milde
And gentle blast did cherish things that grew of owne accorde.
The ground untilde, all kinde of fruits did plenteously avorde.
No mucke nor tillage was bestowde on leane and barren land,
To make the corne of better head and ranker for too stand.
Then streames ran milke, then streames ran wine, and yellow honny flowde
From ech greene tree whereon the rayes of firie *Phebus* glowde.[2]

As the keeping of flocks was deemed to be the original employment of mankind, the life-styles of the denizens of the Golden Age and the shepherds of Arcadia were increasingly equated. This in part encouraged poets to develop the escapist elements of the genre, and indulge in nostalgic dreams of a past happier time. But the myth could also function as a social critique, for, as Harry Levin [*] explains, it can only be defined by the negative formula 'not like now'. Thus many pastoral satires made use of the trope to attack corruptions of State (courtiers are hireling shepherds) or Church (pastors neglect their flocks). Vergil's Eclogue IV stood the myth on its head and celebrated the birth of a child who was to restore the Golden Age in the near future. Its Messianic message, one consistently interpreted as a prophecy of the birth of Christ, is in W. H. Auden's [*] terms Utopian rather than Arcadian, a vision of the future where the 'contradictions of the present . . . have at last been resolved'.

Horace's Epode II is the fountainhead of the third strand of classical pastoral, the great myth of rural retirement:

> Happy the man, who far from town's affairs,
> The life of old-world mortals shares;
> With his own oxen tills his forebears' fields,
> Nor thinks of usury and its yields.
> No soldier he, by the fierce bugle called,
> Nor sailor, at each storm appalled;
> He shuns the forum, and the haughty gate
> Of nobles stronger than the State.
> His business is round poplars tall to twine
> The ripe young layers of the vine;
> Or in some quiet valley to survey
> His lowing heifers as they stray.
> Now with his knife the worthless shoots he lops,
> Grafting instead for richer crops;
> Draws the new honey, in pure jars to keep,
> Or shears the timid staggering sheep.
> When Autumn, with his mellow fruitage gay,

Doth o'er the fields his head display,
What joy it is the grafted pears to try,
And grapes which with sea-purple vie;
Fit gift, Priapus, choosing for thy hand,
Or Silvan, thine, guard of his land!
What joy, beneath some holm-oak old and grey
Or on thick turf, one's limbs to lay;
While streams past toppling banks roll down their flood,
And the birds croon in every wood,
And fountains murmur with their gushing streams
Sounds that shall sooth to sleep and dreams.
Then when the thunderous winter comes again,
Rainstorms and snowdrifts in its train,
This side and that a many hounds he'll set.[3]

The numerous imitations of this piece, such as Katherine Philips's 'A Country-Life', generally ignore Horace's craftily ironic postscript:

Alfius the usurer, when thus he swore
Farmer to be for ever more,
At the mid-month his last transaction ending,
By next new moon is keen for lending.

Alfius the moneylender is a week-end cottager who will soon return to the city despite the charms of the countryside. T. G. Rosenmeyer [*] has objected that the Horatian praise of country life has more in common with *Georgic*, didactic literature on the subject of husbandry, than pastoral. But while it is true that in many cases the shepherd of literary convention does not feature at all in such works, the two traditions are so closely allied that they frequently impinge on one another, for the emotional basis of each is recognisably similar – 'God made the country, and man made the town'.[4]

Few pastorals were written during the Middle Ages, but the form survived in such peripheral genres as *Pastourelle* and vernacular *Bergerie*. The revival of classical scholarship in the Renaissance, however, led to a renewal of interest in the mode, and many of the greatest poets of the period experimented with Latin eclogues. Probably the most influential were a set by Mantuan (1448–1516), which directly inspired the first clumsy attempt at formal pastoral in English, Alexander Barclay's five *Eclogues* (c. 1515–21).

The first English work to rival the achievement of the Continental pastoralists was Edmund Spenser's *The Shepheardes Calender* (1579). Spenser modelled his XII eclogues, one for each month of the year, on the bucolics of Theocritus, Vergil and Mantuan, but attempted to naturalise the form by incorporating within the poem considerable elements of a native realism derived from Chaucer. The extraordinary contemporary popularity of *The Shepheardes Calender*, stemming both from its dazzling technical virtuosity and allegoric subtlety, helped create a vogue for pastoral: it is therefore perhaps ironic that A. C. Hamilton [*] should find its overall argument to be 'the rejection of the pastoral life for the truly dedicated life in the world'. The eclogues of Spenser's prolific followers – Drayton, Browne, Wither and Phineas Fletcher – developed in their own distinctive ways the methods of *The Shepheardes Calender*. But pastoral soon lost its almost exclusive association with the eclogue form, and during the period 1579–1680 came to exercise a pervasive influence, which a short survey such as this can do no more than hint at, over the entire literature and culture of Renaissance England.

Most epics of the period, for example, are studded with pastoral landscapes. Sometimes these take the form of the *locus amoenus*, a set-piece description of an ideal landscape which serves as the backdrop to the development of the plot's romantic interest, but which may, as in the case of Acrasia's Bower of Bliss in Book II of Spenser's *The Faerie Queene* (1596), represent a sensual snare tempting the unwary knight from the path of virtue. On other occasions shepherds are introduced to complicate the value structure of the poem, providing a subversive alternative to the predominant martial and heroic ethos: Calidore's 'truancy' among the herdsmen of Book VI of *The Faerie Queene*, for example, not only allows him to woo fair Pastorella but finally enriches his understanding of the true nature of Courtesy. The popular prose romances of the period, derived from the example of Longus's *Daphnis and Chloe* (c. 350 BC) and Sannazaro's *Arcadia* (1502), also blended the heroic with the bucolic. Sir Philip Sidney's *Arcadia* (1590), for example, intersperses pastoral lyrics within an intricate plot of courtly love and adventure which requires its major protagonists to spend much of their time disguised as shepherds.

Pastoral songs and lyrics not only existed as components of larger works but were popular in their own right. The most famous example, Marlowe's 'The Passionate Shepherd to his Love', was originally published in an anthology of exclusively pastoral verse, *England's Helicon* (1600). Its exploitation of the dissonance between the world of natural simplicity evoked and the artful presentation of the poem itself is characteristic of the genre.

> Come live with mee, and be my love,
> And we will all the pleasures prove,
> That Vallies, groves, hills and fieldes,
> Woods, or steepie mountaine yeeldes.

And wee will sit upon the Rocks,
Seeing the Sheepheards feede theyr flocks,
By shallow Rivers, to whose falls,
Melodious byrds sing Madrigalls.

And I will make thee beds of Roses,
And a thousand fragrant poesies,
A cap of flowers, and a kirtle,
Imbroydred all with leaves of Mirtle.

A gown made of the finest wooll,
Which from our pretty Lambes we pull,
Fayre lined slippers for the cold:
With buckles of the purest gold.

A belt of straw, and Ivie buds,
With Corall clasps and Amber studs,
And if these pleasures may thee move,
Come live with mee, and be my love.

The Sheepheards Swaines shall daunce and sing,
For thy delight each May-morning,
If these delights thy minde may move;
Then live with mee, and be my love.

The speaker may claim to be a simple swain, but his rhetoric marks
him off as a displaced courtier, singing not of cakes and ale but coral
clasps and amber studs amidst an environment which promises birds
that sing complicated part songs and a workforce only too pleased to
put on rustic entertainments for the tourists.

The elements of wish-fulfilment are even more clearly apparent in
the numerous libertine seduction poems which celebrate the promiscuous sexual *mores* of the Golden Age:

Then unconfined each did Tipple
Wine from the Bunch, Milk from the Nipple.[5]

The doctrine that Man was most innocent when pursuing untrammelled instinctual gratification did not, however, go unchallenged.
Milton's Adam and Eve may appear to condone it, since before the
Fall the act of love is both totally satisfying and, because divinely
ordained, completely innocent. But the happy couple live in a state of
married chastity, and Milton is at pains to contrast their lawful
pleasures with 'the bought smile / Of harlots, loveless, joyless,
unendeared, / Casual fruition'. It is unusual to find such explicit
sexuality in the garden literature of the period, which normally
celebrated the joys of contemplative retirement. Marvell's 'The
Garden' is more typical of this strand of pastoral, with its stress on

otium and the recuperative powers of nature: ecstasy is attained not through sexual indulgence but through a withdrawal from the world of the senses towards a *hortus conclusus* of repose:

> Mean while the Mind, from pleasure less,
> Withdraws into its happiness:
> . . .
> Annihilating all that's made
> To a green Thought in a green Shade.

It is equally possible, of course, to view the cultivated garden as a symbol of Man's perversion of an unspoilt Nature. It is entirely typical of Marvell's complex pastoral vision that he explored this central ambiguity. His 'Mower' poems wittily contrive to subvert the traditional pastoral harmony between Man and his environment, and demonstrate the ease with which pastoral conventions could become the vehicle for metaphysical speculation.

The country house poems of the period appear to have a more direct relationship with the realities of the English countryside. Ben Jonson's 'To Penshurst', for example, describes the landed estate where Sidney wrote his *Arcadia*, and celebrates its hierarchical yet harmonious social organisation in which farmers and aristocrats meet on terms of an easy familiarity bred of mutual respect and dependency. The Marxist critic Raymond Williams [*], however, demolishes this aristocratic myth by demonstrating the brutally exploitative economic infra-structure which supported such great houses. In his view, the pastoral themes and images in 'To Penshurst' serve to mystify and thus legitimise the true relationship between the landowning classes and their agricultural workers. Similarly, James Turner [*] is concerned to relate the ideology of 'A Country-Life' to the circumstances of its author: 'Katherine Philips's life was the diametric opposite of what she purports to celebrate. The meaning of "A Country-Life" cannot be adequately grasped without relating it to this matrix of contradiction and suppression.'

The problematic relationship between the reality of life in the countryside and the pastoral myth of rural existence is part of Shakespeare's concern in *As You Like It* (1599). The Duke may find life in the forest of Arden 'more sweet / Than that of painted pomp', but Touchstone is there to remind us that it is a good deal more comfortable in Court, and the aristocrats do not hesitate to return there when given the opportunity. In *The Winter's Tale* (c. 1610) the pastoral life does seem to offer a genuine alternative to that of a court dominated by jealousy and tyranny, but the distinction is by no means clear cut. Perdita is nurtured by the shepherds of Bohemia, but she is in fact a lost princess and her native virtue is genetically determined. Few such complexities trouble John Fletcher's *The Faithful Shepherdess* (1608) [*] which introduced the pastoral tragi-comic mode to the English stage. Fletcher derived the mixed generic form largely from the seminal examples of Tasso's *Aminta* (1573) and Guarini's *Il Pastor Fido* (c. 1580) which had developed the inherent dramatic potential of the dialogue format of most eclogues. The play was a failure in the popular theatre, but was successfully revived at court in 1632. Pastoral themes also infiltrated the semi-dramatic court genre of the masque. Both Milton's *Comus* (1634) and Ben Jonson's *The Golden Age Restored* (1616) for example, consciously blend classical and native pastoral imagery. This form of entertainment, however, ended with the Civil War and was not revived after the Restoration.

Even though its heyday was over, pastoral verse remained a popular medium in the early part of the eighteenth century. Pope made his dazzlingly precocious poetic début with a set of *Pastorals* (1704) modelled with neo-classical propriety on Vergil. Ambrose Philips, on the other hand, attempted to inject into his *Pastorals* (1708) details of life in the contemporary English countryside. His talents were unfortunately limited, so that Pope and his fellow Scriblerians had little difficulty in ridiculing the result. The happiest outcome of the ensuing literary war, which Hoyt Trowbridge [*] traces in some detail, is Gay's *The Shepherd's Week* (1714). It is the earliest and probably the best mock-pastoral, which parodies Philips's style by selectively presenting the grosser aspect of rustic life, yet describes country scenes with a vivacity that many have enjoyed for its own sake.

During the course of the century formal pastoral increasingly came to be regarded as a sentimental masquerade, remote from the affairs of everyday. The trivialisation of its images is best symbolised by the inanities of Marie Antoinette's mock dairy farm, *le Petit Trianon*. Anti-pastoral developed as a response to this state of affairs. George Crabbe, for example, indignantly contrasted empty pastoral rhetoric with the drudgery of actual rural labour in *The Village* (1783):

> I grant indeed that fields and flocks have charms
> For him that grazes or for him that farms
> But when amid such pleasing scenes I trace
> The poor laborious natives of the place
> And see the mid-day sun with fervid ray,
> On their bare heads and dewy temples play;
> While some, with feebler heads and fainter hearts,
> Deplore their fortune, yet sustain their parts –

> Then shall I dare these real ills to hide
> In tinsel trappings of poetic pride?   [I, 39–49]

The increasing dominance of the mode of realism meant that serious poetic efforts were directed towards the nature poetry which romantic sensibility found so convivial. Wordsworth termed 'Michael' (1800) a 'Pastoral' but as Michael Squires [*] notes, the union of realism and sublimity it achieves is incompatible with formal pastoral. With Wordsworth the shepherd of literary convention leaves the stage, returning only for occasional appearances in works such as Arnold's *Thyrsis* (1866).

Although formal pastoral poetry had its origins in classical times, pastoral critical theory did not. Renaissance scholars were disturbed to find that, despite the fact that the genre came into being two generations after his death, Aristotle had not classified the characteristics of pastoral! The earliest serious theoretical discussions, Vida's *Ars Poetica* (1527) and Sebillet's *Art Poétique Françoys* (1548), received no contemporary translation and so fall outside the scope of this volume.[6] Their concerns were reflected, however, in the first extensive consideration of pastoral in English, E.K.'s dedicatory Epistle [*] to Spenser's *The Shepheardes Calender* (1579). E.K. (probably Edward Kirke) praises Spenser both for dignifying the language, and for giving his eclogues a native hue. He picks out, for example, Spenser's deliberate archaisms, claiming 'such old and obsolete wordes' fittest for the 'rusticall rudeness of shepheardes', and thus enunciates the principle of generic decorum which was to dominate many later treatises. His other chief concern is with explicating the allegory of the poem, which he believed unfolded 'great matter of argument covertly'.

Sir Philip Sidney's *An Apologie for Poetrie* (c. 1583) [*] defended imaginative literature from the attacks of the Puritans. His discussion of pastoral is brief, for he believed in a hierarchy of literary genres, with epic and tragedy occupying the most exalted positions, and pastoral the humblest. Its value is primarily didactic, teaching both the 'miserie of people under hard Lords or ravening Souldiours', and also 'what blessedness is derived to them that lye lowest from the goodnesse of them that sit highest'. As Laurence Lerner notes, the potentially radical implications of the first lesson are immediately vitiated by the socially conservative message of the second.[7] George Puttenham's brief discussion of pastoral in his *Arte of English Poesie* (1589) [*] is almost exclusively devoted to the question of its origins. His contention that, although sheep-keeping may have been one of the earliest employments of mankind, pastoral poetry was the product of a later urban culture, is almost universally accepted by modern scholars.

John Fletcher's 'Preface' [*] to his *Faithful Shepherdess* (c. 1609) is a skirmish in the critical war surrounding Guarini's *Il Pastor Fido* (c. 1580). Jason Denores had criticised the latter in his *Discorso* (1587) and thus provoked a lively dispute concerning the legitimacy of such hybrid genres as pastoral tragi-comedy. Ben Jonson also felt constrained to defend his *Sad Shepherd* (c. 1636) from charges of generic mongrelism, and in his 'Prologue' [*] to the play makes a sensible plea for critical flexibility.

Michael Drayton's compact 'To the Reader of his Pastorals' (1619) [*] generally eschews critical squabbles. Drayton leaves such disputes to 'Scaliger and the Nation of Learned Censors', preferring instead to dwell on the well established analogies between Biblical and pastoral themes: 'In the Angels song to Shepheards at our Saviours Nativitie Pastorall Poesie seems consecrated.' He shares with E.K. a concern for decorum and an admiration for Spenser, but displays an empirical bias which leads him to prefer Theocritus's *Idylls*, on account of their realistic detail, to Vergil's *Eclogues*. Thomas Hobbes's 'Answer to the Preface before Gondibert' (1650) [*] is even more frankly empirical, viewing pastoral simply as representation of the countryside. It was the last major critical statement concerning pastoral made before discussion became dominated by the influence of René Rapin (1621–86) and Bernard le Bouvier de Fontenelle (1657–1757).

Rapin's 'Dissertatio de Carmine Pastorali' (1659) [*] was translated by Thomas Creech and prefixed to his *Idylliums of Theocritus* (1684). It is the central document of the neo-classical school of pastoral criticism, providing a systematic description of the genre and prescriptive rules for its composition. These were derived exclusively from the example of the 'Ancients', Theocritus and Vergil, and can be readily summarised. Pastoral should be simple, unpretentious, in brief dialogue form, and describe Golden Age shepherds in love. Aware, however, that swains of those times had a reputation for promiscuousness, Rapin insists that 'no loose expression be allowed', and warns against 'wanton Love-stories on the subject . . . for all sort of lewdness or debauchery are directly contrary to the Innocence of the Golden Age'.

Rapin's veneration for the 'Ancients' was opposed by Fontenelle who refused to treat them as the source of all legitimate authority. While often admiring the works of Theocritus and Vergil, he tried to judge them 'as if they had been some living Authors whom I saw every day': a procedure which many of his contemporaries regarded as tantamount to sacrilege. The methodology of his 'Discours sur la nature de l'eglogue' (1688) [*] – 'Englished by Mr Motteux' in 1695 – is Cartesian rationalism. Fontenelle proposes as a self-evident truth that 'all men would be happy, and that too at an easy Rate', and derives from this proposition the conclusion that pastoral, if it is to please, must present 'a concurrence of the two strongest passions, laziness and love'. His theory is therefore based firmly on the psychology of the reader, rather than on any appeal to literary precedent. It is the central *idea* of pastoral (the 'quiet Life, with no other business but Love') which he considers to be the essential element of the mode. The conventions through which this idea is expressed are relatively unimportant: 'cou'd the scene . . . be placed anywhere but in the country, so that no Goats nor Sheep be brought in; I fancy it would be never the worse'.

Pope claimed to be following both Rapin and Fontenelle in his 'Discourse on Pastoral Poetry' (1704) [*], but both his theory and the practice of his own *Pastorals* derive almost exclusively from the example of the former. Theocritus and Vergil are the 'only undisputed authors of Pastoral' which presents 'an image of what they call the Golden Age'. Realism is therefore out of the question, and the poet must strive to 'use some illusion to render a Pastoral delightful: and this consists in exposing the best side only of a shepherd's life, and in concealing its miseries'. At its subtlest, such a theory approaches a semiotic mode of communication; pastoral conventions provide a system of signifiers which create a 'formal pattern, which, in various guises and in various epochs, may be made to produce a certain complex of meaning'.[8] However, it was relatively easy for the rationalist school of critics – including Addison, Tickell [*], Purney[9] and the anonymous author of 'Recipe for a Pastoral Elegy' [*] – to ridicule the stale clichés of 'lean flocks', 'silver streams', 'blasted oaks' and the like, which inevitably resulted when classical models were slavishly imitated.

Thomas Tickell's *Guardian* essay (No. 30, 1713), however, significantly revised Fontenelle's doctrine by advocating the realistic description of a native countryside and contemporary peasantry. Fontenelle had rejected realism in pastoral, finding low scenes displeasing to the imagination. But Tickell considered 'this our island a proper scene for pastoral', and recommended that poets 'lawfully deviate from the Ancients' and include indigenous folk-customs, rural dialects, and native flora: 'what is proper in Arcadia, or even Italy, might be very absurd in a colder climate'. He therefore took as his model the contemporary poet Ambrose Philips, whose inferior productions he praised fulsomely.

Pope, Gay and Swift attempted to uphold the neo-classical doctrine through ridicule. In a masterly example of sustained irony Pope contrived to damn Philips's *Pastorals* with lavish praise in his *Guardian* essay (No. 40, 1713) [*]. The 'Prologue' [*] to Gay's *The Shepherd's Week* also attempts to burlesque the possibility of realistic pastoral through a *reductio ad absurdum* of the rationalist position. Swift was less active in the debate, but his suggestion for a comic 'Newgate Pastoral' [*] may well have provided the germ of the idea for Gay's masterpiece, *The Beggar's Opera* (1728).

Although Pope's immense prestige bolstered the neo-classical position for some time, the rationalist case was increasingly accepted. Samuel Johnson came down decisively in its favour in his influential *Rambler* essay (No. 37, 1750) [*]. The true definition of pastoral is for him a 'poem in which any action or passion is represented by its effects upon a country life'. This led him to reject firmly any theory of pastoral which made the Golden Age or even shepherds necessary features of the genre. All classes of person could be described 'because persons of all ranks inhabit the country'. It is hardly surprising, therefore, that he found many traditional pastorals trivial and imitative: his acerbic comment on 'Lycidas' [*] – 'its form is that of a pastoral – easy, vulgar, and therefore disgusting' – is only the most notorious of a number of hostile judgements. Johnson equated the conventional features of the poem with personal insincerity; 'where there is leisure for fiction, there is little grief'. However, Northrop Frye [*] eloquently defends the poem by distinguishing between personal and literary sincerity ('one may burst into tears at the news of a friend's death, but one can never spontaneously burst into song. . . . "Lycidas" is a passionately sincere poem, because Milton was deeply interested in the structure and symbolism of funeral elegies') and demonstrates in detail the poem's mythic dimensions.

William Wordsworth's 'Preface' [*] to the 1800 edition of *Lyrical Ballads* is in one sense conventional: both Tickell and Johnson before him had recommended realistic description of rural scenery. However, in another it is revolutionary. Realism before Wordsworth had been largely confined to anti-pastorals such as Crabbe's *The Village* which had emphasised the moral degradation of the poor. But Wordsworth proposed the 'low and rustic life' as a reservoir of elemental passion and purified language where 'the passions of men are incorporated with the beautiful and permanent forms of nature'. His treatment of rural life, therefore, combines realism with idealisation. According to Michael Squires [*] it is a mixture which 'deals the blow that destroys traditional pastoral as a vital source of inspiration to men of letters'.

Few critics of note discussed pastoral seriously during the

nineteenth century. Hazlitt [*] glanced lovingly back at Walton's *Compleat Angler* (1653), but the general critical view could be fairly described by Edmund Gosse (who dissented from it) as one which regarded pastoral as 'cold, unnatural, artificial, . . . the humblest reviewer is free to cast a stone at its dishonoured grave'.[10]

During the course of the twentieth century, however, there has been a resurgence of interest in the mode. To understand why, we need to return to our original working definition: 'pastoral describes literature portraying the life of shepherds, or of the country'. It defines the genre by its subject matter. By and large, all the critics we have considered so far (with the possible exception of Fontenelle) would have agreed, although they would have disagreed among themselves as to which was the *correct* subject matter. But genre, according to Austin Warren and René Wellek, has both an 'Outer' and 'Inner' form.[11] For our purposes, it is convenient to think of the conventions of traditional pastoral as the 'outer' form of the genre: it has been the 'inner' form, or animating impulse, which has preoccupied modern critics.

W. W. Greg inaugurated this trend in his influential historical survey, *Pastoral Poetry and Pastoral Drama* (1906) [*]. He provided a sociological explanation of the origins of pastoral. It occurs when the poet reacts 'against the world which is too much with us' and yearns 'to escape, if it were but in imagination and for a moment, to a life of simplicity and innocence from the bitter luxury of the court and the menial bread of princes'. The constant factor in pastoral, its informing idea, is therefore 'the recognition of a contrast, implicit or expressed, between pastoral life and some more complex type of civilisation'. Almost all modern critics have accepted this point. Frank Kermode [*], for example, considers the opposition between Nature and Art to be the fundamental philosophical basis for pastoral. Laurence Lerner [*] finds it in the contrast between court and country. Harold Toliver [*] argues that there are a variety of possible oppositions (which he tabulates under the headings of Nature *v.* Art, Idyllic Nature *v.* Antipastoral Nature, and Nature *v.* Celestial Paradise) which 'permeate the pastoral from Theocritus to the eighteenth century and create similar tensive structures in pastorals with less definite conventions thereafter'. Using such a schema it is possible to consider as pastorals works which make no mention of the shepherd of literary convention. Hardy's *Tess of the d'Urbervilles*, for example, is structured round the polarities of an anti-pastoral Nature, uncompromisingly depicted at Flintcomb Ash, and an Idyllic Nature, lyrically evoked at Talbothays. J. R. Ebbatson [*] explores the pastoral implications of this contrast, arguing that

Darwin had denied to Hardy the possibility of an innocent nature, and that even the paradisial atmosphere of Talbothays is finally subverted by the iron laws of sexual selection.

Probably the most influential form of the new pastoralism has been the cult of the child. Post-Romantic conceptions of childhood, as a state of natural innocence, joy and wisdom, corrupted by entry into the adult world, allowed the child to usurp the traditional role of the shepherd. Peter Marinelli [*] argues that the association of childhood with pastoral is implicit in the classical tradition, and that the numerous modern novels which survey the hinterland between childhood and adolescence consciously appropriate traditional pastoral imagery. If childhood is an Arcadian existence, it follows that we have all had first-hand experience of the Golden Age. Nostalgia is therefore the emotional core of most pastoral literature: 'We all yearn nostalgically for childhood, and are often deeply moved, both in life and in poetry, by hearing the sudden note of longing, by finding ourselves suddenly caught in the yearnings of memory . . . the Golden Age lies outside history: it is a dream, based perhaps on childhood, perhaps . . . on the dream alone.'[12]

Children are not the only alternative pastoral protagonists. Gaugin's lyrical evocations of life among the South Sea islanders are an extreme example of cultural primitivism – 'the discontent of the civilised with civilisation'. The 'civilised' sixteenth-century 'discoverers' of the Americas held contradictory attitudes towards the indigenous natives, viewing them in some cases as bestial savages, in others as the embodiment of pre-lapsarian Man. Captain Philip Amadas, for example, found them 'most gentle, loving and faithful, void of all guile and treason, such as live after the manner of the Golden Age'.[13] Peter Weston [*] describes the way in which such 'primitive' peoples were accommodated within European ideology through the employment of a pastoral discourse, and how the myth of 'Noble Savage' was instrumental in legitimising, at a crucial moment in the development of a Capitalist society, the 'concept of a free, unitary bourgeois subject'.

The critic most responsible for the extension of the use of the term pastoral is William Empson. His seminal *Some Versions of Pastoral* (1935) [*] proposes as a definition of the 'pastoral process' (and to think of pastoral as a process is inevitably to view it as an animating impulse rather than a set of literary conventions) the paradoxical formula of 'putting the complex into the simple'. Pastoral thus becomes a particular structural relationship which clarifies complex issues by restating them in terms which emphasise the universal at the expense of the accidental. In a sense, of course, all literature simplifies the complexities of experience, but valuable literature for Empson remains in contact with that experience and attempts to resolve its contradictions. Pastoral thus has a unifying social function, 'bridging differences and reconciling social classes'.[14] This can most clearly be seen in Empson's discussion of *The Beggar's Opera*. It qualifies as pastoral because it describes 'the lives of "simple" low people to an audience of refined wealthy people, so as to make them think first "this is true about everyone" and then "this is specially true about us".'[15]

Not all critics have accepted Empson's expansive definition. T. G. Rosenmeyer [*], for example, would prefer to limit the term to literature derived from the Theocritean model. While this would entail a return to an earlier prescriptive concept of genre, it would remove some of the difficulties which have arisen from the extended use of the term. A seventeenth-century poem describing the life of shepherds, for example, would undoubtedly have been classified by contemporary critics as a pastoral; yet it might not exhibit any of the animating contrasts which twentieth-century definitions typically demand. On the other hand, another seventeenth-century poem which no contemporary would have recognised as a pastoral might satisfy all the criteria of modern definitions. Laurence Lerner has proposed, however, a terminology to cope with such awkward cases. The first example is pastoral as *convention*. The second is pastoral as *theme*.

John F. Lynen [*] obviously has some such distinction in mind when he 'recalls the distinction between pastoralism as a kind of poetic structure and pastoralism in the sense of a particular tradition'. Robert Frost is a pastoral poet in the former but not the latter sense, because of his 'regionalism', or ability 'to see in the life of New England a remote, ideal world which could serve the same function as Arcadia'. Lynen's concern with pastoral's special way of seeing the world ('the mode of perception is embodied in the images themselves') is shared by John Bayley [*]. His *Tolstoy and the Novel* (1966) concentrates on the rôle of pastoral within a mimetic framework. Realistic novels, he argues, are pastoral to the extent that they attempt to see their subjects 'in a given frame' which renders everything in the work *characteristic*: 'A coal miner, or a retired colonel in Camberley, are seen by pastoral in their functions and their characters – the fact that they may not feel like or be aware of themselves as a coal miner and a colonel cannot be admitted.' By this definition Balzac's *La Comédie Humaine* is a pastoral enterprise; Tolstoy's *War and Peace*, despite its numerous depictions of rural Russia, is not.

Probably the only recent critic to rival William Empson's influence in the field of pastoral criticism is Renato Poggioli [*]. His essays on the bucolic ideal classify pastoral literature into a number of categories. The most important of these are the *Pastoral of Happiness*, describing works which embody a hedonistic philosophy, and the *Pastoral of Innocence*, where the individual achieves serenity through voluntary retirement from the vanities of the world. While these classifications (and the subsidiary pastorals of *Self*, *Solitude*, *Mirth* and *Melancholy*) provide useful distinctions between the genre's capricious manifestations, Poggioli insists that they all share a common denominator in 'the lyric mode'.[16] His view of pastoral is essentially Freudian: it is a reality substitute which 'embraces both longing and wish-fulfilment', and thus vicariously compensates author and reader for the inevitable deprivations which result from conforming to society's dictates. Laurence Lerner also draws on Freudian terminology to make a similar point. Pastoral is, he believes, an *illusion* in Freud's sense of the term: a 'belief in which wish-fulfilment is a prominent factor in its motivation'.

Pastoral has an ancient pedigree, yet has recently undergone a radical metamorphosis. Inevitably, therefore, the studies collected in this Casebook are diverse and often contradictory. The volume is arranged in two parts. Part One contains a range of pre-twentieth-century criticism. In Part Two, presenting twentieth-century studies, section 1 attempts to define the nature of pastoral; section 2 offers interpretations of individual works in terms of their pastoral themes and conventions. This provides, I hope, a representative selection of the remarkable body of criticism which has attempted to make sense of this most protean of literary modes.

NOTES

1. *OED*: Pastoral, *a.* and *sb.* i, 3.

2. Ovid, *The Metamorphoses*, trans. Arthur Golding (1567): i, 102–31; in W. H. D. Rouse (ed.), *Shakespeare's Ovid* (London, 1961), p. 23.

3. Horace, Epode ii trans. J. Marshall (Everyman edition, London, 1911), pp. 113–14.

4. William Cowper, *The Task*.

5. Richard Lovelace, 'Love Made in the First Age'.

6. For details of these and other early theorists, see J. E. Congleton, *Theories of Pastoral Poetry in England, 1684–1798* (Gainesville, Fl., 1952).

7. L. D. Lerner, *The Uses of Nostalgia* (London, 1972), p. 118.

8. Raman Selden, 'Realism and Country People', in K. Parkinson and M. Priestman (eds), *Peasants and Countrymen in Literature* (Roehampton, 1982),

p. 40. Northrop Frye has speculated that at least one pastoral metaphor – the king as shepherd of his people – is based on sociological observation: 'Perhaps the use of this particular convention is due to the fact that, being stupid, affectionate, gregarious and easily stampeded, the societies formed by sheep are most like human ones'; see *Anatomy of Criticism* (Princeton, N.J., 1957; paperback edn, 1973), p. 143.

9. Thomas Purney, *A Full Enquiry into the True Nature of Pastoral* (London, 1717); reproduced by the Augustan Reprint Society, *Essays on Poetry*, no. 4 (Ann Arbor, 1948).

10. Edmund Gosse, 'An Essay on Pastoral Poetry', in A. Grosart (ed.), *The Complete Works of Edmund Spenser* (London, 1882–84), iii, pp. ix–x.

11. Austin Warren and René Wellek, *A Theory of Literary Criticism* (New York, 1949), p. 231.

12. L. D. Lerner, op. cit., pp. 245–6.

13. Captain Philip Amadas, 'The first voyage made to the coast of America . . .' (1584); in Irwin R. Blacker (ed.), *Hakluyt's Voyages: A Selection* (New York, and London, 1965), p. 293.

14. P. Alpers, 'Empson on Pastoral', *New Literary History*, x, 1 (Autumn 1978), p. 102.

15. W. Empson, *Some Versions of Pastoral* (London, 1935), pp. 195–6.

16. R. Poggioli, *The Oaten Flute* (Cambridge, Mass., 1975), p. 39.

GLOSSARY

Amoebean or *responsive verse*: A specialised form of the débat (see below) where two speakers are given alternating verses or stanzas. The first speaker introduces the theme, while the second attempts to outdo him.

Anti-pastoral: Any work of literature which either explicitly or implicitly rejects pastoral conventions, and refuses to idealise the country life.

Blazon (Fr. 'coat-of-arms' or 'shield'): Verses which praise a woman's beauty by cataloguing the charms of her various physical attributes.

Bucolic (from Gr. βουκόλοs, a herdsman): Now almost a synonym for pastoral, but with a slightly humorous overtone. The Renaissance tended to style Vergil's *Eclogues* and their imitations 'Bucolics'.

Débat: A song or poetic contest in which matters of love, morality, or politics are debated.

Doric: A Greek dialect spoken during the Classical period in the Peloponnese, southern Italy, and Sicily, and thus associated with pastoral. It now denotes the rustic, as opposed to the urban.

Eclogue (from Gr. ἐκλογή, a selection): Originally applied to Vergil's bucolic poems, the term has come to designate any brief poem in dialogue or dramatic soliloquy with a pastoral theme. The eighteenth century employed the term to refer to form only, and there were numerous examples of non-pastoral eclogues: e.g., Swift's *A Town Eclogue*.

Epyllion (from Gr. ἐπύλλιον, 'little epos'): In its classical meaning a 'versicle', the term came to be used in West-European poetic terminology to denote poems (ancient and modern alike) of the short narrative variety, or even brief epics.

Georgic (from the Gr. γεωργικός, 'relating to agriculture'): A didactic poem on the subject of husbandry, which often contains philosophical digressions and praise of rural life.

Hortus conclusus (L. 'enclosed garden'): The traditional setting for contemplative withdrawal.

Idyll (from the Gr. ειδύλλιον, 'brief sketch'): A short poem or episode in a longer work which presents an idealised picture of the countryside and creates a voluptuous atmosphere.

Locus amoenus (L. 'lovely place'): A set-piece description of an ideal landscape which often forms the backdrop for romantic encounters.

Otium (L. ease, leisure).

Pastoral elegy: A lament in which both the poet and the person he mourns are imagined as shepherds.

Pastourelle (Provençal, *pastorela*): A short narrative poem which recounts the chance encounter between a shepherdess and a knight who attempts to seduce her.

Pathetic fallacy: Ruskin's term for the literary trope which ascribes human emotions to the inanimate world.

Primitivism: The discontent of the civilised with civilisation. *Soft primitivism* admires the uncomplicated ease of a life lived in accord with nature. *Hard primitivism* extols the moral virtues promoted by a life of spartan simplicity.

PART ONE

Early Criticism (1579–1818)

'E. K.' (1579)

Uncouthe unkiste, Sayde the olde famous Poete Chaucer: whom for his excellencie and wonderfull skil in making, his scholler Lidgate, a worthy scholler of so excellent a maister, calleth the Loade-starre of our Language: and whom our Colin [C]lout in his Aeglogue calleth Tityrus the God of shepheards, comparing hym to the worthines of the Roman Tityrus Virgile. Which proverbe . . . as in that good old Poete it served well Pandares purpose, for the bolstering of his baudy brocage, so very well taketh place in this our new Poete, who for that he is uncouthe (as said Chaucer) is unkist, and unknown to most men, is regarded but of few. But I dout not, so soone as his name shall come into the knowledg of men, and his worthines be sounded in the tromp of fame, but that he shall be not onely kiste, but also beloved of all, embraced of the most, and wondred at of the best. No lesse I thinke, deserveth his wittinesse in devising, his pithinesse in uttering, his complaints of love so lovely, his discourses of pleasure so pleasantly, his pastorall rudenesse, his morall wisenesse, his dewe observing of Decorum everye where, in personages, in seasons, in matter, in speach, and generally in al seemely simplycitie of handeling his matter, and framing his words: the which of many thinges which in him be straunge, I know will seeme the straungest, the words them selves being so auncient, the knitting of them so short and intricate, and the whole Periode and compasse of speache so delightsome for the roundnesse, and so grave for the straungenesse. And firste of the wordes to speake, I graunt they be something hard, and of most men unused, yet both English, and also used of most excellent Authors and most famous Poetes. In whom whenas this our Poet hath bene much traveiled and throughly redd, how could it be, (as that worthy Oratour sayde) but that walking in the sonne although for other cause he walked, yet needes he mought be sunburnt; and having the sound of those auncient Poetes still ringing in his eares, he mought needes in singing hit out some of theyr tunes. But whether he useth them by such casualtye and custome, or of set purpose and choyse, as thinking them fittest for such rusticall rudenesse of shepheards, eyther for that theyr rough sounde would make his rymes more ragged and rustical, or els because such olde and obsolete wordes are most used of country folke, sure I think, and think I think not amisse, that they bring great grace and, as one would say, auctoritie to the verse. For albe amongst many other faultes it specially be obiected of Valla against Livie, and of other against Saluste, that with over much studie they affect antiquitie, as coveting thereby credence and honor of elder yeeres, yet I am of opinion, and eke the best learned are of the lyke, that those auncient solemne wordes are a great ornament both in the one and in the other; the one labouring to set forth in hys worke an eternall image of antiquitie, and the other carefully discoursing matters of gravitie and importaunce. For if my memory fayle not, Tullie in that booke, wherein he endevoureth to set forth the paterne of a perfect Oratour, sayth that ofttimes an auncient worde maketh the style seeme grave, and as it were reverend: no otherwise then we honour and reverence gray heares for a certein religious regard, which we have of old age. Yet nether every where must old words be stuffed in, nor the commen Dialecte and maner of speaking so corrupted therby, that as in old buildings it seme disorderly and ruinous. But all as in most exquisite pictures they use to blaze and portraict not onely the daintie lineaments of beautye, but also rounde about it to shadow the rude thickets and craggy clifts, that by the basenesse of such parts, more excellency may accrew to the principall; for oftimes we fynde ourselves, I knowe not how, singularly delighted with the shewe of such naturall rudenesse, and take great pleasure in that disorderly order. Even so doe those rough and harsh termes enlumine and make more clearly to appeare the brightnesse of brave and glorious words. So oftentimes a dischorde in Musick maketh a comely concordaunce: so great delight tooke the worthy Poete Alceus to behold a blemish in the ioynt of a wel shaped body. But if any will rashly blame such his purpose in choyse of old and unwonted words, him may I more iustly blame and condemne, or of witlesse headinesse in iudging, or of heedelesse hardinesse in condemning for not marking the compasse of hys bent, he wil iudge of the length of his cast. For in my opinion it is one special prayse, of many whych are dew to this Poete, that he hath laboured to restore, as to theyr rightfull heritage such good and naturall English words, as have ben long time out of use and almost cleane disherited. Which is the onely cause, that our Mother tonge, which truely of it self is both ful enough for prose and stately enough for verse, hath long time ben counted most bare and barrein of both. Which default when as some endevoured to salve and recure, they patched up the holes with peces and rags of other languages, borrowing here of the French, there of the Italian, every where of the Latine, not weighing how il, those tongues accorde with themselves, but much worse with ours: So now they have made our English tongue, a gallimaufray or hodgepodge of al other speches. Other some not so wel seene in the English tonge as perhaps in other languages, if they happen to here an olde word albeit very naturall and significant, crye out streight way, that we speak no English, but gibbrish, or rather such, as in old time Evanders mother spake. Whose first shame is, that they are not ashamed, in their own mother tonge straungers to be counted and alienes. The second shame no lesse then the first, that what so they understand not, they streight way deeme to be sencelesse, and not at all to be understode. Much like to the Mole in Æsopes fable, that being blynd her selfe, would in no wise be perswaded, that any beast could see. The last more shameful then both, that of their owne country and natural speach, which together with their Nources milk they sucked, they have so base regard and bastard iudgement, that they will not onely themselves not labor to garnish and beautifie it, but also repine, that of other it shold be embellished. Like to the dogge in the maunger, that him selfe can eate no hay, and yet barketh at the hungry bullock, that so faine would feede: whose currish kind though it cannot be kept from barking, yet I conne them thanke that they refrain from byting.

Now for the knitting of sentences, whych they call the ioynts and members thereof, and for al the compasse of the speach, it is round without roughnesse, and learned wythout hardnes, such indeede as may be perceiued of the leaste, understoode of the moste, but iudged onely of the learned. For what in most English wryters useth to be loose, and as it were ungyrt, in this Authour is well grounded, finely framed, and strongly trussed up together. In regard whereof, I scorne and spue out the rakehellye route of our ragged rymers (for so themselves use to hunt the letter) which without learning boste, without iudgement iangle, without reason rage and fome, as if some instinct of Poeticall spirite had newly ravished them above the meanenesse of commen capacitie. And being in the middest of all theyr bravery, sodenly eyther for want of matter, or of ryme, or having forgotten theyr former conceipt, they seeme to be so pained and traveiled in theyr remembrance, as it were a woman in childebirth or as that same Pythia, when the traunce came upon her.

Os rabidum fera corda domans &c.

Nethelesse let them a Gods name feede on theyr owne folly, so they seeke not to darken the beames of others glory. As for Colin, under whose person the Author selfe is shadowed, how farre he is from such vaunted titles and glorious showes, both him selfe sheweth, where he sayth.

Of Muses Hobbin. I conne no skill.   And,
Enough is me to paint out my unrest, &c.

And also appeareth by the basenesse of the name, wherein, it semeth, he chose rather to unfold great matter of argument covertly, then professing it, not suffice thereto accordingly. Which moved him rather in Æglogues, then other wise to write, doubting perhaps his habilitie, which he little needed, or mynding to furnish our tongue with this kinde, wherein it faulteth, or following the example of the best and most auncient Poetes, which devised this kind of wryting, being both so base for the matter, and homely for the manner, at the first to trye theyr habilities: and as young birdes, that be newly crept out of the nest, by little first to prove theyr tender wyngs, before they make a greater flyght. So flew Theocritus, as you may perceive he was all ready full fledged. So flew Virgile, as not yet well feeling his winges. So flew Mantuane, as being not full somd. So Petrarque. So Boccace; So Marot, Sanazarus, and also divers other excellent both Italian and French Poetes, whose foting this Author every where followeth, yet so as few, but they be wel sented can trace him out. So finally flyeth this our new Poete, as a bird, whose principals be scarce growen out, but yet as that in time shall be hable to keepe wing with the best.

Now as touching the generall dryft and purpose of his Æglogues, I mind not to say much, him selfe labouring to conceale it. Onely this appeareth, that his unstayed yougth had long wandred in the common Labyrinth of Love, in which time to mitigate and allay the heate of his passion, or els to warne (as he sayth) the young shepheards his equalls and companions of his unfortunate folly, he compiled these xij. Æglogues, which for that they be proportioned to the state of the xij. monethes, he termeth the SHEPHEARDS CALENDAR, applying an olde name to a new worke. Hereunto have I added a certain Glosse or scholion for thexposition of old wordes and harder phrases: wich maner of glosing and commenting, well I wote, wil seeme straunge and rare in our tongue: yet for somuch as I knew many excellent and proper devises both in wordes and matter would passe in the speedy course of reading, either as unknowen, or as not marked, and that in this kind, as in other we might be equal to the learned of other nations, I thought good to take the paines upon me, the rather for that by meanes of some familiar acquaintaunce I was made privie to his counsell and secret meaning in them, as also in sundry other works of his. Which albeit I know he nothing so much hateth, as to promulgate, yet thus much have I adventured upon his frendship, him selfe being for long time farre estraunged, hoping that this will the rather occasion him, to put forth divers other excellent works of his, which slepe in silence, as his Dreames, his Legendes, his Court of Cupide, and sondry others; whose commendations to set out, were verye vayne; the thinges though worthy of many, yet being knowen to few. These my present paynes if to any they be pleasurable or profitable, be you iudge, mine own good Maister Harvey, to whom

I have both in respect of your worthinesse generally, and otherwyse upon some particular and special considerations voued this my labour, and the maydenhead of this our commen frends Poetrie, himselfe having already in the beginning dedicated it to the Noble and worthy Gentleman, the right worshipfull Ma. Phi. Sidney, a special favourer and maintainer of all kind of learning. Whose cause I pray you Sir, yf Envie shall stur up any wrongful accusasion, defend with your mighty Rhetorick and other your rare gifts of learning, as you can, and shield with your good wil, as you ought, against the malice and outrage of so many enemies, as I know wilbe set on fire with the sparks of his kindled glory. And thus recommending the Author unto you, as unto his most special goodfrend, and my selfe unto you both, as one making singuler account of two so very good and so choise frends, I bid you both most hartely farwel, and commit you and your most commendable studies to the tuicion of the greatest.

Your owne assuredly to
be commaunded E. K.

SOURCE: The Epistle Dedicatory ('To the most excellent and learned . . . Mayster Gabriell Harvey'), prefixed to Edmund Spenser's *The Shepheards Calendar* (1579); reproduced in G. Gregory Smith (ed.), *Elizabethan Critical Essays* (Oxford, 1904), vol. I, pp. 127–34

NOTE

[Ed.]. 'E.K.' is probably Edward Kirke (1553–1613), a friend of Spenser's at Pembroke Hall, Cambridge.

The orthography of the original is retained, save that its u / v variations have been regularised to present received usage. This convention has been followed, where appropriate, in subsequent excerpts.

Sir Philip Sidney (c. 1580)

. . . Nature never set forth the earth in so rich tapistry as divers Poets have done, neither with plesant rivers, fruitful trees, sweet smelling flowers, nor whatsoever els may make the too much loved earth more lovely. Her world is brasen, the Poets only deliver a golden. . . .

Is it then the Pastorall Poem which is misliked? (for perchance, where the hedge is lowest they will soonest leape over). Is the poore pype disdained, which sometimes out of *Melibeus* mouth can shewe the miserie of people under hard Lords or ravening Souldiours? and again, by *Titirus*, what blessednes is derived to them that lye lowest from the goodnesse of them that sit highest? sometimes, under the prettie tales of Wolves and Sheepe, can include the whole considerations of wrong dooing and patience; sometimes shew that contention for trifles can get but a trifling victorie. . . .

SOURCE: extracts from *An Apologie for Poetrie* (c. 1580, published 1595), alternatively entitled *A Defence of Poesie*: reproduced in G. Gregory Smith (ed.), *Elizabethan Critical Essays* (Oxford, 1904), I, pp. 156, 175–6.

George Puttenham   (1589)

. . . Some be of opinion, and the chiefe of those who have written in this Art among the Latines, that the pastorall Poesie which we commonly call by the name of *Eglogue* and *Bucolick*, a tearme brought in by the Sicilian Poets, should be the first of any other, and before the *Satyre*, *Comedie*, or *Tragedie*, because, say they, the shepheards and haywards assemblies & meetings when they kept their cattell and heards in the common fields and forests was the first familiar conversation, and their babble and talk under bushes and shadie trees the first disputation and contentious reasoning, and their fleshly heates growing of ease the first idle wooings, and their songs made to their mates or paramours either upon sorrow or iolity of courage the first amorous musicks; sometime also they sang and played on their pipes for wages, striving who should get the best game and be counted cunningest. All this I do agree unto, for no doubt the shepheards life was the first example of honest felowship, their trade the first art of lawfull acquisition or purchase, for at those daies robbery was a manner of purchase. So saith *Aristotle* in his bookes of the Politiques; and that pasturage was before tillage, or fishing, or fowling, or any other predatory art or chevisance. And all this may be true, for before there was a shepheard keeper of his owne or of some other bodies flocke, there was none owner in the world, quick cattel being the first property of any forreine possession. I say forreine, because alway men claimed property in their apparell and armour, and other like things made by their owne travel and industry, nor thereby was there yet any good towne, or city, or Kings palace, where pageants and pompes might be shewed by Comedies or Tragedies. But for all this, I do deny that the *Eglogue* should be the first and most auncient forme of artificiall Poesie, being perswaded that the Poet devised the *Eglogue* long after the other *drammatick* poems, not of purpose to counterfait or represent the rusticall manner of loves and communication, but under the vaile of homely persons and in rude speeches to insinuate and glaunce at greater matters, and such as perchance had not bene safe to have beene disclosed in any other sort, which may be perceived by the Eglogues of *Virgill*, in which are treated by figure matters of greater importance then the loves of *Titirus* and *Corydon*. These Eglogues came after to containe and enforme morall discipline, for the amendment of mans behaviour, as be those of *Mantuan* and other moderne Poets. . . .

SOURCE: extract from *The Arte of English Poesie* (1589); reproduced in G. Gregory (ed.), *Elizabethan Critical Essays* (Oxford, 1904), II, pp. 39–40.

John Fletcher   (1609)

If you be not reasonably assurde of your knowledge in this kinde of Poeme, lay downe the booke or read this, which I would wish had bene the prologue. It is a pastorall Tragie-comedie, which the people seeing when it was plaid, having ever had a singuler guift in defining, concluded to be a play of country hired Shepheards, in gray cloakes, with curtaild dogs in strings, sometimes laughing together, and sometimes killing one another: And missing whitsun ales, creame, wassel and morris-dances, began to be angry. In their error I would not have you fall, least you incurre their censure. Understand therefore a pastorall to be a representation of shepheards and shephearddesses, with their actions and passions, which must be such as may agree with their natures, at least not exceeding former fictions, and vulgar traditions: they are not to be adorn'd with any art, but such improper ones as nature is said to bestow, as singing and Poetry, or such as experience may teach them, as the vertues of hearbs, and fountaines: the ordinary course of the Sun, moone, and starres, and such like. But you are ever to remember Shepherds to be such, as all the ancient Poets and moderne of understanding have receaved them: that is, the owners of flockes and not hyerlings. A tragie-comedie is not so called in respect of mirth and killing, but in respect it wants deaths, which is inough to make it no tragedie, yet brings some neere it, which is inough to make it no comedie: which must be a representation of familiar people, with such kinde of trouble as no life be questiond, so that a God is as lawfull in this as in a tragedie, and meane people as in a comedie. Thus much I hope will serve to justifie my Poeme, and make you understand it, to teach you more for nothing, I do not know that I am in conscience bound.

SOURCE: 'To the Reader', prefacing *The Faithful Shepherdess* (printed c. 1609); reproduced in F. Bowers (ed.), *The Dramatic Works in the Beaumont and Fletcher Canon* (London, 1976), p. 21.

Michael Drayton   (1619)

Somewhat is to be said, by way of generall preparative, touching the name, and nature of Pastorall Poesie, before I give thee my Pastorals. Pastorals, as they are a *Species* of Poesie, signifie fained Dialogues, or other speeches in Verse, fathered upon Heardsmen, whether *Opiliones, bubulci, &c.* that is to say, *Shepheards, Neat-heards*, &c. who are ordinarie persons in this kind of Poeme, worthily therefore to be called base, or low. This, as all other formes of Poesie (excepting perhaps the admirable Latine *Piscatories* of that noble *Neapolitan*, SANAZARA) hath beene received from the *Greekes*, and as at the second hand, from the *Romanes*. The subject of Pastorals, as the language of it ought to be poor, silly, & of the coursest Woofe in appearance. Neverthelesse, the most High, and most Noble Matters of the World may bee shaddowed in them, and for certaine sometimes are: but he who hath almost nothing Pastorall in his Pastorals, but the name (which is my Case) deales more plainly, because *detracto velamine*, he speaks of most weightie things. The *Greek* Pastorals of THEOCRITUS, have the chiefe praise. Whether VIRGIL in his *Bucolicks*, hath kept within Pastorall humblenesse, let SCALIGER and the Nation of Learned *Censors* dispute: the Blessing which came in them to the testimoniall Majestie of the Christian Name, out of SIBYLS Moniments, cited before CHRIST's Birth, must ever make VIRGIL venerable with me: and in the *Angels* Song to Shepheards at our Saviours Nativitie Pastorall Poesie seemes consecrated. It is not of this time and place, to shew the Originals of this Invention: let it here suffice to have pointed out the best, and them so old, as may serve for prescription. The chiefe Law of Pastorals is the same which is of all Poesie, and of all wise carriage, to wit DECORUM, and that not to be exceeded without leave, or without at least faire warning. For so did Virgil, when he wrote,

— *Paulò maiora canamus.*

Master EDMUND SPENSER had done enough for the immortalitie of his Name, had he only given us his *Shepheards Kalendar*, a Master-piece if any. The *Colin Clout* of SKOGAN, under King HENRY the Seventh, is prettie: but BARKLEY's *Ship of Fooles* hath twentie wiser in it. SPENSER is the prime *Pastoralist* of England. My Pastorals bold upon a new straine, must speake for themselves, and the Taber striking up, if thou hast in thee any Country-Quicksilver, thou hadst rather be at the sport, then heare thereof. Farewell.

SOURCE: 'To the Reader of His Pastorals', prefacing Drayton's *Pastorals* (1619); reproduced in J. William Hebel (ed.), *The Works of Michael Drayton* (Oxford, 1931), pp. 517–18.

Ben Jonson (c. 1636)

. . .
But here's an Heresie of late let fall;
That Mirth by no meanes fits a *Pastorall*;
Such say so, who can make none, he presumes:
Else, there's no *Scene*, more properly assumes
The Sock. For whence can sport in kind arise,
But from the Rurall Routs and Families?
Safe on this ground then, wee not feare to day,
To tempt your laughter by our rustick *Play*.
Wherein if we disaste, or be cry'd downe,
Wee thinke wee therefore shall not leave the Towne;
Nor that the Fore-wits, that would draw the rest
Unto their liking, alwayes like the best.
The wise, and knowing *Critick* will not say,
This worst, or better is, before he weigh,
Where every piece be perfect in the kind:
And then, though in themselves he difference find,
Yet if the place require it where they stood,

The equall fitting makes them equall good.
You shall have Love and Hate, and Iealousie,
As well as Mirth, and Rage, and Melancholy:
Or whatsoever else may either move,
Or stirre affections, and your likings prove.
But that no stile for *Pastorall* should goe
Current, but what is stamp'd with *Ah* and *O*;
Who judgeth so, may singularly erre;
As if all *Poesie* had one Character:
In which what were not written, were not right,
Or that the man who made such one poore flight,
In his whole life, had with his winged skill
Advanc'd him upmost on the *Muses* hill.
When he like *Poet* yet remaines, as those
Are *Painters* who can only make a *Rose*.
From such your wits redeeme you, or your chance,
Lest to a greater height you doe advance
Of Folly, to contemne those that are knowne
Artificers, and trust such as are none.

SOURCE: excerpt from the Prologue to *The Sad Shepherd; or, A Tale of Robin-Hood* (c. 1636; published in the folio edn of 1641); reproduced in C. H. Herford, P. and E. Simpson (eds), *The Works of Ben Jonson* (Oxford, 1925–41): VII (1941), pp. 9–10.

Thomas Hobbes   (1650)

. . . As Philosophers have divided the Universe (their subject) into three Regions, *Celestiall*, *Aëriall*, and *Terrestriall*; so the Poets, (whose worke it is by imitating humane life, in delightfull and measur'd lines, to avert men from vice, and encline them to vertuous and honorable actions) have lodg'd themselves in the three Regions of mankind, *Court*, *Citty*, and *Country*, correspondent in some proportion, to those three Regions of the World. For there is in Princes, and men of conspicuous power (anciently called *Heroes*) a lustre and influence upon the rest of men, resembling that of the Heavens; and an insincerenesse, inconstancy, and troublesome humor of those that dwell in populous Citties, like the mobility, blustring, and impurity of the Aire; and a plainesse, and (though dull) yet a nutritive faculty in rurall people, that endures a comparison with the Earth they labour.

From hence have proceeded three sorts of Poesy. *Heroique, Scommatique*, and *Pastorall*. Every one of these is distinguished againe in the manner of *Representation*, which sometimes is *Narrative*, wherein the Poet himselfe relateth, and sometimes *Dramatique*, as when the persons are every one adorned and brought upon the Theater, to speake and act their owne parts. There is therefore neither more nor lesse then six sorts of Poesy. For the Heroique Poeme narrative (such as is yours) is called an *Epique Poeme*; The Heroique Poeme Dramatique, is *Tragedy*. The Scommatique Narrative, is *Satyre*, Dramatique is *Comedy*. The Pastorall narrative, is called simply *Pastorall* (anciently *Bucolique*) the same Dramatique, *Pastorall comedy*. The Figure therefore of an Epique Poeme, and of a Tragedy, ought to be the same, for they differ no more but in that they are pronounced by one, or many persons. Which I insert to justify the figure of yours, consisting of five bookes divided into Songs, or Cantoes, as five Acts divided into Scenes has ever bene the approved figure of a Tragedy. . . .

SOURCE: extract from *The Answer of Mr Hobbes to Sir Will. D'Avenant's Preface before Gondibert* (Paris, 1650); reproduced in D. F. Gladish (ed.), *Gondibert* (Oxford, 1971), pp. 45–6.

René Rapin   (1659)

In delivering Rules for writing *Pastorals*, I shall not point to the *streams*, which to look after argues a small creeping *Genius*, but lead you to the *fountains*. But first I must tell you, how difficult it is to write *Pastorals*, which many seem not sufficiently to understand. For since its matter is low, and humble, it seems to have nothing that is troublesome, and difficult. But this is a great mistake, for, as *Horace* says of *Comedy*, 'It is by so much the more difficult, by how much the less pardonable are the mistakes committed in its composure': and the same is to be thought of every thing, whose end is to please, and delight. For whatsoever is contriv'd for pleasure, and not necessarily requir'd, unless it be exquisite, must be nauseous, and distastful; as at a Supper, scraping Musick, thick Oyntment, or the like, because the Entertainment might have been without all these. For the sweetest things, and most delicious, are most apt to satiate; for tho the sense may sometimes be pleas'd, yet it presently disgusts that which is luscious, and, as *Lucretius* phraseth it,

> *E'en in the midst and fury of the Joys,*
> *Some thing that's better riseth, and destroys.*

Beside, since *Pastoral* is of that nature, that it cannot endure too much of negligence, nor too scrupulous diligence, it must be very difficult to be compos'd, especially since the expression must be neat, but not too exquisite, and fine. It must have a simple native beauty, but not too mean; it must have all sorts of delicacies, and surprizing fancies, yet not be flowing, and luxuriant. And certainly, to hit all these excellencies is difficult enough, since Wit, whose nature is to pour itself forth, must rather be restrained than indulg'd; and that force of the Mind, which of it self is so ready to run on, must be checkt, and bridled: Which cannot be easily perform'd by any, but those who have a very good Judgment, and practically skill'd in Arts, and Sciences. And lastly, a neat, and as it were a happy Wit; not that curious sort, I mean, which *Petronius* allows *Horace*, lest too much *Art* should take off the Beauty of the *Simplicity*. And therefore I would not have any one undertake this task, that is not very polite by *Nature*, and very much at leisure. For what is more hard than to be always in the *Country*, and yet never to be *Clownish*? to sing of *mean*, and *trivial* matters, yet not *trivially*, and *meanly*? to pipe on a *slender* reed, and yet keep the sound from being *harsh* and *squeaking*? to make every thing *sweet*, and yet never *satiate*? And this I thought necessary to premise, in order to the better laying down of such Rules as I design. For the naked *simplicity* both of the Matter and Expression of a *Pastoral*, upon bare Contemplation, might seem easily to be hit, but upon trial 'twill be found a very hard task. Nor was the difficulty to be dissembled, lest *Ignorance* should betray some into a rash attempt. Now I must come to the very Rules; for as nothing excellent can be brought to perfection without *Nature*, (for *Art* unassisted by that, is vain, and ineffectual) so there is no *Nature* so excellent, and happy, which by its own strength, and without *Art* and *Use* can make any thing excellent, and great.

But 'tis hard to give *Rules* for that, for which there have been none already given; for where there are no footsteps nor path to direct, I cannot tell how any one can be certain of his way. Yet in this difficulty I will follow *Aristotle*'s Example, who being to lay down Rules concerning *Epicks*, propos'd *Homer* as a Pattern, from whom he deduc'd the whole Art. So I will gather from *Theocritus* and *Virgil*, those Fathers of *Pastoral*, what I shall deliver on this account. For all the Rules that are to be given of any Art, are to be given of it as excellent, and perfect, and therefore ought to be taken from them in whom it is so.

The first Rule shall be about the *Matter*, which is either the *Action* of a *Shepherd*, or contriv'd and fitted to the *Genius* of a Shepherd; for tho *Pastoral* is simple, and bashful, yet it will entertain lofty subjects, if it can be permitted to turn and fashion them to its own proper Circumstances, and Humor: which tho *Theocritus* hath never done, but kept close to *pastoral* simplicity, yet *Virgil* hath happily attempted; of whom almost the same *Character* might be given, which *Quintilian* bestow'd on *Stesichorus*, who *with his Harp bore up the most weighty subjects* of Epick *Poetry*; for *Virgil* sang great and lofty things to his Oaten Reed, but yet suited to the Humor of a Shepherd, for every thing that is not agreeable to that, cannot belong to *Pastoral*: of its own nature it cannot treat of lofty and great matters.

Therefore let *Pastoral* be smooth and soft, not noisy and bombast; lest while it raiseth its voice, and opens its mouth, it meet with the same fate that, they say, an *Italian* Shepherd did, who having a very large mouth, and a very strong breath, brake his Pipe as often as he blow'd it. This is a great fault in one that writes *Pastorals*: for if his words are too sounding, or his sense too strong, he must be absurd, because indecently loud. . . .

Concerning the Form, or mode of *Imitation*, I shall not repeat what I have already said, *viz*. that this is in it self *mixt*; for *Pastoral* is either *Alternate*, or hath but *one Person*, or is *mixt* of both: yet 'tis properly and chiefly *Alternate*, as is evident from that of *Theocritus*.

> *Sing* Rural *strains, for as we march along*
> *We may delight each other with a Song.*

In which the *Poet* shows that *alternate* singing is proper to a *Pastoral*. But as for the *Fable*, 'tis requisite that it should be simple, lest in stead of *Pastoral* it put on the form of a *Comedy*, or *Tragedy* if the *Fable* be great, or intricate. It must be *one*; this *Aristotle* thinks necessary in every *Poem*, and *Horace* lays down this general Rule,

> *Be every* Fable *simple, and but one.*

For every Poem, that is not *One*, is imperfect, and this *Unity* is to be taken from the *Action*: for if that is *One*, the Poem will be so too. . . .

Let the third Rule be concerning the *Expression*, which cannot be in this kind excellent unless borrow'd from *Theocritus*'s *Idylliums*, or *Virgil*'s *Eclogues*; let it be chiefly simple, and ingenuous: such as that of *Theocritus*,

> *A Kid belongs to thee, and Kids are good,*

or that in *Virgil*'s Seventh Eclogue,

> *This Pail of Milk, these Cakes* (Priapus) *every year*
> *Expect; a little Garden is thy care:*
> *Thou'rt Marble now, but if more Land I hold,*
> *If my Flock thrive, thou shalt be made of Gold,*

than which I cannot imagine more simple and more ingenuous expressions. To which may be added that out of his *Palæmon*,

> *And I love* Phyllis, *for her Charms excell;*
> *At my departure O what tears there fell!*
> *She sigh'd, Farewell Dear Youth, a long Farewell.*

Now, that I call an ingenuous Expression which is clear and smooth, that swells with no insolent words, or bold metaphors, but hath something familiar, and as it were obvious in its Composure, and not disguis'd by any study'd and affected dress. All its Ornament must be like the Corn and fruit in the Country, easy to be gotten, and ready at hand, not such as requires Care, Labor, and Cost to be obtain'd: as *Hermogenes* on *Theocritus* observes, *See how easie and unaffected this sounds*,

> *Pines murmurings, Goatherd, are a pleasing sound,*

and most of his expressions, not to say all, are of the same nature: for the ingenuous simplicity both of Thought and Expression is the natural *Characteristick* of *Pastoral*. In this *Theocritus* and *Virgil* are admirable, and excellent, the others despicable, and to be pitied: for they being enfeebled by the meaness of their subject, either creep, or fall flat. *Virgil* keeps himself up by his choice and curious words, and tho his matter for the most (and *Pastoral* requires it) is mean, yet his expressions never flag, as is evident from these lines in his *Alexis*:

> *The glossy Plums I'le bring, and juicy Pear,*
> *Such as were once delightful to my Dear:*
> *I'le crop the Laurel, and the Myrtle tree,*
> *Confus'dly set, because their Sweets agree.*

For since the matter must be low, to avoid being abject, and despicable, you must borrow some light from the Expression: not such as is dazling, but pure, and lambent, such as may shine thro the whole matter, but never flash, and blind. . . .

. . . tho *Pastoral* does not admit any violent passions, such as proceed from the greatest extremity, and usually accompany despair; yet because Despairing Love is not attended with those frightful and horrible consequences, but looks more like *grief to be pittied*, and a *pleasing madness*, than *rage* and *fury*, *Eclogue* is so far from refusing, that it rather loves, and passionately requires them. Therefore an unfortunate *Shepherd* may be brought in, complaining of his succesless Love to the *Moon*, *Stars*, or *Rocks*, or to the Woods, and purling Streams, mourning the unsupportable anger, the frowns and coyness of his proud *Phyllis*; singing at his *Nymphs* door, (which *Plutarch* reckons among the signs of Passion) or doing any of those fooleries, which are familiar to Lovers. Yet the Passion must not rise too high, as *Polyphemus*'s, *Galateas*'s mad Lover, of whom *Theocritus* divinely thus, as almost of everything else:

> *His was no common flame, nor could he move*
> *In the old Arts, and beaten paths of Love,*
> *No Flowers nor Fruits sent to oblige the Fair,*
> *His was all Rage, and Madness.*

For all violent Perturbations are to be diligently avoided by *Bucolicks*, whose nature it is to be *soft* and *easie*. For in small matters, and such must all the strifes and contentions of Shepherds be, to make a great deal of adoe, is as unseemly, as to put *Hercules*'s Vizard and Buskins on an Infant, as *Quintilian* hath excellently observ'd. For since *Eclogue* is but weak, it seems not capable of those Commotions which belong to the *Theater*, and *Pulpit*; they must be soft, and gentle, and all its Passion must seem to flow only, and not break out: as in *Virgil*'s *Gallus*:

> *Ah, far from home and me You wander o're*
> *The* Alpine *snows, the farthest Western shore,*
> *And frozen* Rhine. *When are we like to meet?*
> *Ah gently, gently, lest thy tender feet*
> *Sharp ice may wound.*

To these he may sometimes joyn some short Interrogations made to *inanimate Beings*, for those spread a strange life and vigor thro the whole Composure. Thus in *Daphnis*,

> *Did not You Streams, and Hazels, hear the Nymphs?*

Or give the very Trees, and Fountains sense, as in *Tityrus*,

> *Thee* (Tityrus) *the Pines, and every Vale,*
> *The Fountains, Hills, and every Shrub did call:*

for by this the Concernment is express'd; and of the like nature is that of *Thyrsis*, in *Virgil*'s *Melibœus*,

> *When* Phyllis *comes, my wood will all be green.*

And this sort of Expression is frequent in *Theocritus*, and *Virgil*, and in these the delicacy of *Pastoral* is principally contain'd, as one of the old *Interpreters* of *Theocritus* hath observ'd on this line, in the eighth *Idyllium*,

> *Ye Vales, and Streams, a race Divine.*

But let them be so, and so seldom us'd, that nothing appear vehement, and bold, for Boldness and Vehemence destroy the sweetness which peculiarly commends *Bucolicks*, and in those Composures a constant care to be soft and easie should be chief. . . .

Concerning the *Numbers*, in which *Pastoral* should be written, this is my opinion; the *Heroick* Measure, but not so strong and sounding as in *Epicks*, is to be chosen. *Virgil* and *Theocritus* have given us examples; for tho *Theocritus* hath in one *Idyllium* mixt other Numbers, yet that can be of no force against the rest; and *Virgil* useth no Numbers but *Heroick*, from whence it may be inferr'd, that those are the fittest. . . .

. . . tho you must be sparing in your *Descriptions*, yet your *Comparisons* must be frequent, and the more often you use them, the better and more graceful will be the Composure; especially if taken from such things, as the Shepherds must be familiarly acquainted with. They are frequent in *Theocritus*, but so proper to the Country, that none but a *Shepherd* dare use them. Thus *Menalcas* in the eighth *Idyllium*:

> *Rough Storms to Trees, to Birds the treacherous Snare,*
> *Are frightful Evils; Springes to the Hare,*
> *Soft Virgins Love to Man,*   &c.

And *Dametas* in *Virgil*'s *Palæmon*,

> *Woolves sheep destroy, Winds Trees when newly blown,*
> *Storms Corn, and me my* Amaryllis *frown.*

And that in the eighth *Eclogue*,

> *As Clay grows hard, Wax soft in the same fire,*
> *So* Daphnis *does in one extream desire.*

And such *Comparisons* are very frequent in him, and very suitable to the Genius of a Shepherd; as likewise often *repetitions*, and doublings of some words: which, if they are luckily plac'd, have an unexpressible quaintness, and make the Numbers extream sweet, and the turns ravishing and delightful. An instance of this we have in *Virgil*'s *Melibœus*,

> Phyllis *the Hazel loves; whilst* Phyllis *loves that Tree,*
> *Myrtles than Hazels of less fame shall be.*

As for the *Manners* of your *Shepherds*, they must be such as theirs who liv'd in the Islands of the Happy or Golden Age. They must be candid, simple, and ingenuous; lovers of Goodness, and Justice, affable, and kind; strangers to all fraud, contrivance, and deceits; in their Love modest, and chast, not one suspitious word, no loose expression to be allow'd: and in this part *Theocritus* is faulty, *Virgil* never; and this difference is perhaps to be ascrib'd to their Ages, the time in which the latter liv'd being more polite, civil, and gentile. And therefore those who make wanton Love-stories the subject of Pastorals, are in my opinion very unadvis'd; for all sort of lewdness or debauchery are directly contrary to the *Innocence* of the *golden* Age. There is another thing in which *Theocritus* is faulty, and that is making his Shepherds too sharp, and abusive to one another; *Comatas* and *Lacon* are ready to fight, and the railing between these two is as bitter as *Billingsgate*. Now certainly such raillery cannot be suitable to those sedate times of the Happy Age.

As for *Sentences*,[1] if weighty, and Philosophical, common Sense tells us they are not fit for a *Shepherd*'s mouth. Here *Theocritus* cannot be altogether excus'd, but *Virgil* deserves no reprehension. But *Proverbs* justly challenge admission into *Pastorals*, nothing being more common in the mouths of Countrymen than old Sayings. . . .

SOURCE: extracts from Thomas Creech's translation of Rapin's *Dissertatio de Carmine Pastorali* (1659), prefixed (as 'A Treatise de Carmine Pastorali') to Creech's *Idylliums of Theocritus* (Oxford, 1684); reproduced by the Augustan Reprint Society (Ann Arbor, 1947), pp. 50–3, 55, 56–7, 61–3, 66–8.

NOTE

1. [Ed.] *Sentences*: sage observations, maxims (cf. modern 'sententious').

Bernard le Bouvier de Fontenelle (1688)

. . . I am . . . of opinion, that Pastoral Poetry cannot be very charming, if it is as low and clownish as Shepherds naturally are; or if it precisely runs upon nothing but rural Matters. For, to hear one speak of Sheep and Goats, and of the Care that ought to be taken of those Animals, has nothing which in it self can please us; what is pleasing is the Idea of Quietness, which is inseparable from a Pastoral Life. Let a Shepherd say, *My Sheep are in good Case, I conduct them on the best Pastures, they feed on nothing but the best Grass*, and let him say this in the best Verse in the World, I am sure that your Imagination will not be very delighted with it. But let him say, *How free from anxious Care is my Life! In what a quiet state I pass my Days! All my Desires rise no higher than that I may see my Flocks in a thriving Condition, and the Pastures wholesome and pleasing; I envy no Man's Happiness,* &c. You perceive that this begins to become more agreeable. The Reason of it is, that the Idea runs no longer immediately upon Country Affairs, but upon the little share of Care which Shepherds undergo, and upon the Quietness and Leisure which they enjoy; and what is the chiefest Point, upon the Cheapness of their Happiness.

For, all Men would be happy, and that too at an easy Rate. A quiet Pleasure is the common Object of all their Passions, and we are all controuled by a certain Laziness. Even those who are most stirring, are not precisely such for Business sake, or because they love to be in Action, but because they cannot easily satisfy themselves.

Ambition, as it is too much an Enemy to this natural Laziness, is neither a general Passion nor very delicious. A considerable part of Mankind is not ambitious; many have began to be such but by the means of some Undertakings and Ties that have determin'd them before they seriously reflected on what they did, and that have made them unfit ever to return to calmer Inclinations; and even those who have most Ambition, do often complain of the Cares which it exacts, and the Pains that attend it. The Reason of this is, that the native Laziness of which we were speaking, is not wholly suppress, tho' it has been sacrificed to that presumptuous Tyrant of the Mind; it prov'd the weakest, and could not over-balance its Rival; yet it still subsists and continually opposes the Motions of Ambition. Now no Man can be happy while he is divided by two warring Inclinations.

However, I do not say that Men can relish a State of absolute Laziness and Idleness; no, they must have some Motion, some Agitations, but it must be such a Motion and Agitation as may be reconcil'd, if possible, to the kind of Laziness that possesses 'em; and this is most happily to be found in Love, provided it be taken in a certain manner. It must neither be a hot, jealous, touchy, furious, desperate Love, but tender, pure, simple, delicate, faithful, and, that it may preserve it self in this State, attended with Hopes: Then the Heart is taken up, but not disturb'd; we have Cares, but no Uneasinesses; we are mov'd, but not torn, and this soft Motion is just such, as the love of Rest, and our native Laziness can bear it.

Besides, 'tis most certain that Love is the most general and the most agreeable of all the Passions. So, in the State of Life which we have now describ'd, there is a Concurrence of the two strongest Passions,

Laziness and Love; which thus are both satisfied at once; and that we may be as happy as 'tis possible we should by the Passions, 'tis necessary that all those by which we are moved, agree together in us.

This is properly what we conceive of a Pastoral Life. For it admits of no Ambition, nor of any thing that moves the Heart with too much Violence; therefore our Laziness has cause to be contented. But this way of living, by reason of its Idleness and Tranquillity, creates Love more easily than any other, or at least indulges it more. But after all, what Love! A Love more innocent, because the Mind is not so dangerously refin'd; more assiduous, because those who feel it are not diverted by any other Passions; more full of Discretion, because they hardly have any Acquaintance with Vanity; more faithful, because with a Vivacity of Imagination less used, they have also less Uneasiness, less Distaste, and less Fickleness; that is to say, in short, a Love purg'd of whatever the Excesses of human Fancy have sophisticated it with.

This consider'd, 'tis not to be admir'd why the Pictures which are drawn of a Pastoral Life, have always something so very smiling in them, and indulge our Fancies more than the pompous Description of a splendid Court, and of all the Magnificence that can shine there. A Court gives us no Idea but of toilsome and constrain'd Pleasures: For, as we have observ'd, the Idea is all in all: Cou'd the Scene of this quiet Life, with no other Business but Love, be plac'd any where but in the Country, so that no Goats nor Sheep shou'd be brought in; I fansy it would be never the worse; for the Goats and Sheep add nothing to its Felicity; but as the Scene must lye either in the Country or in Towns, it seems more reasonable to chuse the first.

As the Pastoral Life is the most idle of all others, 'tis also the most fit to be the Ground-work of those ingenious Representations of which we are speaking. So that no Plough-men, Reaper, Vine-dressers, or Hunts-men, can by any means be so properly introduc'd in Eclogues, as Shepherds: Which confirms what I said, that what makes this kind of Poetry please, is not its giving an Image of a Country Life, but rather the Idea which it gives of the Tranquillity and Innocence of that Life.

Yet there is an *Idyllium* of *Battus* and *Milo*, two Reapers in *Theocritus*, which has Beauties. *Milo* asks *Battus* why he does not reap as fast as he used to do? He answers, that he is in Love, and then sings something that's very pretty about the Woman that he loves. But *Milo* laughs at him, and tells him he is a Fool, for being so idle as to be in love; that this is not an Imployment fit for one who works for Food; and that, to divert himself, and excite one another to work, he should sing some Songs which he denotes to him, and which altogether relate to the

Harvest. I must needs own that I do not so well like this Conclusion. For I would not be drawn from a pleasing and soft Idea to another that is low and without Charms.

Sannazarius has introduced none but Fishermen in his Eclogues; and I always perceive, when I read those Piscatory Poems, that the Idea I have of Fishermen's hard and toilsome way of living, shocks me. I don't know what mov'd him to bring in Fishermen instead of Shepherds, who were in Possession of the Eclogue time out of mind; but had the Fishermen been in Possession of it, it had been necessary to put the Shepherds in their place: For singing, and above all, an idle Life becomes none but Shepherds: Besides methinks 'tis prettier and more genteel to send Flowers or Fruit to one's Mistress, than send her Oysters, as *Sannazarius*'s *Lyco* doth to his.

'Tis true that *Theocritus* hath an *Idyllium* of two Fishermen; but it doth not seem to me so beautiful as to have deserv'd to tempt any Man to write one of that kind. The subject of it is this; Two old Fishermen had but sparingly supp'd together in a wretched little thatcht House, by the Sea-side: One of them wakes his Bedfellow to tell him, he had just dreamt that he was catching a golden Fish; and the other answers him, that he might starve though he had really caught such a one. Was this worth writing an Eclogue!

However, though none but Shepherds were introduc'd in Eclogues, 'tis impossible but that the Life of Shepherds which after all is yet very clownish, must lessen and debase their Wit, and hinder their being as ingenious, nice, and full of Gallantry, as they are commonly represented in Pastorals. The famous Lord *D'urfe*'s *Astræa* seems a less fabulous Romance than *Amadis de gaule*; yet I fansy that in the main it is as incredible, as to the Politeness and Graces of his Shepherds, as *Amadis* can be as to all its Enchantments, all its Fairies, and the Extravagance of its Adventures. How comes it then that Pastorals please in spight of the falsity of the Characters, which ought always to shock us? Could we be pleased with seeing some Courtiers represented as having a Clownishness which should resemble that of real Shepherds, as much as the Gallantry which Shepherds have in Pastorals resembles that of Courtiers? No, doubtless; but indeed that Character of the Shepherds is not false after all, if we look upon it one way: For we do not mind the Meanness of the Concerns that are their real Employment, but the little Trouble those Concerns bring. This Meanness would wholly exclude Ornaments and Gallantry, but on the other hand the quiet State promotes them; and 'tis only on that Tranquillity that whatever pleases in a Pastoral Life is grounded.

Our Imagination is not to be pleased without Truth; but it is not very hard to please it; for often 'tis satisfied with a kind of half Truth.

Let it see only the half of a thing, but let that half be shown in a lively manner, then it will hardly bethink it self that you hide from it the other half, and you may thus deceive it as long as you please, since all the while it imagines that this single Moiety, with the Thoughts of which it is taken up, is the whole thing. The Illusion, and at the same time the pleasingness of Pastorals therefore consists, in exposing to the Eye only the Tranquillity of a Shepherd's Life, and in dissembling or concealing its Meanness, as also in showing only its Innocence, and hiding its Miseries; so that I do not comprehend why *Theocritus* dwelt so much upon its Miseries and Clownishness.

If those who are resolved to find no Faults in the Ancients, tell us that *Theocritus* had a mind to draw Nature just such as it is, I hope that according to those Principles, we shall have some *Idyllia* of Porters or Watermen discoursing together of their particular Concerns: Which will be every whit as good as some *Idyllia* of Shepherds speaking of nothing but their Goats or their Cows.

The Business is not purely to describe, we must describe such Objects as are delightful: When the Quiet that reigns in the Country, and the Simplicity and Tenderness which are discover'd there in making Love, are represented to me, my Imagination, mov'd and affected with these pleasing Ideas, is fond of a Shepherd's Life; but tho' the vile and low Employments of Shepherds, were describ'd to me with all the Exactness possible, I shou'd never be taken with 'em, and my Imagination wou'd not in the least be touched. The chief Advantage of Poetry consists in representing to us in a lively manner the things that concern us, and in striking strongly a Heart which is pleas'd with being mov'd . . .

SOURCE: extract from Fontenelle's discussion of Pastorals in *Digression sur les Anciens et les Modernes* (1688), translated by 'Mr. Motteux' and included as the chapter 'Of Pastorals' in Bossu's *Treatise of the Epick Poem* (London, 1695), pp. 325–33.

Alexander Pope   (?1704)*

There are not, I believe, a greater number of any sort of verses than of those which are called Pastorals, nor a smaller, than of those which are truly so. It therefore seems necessary to give some account of this kind of Poem, and it is my design to comprize in this short paper the substance of those numerous dissertations the Criticks have made on the subject, without omitting any of their rules in my own favour. You will also find some points reconciled, about which they seem to differ, and a few remarks which I think have escaped their observation.

The original of Poetry is ascribed to that age which succeeded the creation of the world: And as the keeping of flocks seems to have been the first employment of mankind, the most ancient sort of poetry was probably pastoral. 'Tis natural to imagine, that the leisure of those ancient shepherds requiring some diversion, none was so proper to that solitary life as singing; and that in their songs they took occasion to celebrate their own felicity. From hence a Poem was invented, and afterwards improv'd to a perfect image of that happy time; which by giving us an esteem for the virtues of a former age, might recommend them to the present. And since the life of shepherds was attended with more tranquillity than any other rural employment, the Poets chose to introduce their Persons, from whom it receiv'd the name of Pastoral.

A Pastoral is an imitation of the action of a shepherd; the form of this imitation is dramatic, or narrative, or mix'd of both; the fable simple, the manners not too polite nor too rustic: The thoughts are plain, yet admit a little quickness and passion, but that short and flowing: The expression humble, yet as pure as the language will afford; neat, but not florid; easy, and yet lively. In short, the fable, manners, thoughts, and expressions, are full of the greatest simplicity in nature.

The complete character of this poem consists in simplicity, brevity, and delicacy; the two first of which render an eclogue natural, and the last delightful.

If we would copy Nature, it may be useful to take this consideration along with us, that pastoral is an image of what they call the Golden age. So that we are not to describe our shepherds as shepherds at this

---

* [Ed.] Pope himself assigned the composition of this discourse (included in the 1717 edition of his *Works*) to 1704. An early version, 'An Essay on Pastoral', still exists in his autograph. However, there is no external evidence to corroborate the poet's claim that this was written in 1704, at the age of sixteen.

day really are, but as they may be conceiv'd then to have been; when a notion of quality was annex'd to that name, and the best of men follow'd the employment. To carry this resemblance yet farther, that Air of piety to the Gods should shine thro' the Poem, which so visibly appears in all the works of antiquity: And it ought to preserve some relish of the old way of writing; the connections should be loose, the narrations and descriptions short, and the periods concise. Yet it is not sufficient that the sentences only be brief, the whole Eclogue should be so too. For we cannot suppose Poetry to have been the business of the ancient shepherds, but their recreation at vacant hours.

But with a respect to the present age, nothing more conduces to make these composures natural, than when some Knowledge in rural affairs is discover'd. This may be made to appear rather done by chance than on design, and sometimes is best shewn by inference; lest by too much study to seem natural, we destroy the delight. For what is inviting in this sort of poetry (as *Fontenelle* observes)[1] proceeds not so much from the Idea of a country life itself, as from that of its Tranquillity. We must therefore use some illusion to render a Pastoral delightful; and this consists in exposing the best side only of a shepherd's life, and in concealing its miseries. Nor is it enough to introduce shepherds discoursing together, but a regard must be had to the subject; that it contain some particular beauty in itself, and that it be different in every Eclogue. Besides, in each of them a design'd scene or prospect is to be presented to our view, which should likewise have its variety. This Variety is obtain'd in a great degree by frequent comparisons, drawn from the most agreeable objects of the country; by interrogations to things inanimate; by beautiful digressions, but those short; sometimes by insisting a little on circumstances; and lastly by elegant turns on the words, which render the numbers extremely sweet and pleasing. As for the numbers themselves, tho' they are properly of the heroic measure, they should be the smoothest, the most easy and flowing imaginable.

It is by rules like these that we ought to judge of Pastoral. And since the instructions given for any art are to be deliver'd as that art is in perfection, they must of necessity be deriv'd from those in whom it is acknowledg'd so to be. 'Tis therefore from the practice of *Theocritus* and *Virgil*, (the only undisputed authors of Pastoral) that the Criticks have drawn the foregoing notions concerning it.

Theocritus excells all others on nature and simplicity. The subjects of his *Idyllia* are purely pastoral, but he is not so exact in his persons, having introduced Reapers and fishermen as well as shepherds. He is apt to be long in his descriptions, of which that of the Cup in the first pastoral·is a remarkable instance. In the manners he seems a little defective, for his swains are sometimes abusive and immodest, and perhaps too much inclining to rusticity; for instance, in his fourth and fifth *Idyllia*. But 'tis enough that all others learn'd their excellencies from him, and that his Dialect alone has a secret charm in it which no other could ever attain.

Virgil who copies *Theocritus*, refines upon his original: and in all points where Judgment has the principal part, is much superior to his master. Tho' some of his subjects are not pastoral in themselves, but only seem to be such; they have a wonderful variety in them which the *Greek* was a stranger to. He exceeds him in regularity and brevity, and falls short of him in nothing but simplicity and propriety of style; the first of which perhaps was the fault of his age, and the last of his language.

Among the moderns, their success has been greatest who have most endeavour'd to make these ancients their pattern. The most considerable Genius appears in the famous *Tasso*, and our *Spenser*. *Tasso* in his *Aminta* has as far excell'd all the Pastoral writers, as in his *Gierusalemme* he has outdone the Epic Poets of his country. But as this piece seems to have been the original of a new sort of poem, the Pastoral Comedy, in *Italy*, it cannot so well be consider'd as a copy of the ancients. *Spenser*'s *Calender*, in Mr *Dryden*'s opinion, is the most complete work of this kind which any Nation has produc'd ever since the time of *Virgil*. Not but he may be thought imperfect in some few points. His Eclogues are somewhat too long, if we compare them with the ancients. He is sometimes too allegorical, and treats of matters of religion in a pastoral style as *Mantuan* had done before him. He has employ'd the Lyric measure, which is contrary to the practice of the old Poets. His Stanza is not still the same, nor always well chosen. This last may be the reason his expression is sometimes not concise enough: for the Tetrastic has oblig'd him to extend his sense to the length of four lines, which would have been more closely confin'd in the Couplet.

In the manners, thoughts, and characters, he comes near *Theocritus* himself; tho' notwithstanding all the care he has taken, he is certainly inferior in his Dialect: For the *Doric* had its beauty and propriety in the time of *Theocritus*; it was used in part of *Greece*, and frequent in the mouths of many of the greatest persons; whereas the old *English* and country phrases of *Spenser* were either entirely obsolete, or spoken only by people of the basest condition. As there is a difference betwixt simplicity and rusticity, so the expression of simple thoughts should be plain, but not clownish. The addition he has made of a Calendar to his Eclogues is very beautiful: since by this, besides that general moral of innocence and simplicity, which is common to other authors of pastoral, he has one peculiar to himself; he compares human Life to the several Seasons, and at once exposes to his readers a view of the great and little worlds, in their various changes and aspects. Yet the scrupulous division of his Pastorals into Months, has oblig'd him either to repeat the same description, in other words, for three months together; or when it was exhausted before, entirely to omit it: whence it comes to pass that some of his Eclogues (as the sixth, eighth, and tenth for example) have nothing but their Titles to distinguish them. The reason is evident, because the year has not that variety in it to furnish every month with a particular description, as it may every season.

Of the following Eclogues I shall only say, that these four comprehend all the subjects which the Criticks upon *Theocritus* and *Virgil* will allow to be fit for pastoral: That they have as much variety of description, in respect of the several seasons, as *Spenser*'s: That in order to add to this variety, the several times of the day are observ'd, the rural employments in each season or time of day, and the rural scenes or places proper to such employments; not without some regard to the several ages of man, and the different passions proper to each age.

But after all, if they have any merit, it is to be attributed to some good old Authors, whose works as I had leisure to study, so I hope I have not wanted care to imitate.

SOURCE: 'A Discourse on Pastoral Poetry', included in *The Works* of *Mr Alexander Pope* (1717); reproduced in Norman Ault (ed.), *The Prose Works of Alexander Pope* (Oxford, 1936), I, pp. 297–302. (See footnote on the opening page, above, of this Discourse.)

NOTE

1. [Ed.] See the preceding excerpt herein.

Thomas Tickell (1713)

The Italians and French being dispatched [in a previous essay – Ed.] I come now to the English, whom I shall treat with such meekness as becomes a good patriot; and shall so far recommend this our island as a proper scene for pastoral, under certain regulations, as will satisfy the courteous reader that I am in the landed interest.[1]

I must in the first place observe, that our countrymen have so good an opinion of the ancients, and think so modestly of themselves, that the generality of pastoral-writers have either stolen all from the Greeks and Romans, or so servilely imitated their manners and customs, as makes them very ridiculous. In looking over some English pastorals a few days ago, I perused at least fifty lean flocks, and reckoned up an hundred left-handed ravens, besides blasted oaks, withering meadows, and weeping deities. Indeed most of the occasional pastorals we have, are built upon one and the same plan. A shepherd asks his fellow, 'Why he is so pale? if his favourite sheep hath strayed? if his pipe be broken? or Phyllis unkind?' He answers, 'None of these misfortunes have befallen him, but one much greater, for Damon (or sometimes the god Pan) is dead.' This immediately causes the other to make complaints, and call upon the lofty pines and silver streams to join in the lamentation. While he goes on, his friend interrupts him, and tells him that Damon lives, and shews him a track of light in the skies to confirm it; then invites him to chesnuts and cheese. Upon this scheme most of the noble families in Great-Britain have been comforted; nor can I meet with any right honourable shepherd that doth not die and live again, after the manner of the aforesaid Damon.

Having already informed my reader wherein the knowledge of antiquity may be serviceable, I shall now direct him where he may lawfully diviate from the ancients. There are some things of an established nature in pastoral, which are essential to it, such as a country scene, innocence, simplicity. Others there are of a changeable kind, such as habits, customs, and the like. The difference of the climate is also to be considered, for what is proper in Arcadia, or even in Italy, might be very absurd in a colder country. By the same rule the difference of the soil, of fruits and flowers, is to be observed. And in so fine a country as Britain, what occasion is there for that profusion of hyacinths and Pæstan roses, and that cornucopia of foreign fruits which the British shepherds never heard of? How much more pleasing is the following scene to an English reader!

> This place may seem for shepherds' leisure made,
> So lovingly these elms unite their shade.
> Th' ambitious woodbine, how it climbs to breathe
> Its balmy sweets around on all beneath!
> The ground with grass of chearful green bespread,
> Thro' which the springing flow'r up-rears its head!
> Lo here the king-cup of a golden hue

> Medley'd with daisies white, and endive blue!
> Hark, how the gaudy goldfinch and the thrush,
> With tuneful warblings fill that bramble-bush!
> In pleasing concert all the birds combine,
> And tempt us in the various song to join.²

The theology of the ancient pastoral is so very pretty, that it were pity intirely to change it; but I think that part only is to be retained which is universally known, and the rest to be made up out of our own rustical superstition of hobthrushes, fairies, goblins, and witches. The fairies are capable of being made very entertaining persons, as they are described by several of our poets; and particularly by Mr Pope:

> About this spring (if ancient fame say true)
> The dapper elves their moon-light sports pursue,
> Their pigmy king, and little fairy queen,
> In circling dances gambol'd on the green,
> While tuneful springs a merry concert made,
> And airy music warbled through the shade.

What hath been said upon the difference of climate, soil, and theology, reaches the proverbial sayings, dress, customs and sports of shepherds. The following examples of our pastoral sports are extremely beautiful:

> Whilome did I, tall as this poplar fair,
> Up-raise my heedless head, devoid of care,
> 'Mong rustic routs the chief for wanton game;
> Nor could they merry make till Lobbin came.
> Who better seen than I in shepherds arts,
> To please the lads, and win the lasses hearts?
> How deftly to mine oaten reed, so sweet,
> Wont they upon the green to shift their feet?
> And weary'd in the dance, how would they yearn
> Some well devised tale from me to learn?
> For many songs and tales of mirth had I,
> To chace the lingring sun a-down the sky.
>
> ———O now! if ever, bring
> The laurel green, the smelling eglantine,
> And tender branches from the mantling vine,
> The dewy cowslip that in meadow grows,
> The fountain violet, and garden rose:
> Your hamlet straw, and every public way,
> And consecrate to mirth Albino's day.
> Myself will lavish all my little store:
> And deal about the goblet flowing o'er:

Old Moulin there shall harp, your Mico sing,
And Cuddy dance the round amidst the ring,
And Hobbinol his antic gambols play.[3]

The reason why such changes from the ancients should be introduced is very obvious; namely, that poetry being imitation, and that imitation being the best which deceives the most easily, it follows that we must take up the customs which are most familiar or universally known, since no man can be deceived or delighted with the imitation of what he is ignorant of.

It is easy to be observed that these rules are drawn from what our countrymen Spenser and Philips have performed in this way. I shall not presume to say any more of them, than that both have copied and improved the beauties of the ancients, whose manner of thinking I would above all things recommend. As far as our language would allow them, they have formed a pastoral style according to the Doric of Theocritus, in which I dare not say they have excelled Virgil! but I may be allowed, for the honour of our language, to suppose it more capable of that pretty rusticity than the Latin. To their works I refer my reader to make observations upon the pastoral style: where he will sooner find that secret than from a folio of criticisms.

SOURCE: essay in *The Guardian*, No. 30 (Monday, 15 April 1713); reprinted in the collected edition of *Guardian Essays* (London, 1797), pp. 171–5.

NOTES

1. [Ed.] Though assigned to Steele in the 1797 edition, the latter's editor inserts a note: 'Probably by Mr T. Tickell, with some slight assistance from Addison, who about this time was giving the last politure to his *Cato*. See nos 15, 22, 23, 28, 33 and 40, and notes.'

2. [Annotation, 1797 edn] Philips's Fourth Pastoral, *ab initio*. [Tickell quotes from Ambrose Philips, *Pastorals* (1708); in M. G. Segar (ed.), *Philips: Poems* (Oxford, 1937) – Ed.]

3. [Annotation, 1797 edn] Philips's First Pastoral, l. 31 &c.; Third Part, l. 106 &c.

Alexander Pope (1713)

[This *Guardian* essay was written by Pope to ridicule Philips's poetry and the theories of the rationalist school of criticism, at that time being expounded in the journal: see the preceding essay by Tickell. Pope is writing with the archness of anonymity; his essay was unsigned, though its authorship was not a secret – Ed.]

I designed to have troubled the reader with no farther discourses of pastorals; but, being informed that I am taxed of partiality in not mentioning an author, whose eclogues are published in the same volume with Mr Philips's, I shall employ this paper in observations upon him, written in the free spirit of criticism, and without apprehension of offending that gentleman, whose character it is, that he takes the greatest care of his works before they are published, and has the least concern for them afterwards.

I have laid it down as the first rule of pastoral, that its idea should be taken from the manners of the golden age, and the moral formed upon the representation of innocence; it is therefore plain that any deviations from that design degraded a poem from being true pastoral. In this view it will appear that Virgil can only have two of his eclogues allowed to be such. His first and ninth must be rejected, because they describe the ravages of armies, and oppressions of the innocent; Corydon's criminal passion for Alexis throws out the second; the calumny and railing in the third are not proper to that state of concord; the eighth represents unlawful ways of procuring love by enchantments, and introduces a shepherd whom an inviting precipice tempts to self-murder. As to the fourth, sixth and tenth, they are given up by Heinsius, Salmasius, Rapin, and the critics in general.[1] They likewise observe that but eleven of the Idyllia of Theocritus are to be admitted as pastorals; and even out of that number the greater part will be excluded, for one or other of the reasons above-mentioned. So that when I remarked in a former paper, that Virgil's eclogues, taken altogether, are rather select poems than pastorals, I might have said the same thing, with no less truth, of Theocritus. The reason of this I take to be yet unobserved by the critics, viz. 'They never meant them all for pastorals.' Which it is plain Philips hath done, and in that particular excelled both Theocritus and Virgil.

As simplicity is the distinguishing characteristic of pastoral, Virgil has been thought guilty of too courtly a style: his language is perfectly pure, and he often forgets he is among peasants. I have frequently wondered that since he was so conversant in the writings of Ennius, he had not imitated the rusticity of the Doric, as well, by the help of the old obsolete Roman language, as Philips hath the antiquated English. For example, might he not have said *quoi* instead of *cui*; *quoijum* for *cujum*; *volt* for *vult*, &c. as well as our modern hath *welladay* for *alas*, *whilome* for *of old*, *make mock* for *deride*, and *whitless younglings* for *simple lambs*, &c. by which means he had attained as much of the air of Theocritus, as Philips hath of Spenser?

Mr Pope hath fallen into the same error with Virgil. His clowns do not converse in all the simplicity proper to the country. His names are borrowed from Theocritus and Virgil, which are improper to the scene of his pastorals. He introduces Daphnis, Alexis, and Thyrsis on British plains, as Virgil had done before him on the Mantuan: whereas Philips, who hath the strictest regard to propriety, makes choice of names peculiar to the country, and more agreeable to a reader of delicacy; such as Hobbinol, Lobbin, Cuddy and Colin Clout.

So easy as pastoral writing may seem (in the simplicity we have described it), yet it requires great reading, both of the ancients and moderns, to be a master of it. Philips hath given us manifest proofs of his knowledge of books; it must be confessed his competitor hath imitated some single thoughts of the ancients well enough, if we consider he had not the happiness of an university education; but he hath dispersed them here and there, without that order and method which Mr Philips observes, whose whole third pastoral is an instance how well he hath studied the fifth of Virgil, and how judiciously reduced Virgil's thoughts to the standard of pastoral; as his contention of Colin Clout and the Nightingale, shows with what exactness he hath imitated Strada.

When I remarked it as a principal fault to introduce fruits and flowers of a foreign growth in descriptions where the scene lies in our country, I did not design that observation should extend also to animals, or the sensitive life; for Philips hath with great judgement described wolves in England, in his first pastoral.[2] Nor would I have a poet slavishly confine himself (as Mr Pope hath done) to one particular season of the year, one certain time of the day, and one unbroken scene in each eclogue. It is plain Spenser neglected this pedantry, who in his pastoral of November, mentions the mournful song of the nightingale.

> Sad Philomel her song in tears doth steep.

And Mr Philips, by a poetical creation, hath raised up finer beds of flowers than the most industrious gardener; his roses, lilies and daffodils, blow in the same season.

But the better to discover the merits of our two contemporary pastoral writers, I shall endeavour to draw a parallel of them, by setting several of their particular thoughts in the same light, whereby it will be obvious how much Philips hath the advantage. With what simplicity he introduces two shepherds singing alternately:

> *Hobb.* Come, Rosalind, O come, for without thee
> What pleasure can the country have for me.
> Come, Rosalind, O come: My brinded kine,
> My snowy sheep, my farm, and all, is thine.
> *Lanq.* Come, Rosalind, O come: here shady bowers,
> Here are cool fountains, and here springing flow'rs.
> Come, Rosalind; here ever let us stay,
> And sweetly waste our live-long time away.

Our other pastoral writer, in expressing the same thought, deviates into downright poetry.

> *Streph.* In spring the fields, in autumn hills I love,
> At morn the plains, at noon the shady grove,
> But Delia always; forc'd from Delia's sight,
> Nor plains at morn, nor groves at noon delight.
> *Daph.* Sylvia's like autumn ripe, yet mild as May,
> More bright than noon, yet fresh as early day:
> Ev'n spring displeases when she shines not here:
> But, blest with her, 'tis spring throughout the year.

In the first of these authors, two shepherds thus innocently describe the behaviour of their mistresses.

> *Hobb.* As Marian bath'd, by chance I passed by;
> She blush'd, and at me cast a side-long eye:
> Then swift beneath the crystal wave she try'd
> Her beauteous form, but all in vain, to hide.
> *Lanq.* As I to cool me bath'd one sultry day,
> Fond Lydia lurking in the surges lay:
> The wanton laugh'd and seem'd in haste to fly;
> Yet often stopp'd, and often turn'd her eye.

The other modern (who it must be confessed hath a knack of versifying) hath it as follows:

> *Streph.* Me gentle Delia beckons from the plain,
> Then, hid in shades, eludes her eager swain:
> But feigns a laugh, to see me search around,
> And by that laugh the willing fair is found.

> *Daph.* The sprightly Sylvia trips along the green;
> She runs, but hopes she does not run unseen;
> While a kind glance at her pursuer flies,
> How much at variance are her feet and eyes!

There is nothing the writers of this kind of poetry are fonder of, than descriptions of pastoral presents. Philips says thus of a sheep-hook:

> Of season'd elm; where studs of brass appear,
> To speak the giver's name, the month, and year,
> The hook of polish'd steel, the handle turn'd,
> And richly by the graver's skill adorn'd.

The other of a bowl embossed with figures:

> ————where wanton ivy twines;
> And swelling clusters bend the curling vines;
> Four figures rising from the work appear,
> The various seasons of the rolling year;
> And what is that which binds the radiant sky,
> Where twelve bright signs in beauteous order lie?

The simplicity of the swain in this place, who forgets the name of the Zodiac, is no ill imitation of Virgil; but how much more plainly and unaffected would Philips have dressed this thought in his Doric?

> And what That height, which girds the Welkin sheen,
> Where twelve gay signs in meet array are seen?

If the reader would indulge his curiosity any farther in the comparison of particulars, he may read the first pastoral of Philips with the second of his contemporary, and the fourth and sixth of the former, with the fourth and first of the latter; where several parallel places will occur to every one.

Having now shown some parts, in which these two writers may be compared, it is a justice I owe to Mr Philips, to discover those in which no man can compare with him. First, that beautiful rusticity, of which I shall only produce two instances, out of a hundred not yet quoted:

> O woful day! O day of woe, quoth he,
> And woful I, who live the day to see?

That simplicity of diction, the melancholy flowing of the numbers, the solemnity of this sound, and the easy turn of the words, in this dirge (to make use of our author's expression) are extremely elegant.

In another of his pastorals a shepherd utters a dirge not much inferior to the former, in the following lines:

> Ah me the while! ah me, the luckless day!
> Ah luckless lad, the rather might I say;
> Ah silly I! more silly than my sheep,
> Which on the flow'ry plains I once did keep.

How he still charms the ear with these artful repetitions of the epithets; and how significant is the last verse! I defy the most common reader to repeat them without feeling some motions of compassion.

In the next place I shall rank his proverbs, in which I formerly observed he excels. For example,

> A rolling stone is ever bare of moss;
> And, to their cost, green years old proverbs cross.

> ———He that late lies down, as late will rise,
> And, sluggard-like, till noon-day snoring lies,
> Against ill luck all cunning foresight fails;
> Whether we sleep or wake it nought avails.
> Nor fear, from upright sentence, 'wrong.'

Lastly his elegant dialect, which alone might prove him the eldest born of Spenser, and our only true Arcadian. I should think it proper for the several writers of pastoral, to confine themselves to their several counties: Spenser seems to have been of this opinion; for he hath laid the scene of one of his pastorals in Wales, where, with all the simplicity natural to that part of our island, one shepherd bids the other good-morrow in an unusual and elegant manner.

> Diggon Davey, I bid her God-day;
> Or Diggon hur is, or I mis-say.

Diggon answers,

> Hur was her while it was day-light:
> But now hur is a most wretched wight,   &c.

But the most beautiful example of this kind that I ever met with, is a very valuable piece which I chanced to find among some old manuscripts, entituled, A Pastoral Ballad; which I think, for its nature and simplicity, may (notwithstanding the modesty of the title) be allowed a perfect pastoral. It is composed in the Somersetshire dialect, and the names such as are proper to the country people. It may be observed, as a farther beauty of this pastoral, the words Nymph, Dryad, Naiad, Faun, Cupid, or Satyr, are not once mentioned through the whole. I shall make no apology for inserting some few lines of this excellent piece. Cicily breaks thus into the subject, as she is going a milking;

> *Cicily*. Rager go vetch tha kee,[3] or else tha zun
> Will quite be go, beyore c'have half a don.
> *Roger*. Thou shouldst not ax ma tweece, but I've a be
> To dreave our bull to bull the parson's kee.

It is to be observed, that this whole dialogue is formed upon the passion of jealousy; and his mentioning the parson's kine naturally revives the jealousy of the shepherdess Cicily, which she expresses as follows:

> *Cicily*. Ah Rager, Rager, chee was zore avraid
> When in yond vield you kiss'd tha parson's maid:
> Is this the love that once to me you zed
> When from the wake thou broughtst me gingerbread?
> *Roger*. Cicily thou charg'st me false – I'll zwear to thee,
> Tha parson's maid is still a maid for me.

In which answer of his are expressed at once that 'spirit of religion,' and that 'innocence of the golden age,' so necessary to be observed by all writers of pastoral.

At the conclusion of this piece, the author reconciles the lovers, and ends the eclogue the most simply in the world:

> So Rager parted vor to vetch tha kee,
> And vor her bucket in went Cicily.

I am loth to shew my fondness for antiquity so far as to prefer this ancient British author to our present English writers of pastoral; but I cannot avoid making this obvious remark, that both Spenser and Philips have hit into the same road with this old west country bard of ours.

After all that hath been said I hope none can think it any injustice to Mr Pope, that I forbore to mention him as a pastoral-writer; since upon the whole he is of the same class with Moschus and Bion, whom we have excluded that rank; and of whose eclogues, as well as some of Virgil's, it may be said, that according to the description we have given of this sort of poetry, they are by no means pastorals, but 'something better.'

SOURCE: essay in *The Guardian*, No. 40 (Monday, 27 April 1713); reprinted in the collected edition of *Guardian Essays* (London, 1797), pp. 226–34.

NOTES

[These annotations are from the 1797 edn of *Guardian Essays* – Ed.]

1. See Rapin, *de Carm. Past.*, *pars* 3.
2. Ossian has forgot them, as Mr Pennant acutely observes.
3. That is the kine or cows.

John Gay   (1714)

[Gay here burlesques the theories of Tickell and Philips: see the preceding excerpts. – Ed.]

Great Marvell hath it been, (and that not unworthily) to diverse worthy Wits, that in this our Island of *Britain*, in all rare Sciences so greatly abounding, more especially in all kinds of Poesie flourishing, no Poet (though otherways of notable Cunning in Roundelays) hath hit on the right simple Eclogue after the true ancient guise of *Theocritus*, before this mine Attempt.

Other Poet travailing in this plain High-way of Pastoral know I none. Yet, certes, such it behoveth a Pastoral to be, as Nature in the Country affordeth; and the Manners also meetly copied from the rustical Folk therein. In this also my Love to my native Country *Britain* much pricketh me forward, to describe aright the Manners of our own honest and laborious Plough-men, in no wise sure more unworthy a *British* Poet's imitation, than those of *Sicily* or *Arcadie*; albeit, not ignorant I am, what a Rout and Rabblement of Critical Gallimawfry hath been made of late Days by certain young Men of insipid Delicacy, concerning, I wist not what, *Golden Age*, and other outragious Conceits, to which they would confine Pastoral. Whereof, I avow, I account nought at all, knowing no Age so justly to be instiled *Golden*, as this of *our Soveraign Lady Queen* ANNE.

This idle Trumpery (only fit for Schools and Schoolboys) unto that ancient *Dorick* Shepherd *Theocritus*, or his Mates, was never known; he rightly, throughout his fifth *Idyll*, maketh his Louts give foul Language, and behold their Goats at Rut in all Simplicity. [Quotes relevant verse in Greek – Ed.] . . .

Verily, as little Pleasance receiveth a true homebred Tast, from all the fine finical new-fangled Foolcries of this gay Gothic Garniture, wherewith they so nicely bedeck their Court Clowns, or Clown

Courtiers, (for, which to call them rightly, I wot not) as would a prudent Citizen journeying to his Country Farms, should he find them occupied by People of this motley Make, instead of plain downright hearty cleanly Folk: such as be now Tenants to the Burgesses of this Realme.

Furthermore, it is my Purpose, gentle Reader, to set before thee, as it were, a Picture, or rather lively Landscape of thy own Country, just as thou mightest see it, didest thou take a Walk in the Fields at the proper Season; even as Maister *Milton* hath elegantly set forth the same.

> *As one who long in populous City pent,*
> *Where Houses thick and Sewers annoy the Aire,*
> *Forth issuing on a Summer's Morn to breathe*
> *Among the pleasant Villages and Farms*
> *Adjoin'd, from each thing met conceives Delight;*
> *The Smell of Grain or tedded Grass or Kine*
> *Or Dairie, each rural Sight, each rural Sound.*

Thou wilt not find my Shepherdesses idly piping on oaten Reeds, but milking the Kine, tying up the Sheaves, or if the Hogs are astray driving them to their Styes. My Shepherd gathereth none other Nosegays but what are the growth of our own Fields, he sleepeth not under Myrtle shades, but under a Hedge, nor doth he vigilantly defend his Flock from Wolves, because there are none, as Maister *Spenser* well observeth.

> *Well is known that since the* Saxon *King*
> *Never was Wolf seen, many or some*
> *Nor in all* Kent *nor in Christendom.*

For as much, as I have mentioned Maister *Spenser*, soothly I must acknowledge him a Bard of sweetest Memorial. Yet hath his Shepherds Boy at some times raised his rustick Reed to Rhimes more rumbling than rural. Diverse grave Points also hath he handled of Churchly Matter and Doubts in Religion daily arising, to great Clerkes only appertaining. What liketh me best are his Names, indeed right simple and meet for the Country, such as *Lobbin, Cuddy, Hobbinol, Diggon*, and others, some of which I have made bold to borrow. Moreover, as he called his Eclogues *the Shepherd's Calendar*, and divided the same into the twelve Months, I have chosen (paradventure not overrashly) to name mine by the Days of the Week, omitting *Sunday* or the *Sabbath*, Ours being supposed to be Christian Shepherds, and to be then at Church worship. Yet further of many of Maister *Spenser*'s Eclogues it may be observed; though Months they be called, of the said Months therein, nothing is specified; wherein I have also esteemed him worthy mine Imitation.

That principally, courteous Reader, whereof I would have thee to be advised, (seeing I depart from the vulgar Usage) is touching the Language of my Shepherds; which is, soothly to say, such as is neither spoken by the country Maiden nor the courtly Dame; nay, not only such as in the present Times is not uttered, but was never uttered in Times past; and, if I judge aright, will never be uttered in Times future. It having too much of the Country to be fit for the Court; too much of the Court to be fit for the Country, too much of the Language of old Times to be fit for the Present, too much of the Present to have been fit for the Old, and too much of both to be fit for any time to come. Granted also it is, that in this my Language, I seem unto my self, as a *London* mason, who calculateth his Work for a Term of Years, when he buildeth with old Materials upon a Ground-rent that is not his own, which soon turneth to Rubbish and Ruins. For this point, no Reason can I alledge, only deep learned Ensamples having led me thereunto.

But here again, much Comfort ariseth in me, from the Hopes, in that I conceive, when these Words in the course of transitory Things shall decay, it may so hap, in meet time that some Lover of *Simplicity* shall arise, who shall have the Hardiness to render these mine Eclogues into such more modern Dialect as shall be then understood, to which end, Glosses and Explications of uncouth Pastoral Terms are annexed.

Gentle Reader, turn over the Leaf, and entertain thyself with the Prospect of thine own Country, limned by the painful Hand of
thy Loving Countryman

JOHN GAY

SOURCE: 'The Proeme' to *The Shepherd's Week* (1714); reproduced in V. A. Dearing (ed.), *John Gay: Poetry and Prose* (Oxford, 1974), I, pp. 90–2.

Jonathan Swift (1716)

... There is a young ingenious Quaker in this town who writes verses to his mistress, not very correct, but in a strain purely what a poetical Quaker should do, commending her look and habit, etc. It gave me a hint that a set of Quaker pastorals might succeed, if our friend Gay could fancy it, and I think it a fruitful subject; pray hear what he says. I believe farther, the pastoral ridicule is not exhausted, and that a porter, footman, or chairman's pastoral might do well. Or what think you of a Newgate pastoral, among the whores and thieves there?[1] . . .

SOURCE: Letter from Swift to Pope (30 Aug. 1716); in F. Elrington Ball (ed.), *The Correspondence of Jonathan Swift* (London, 1911), II, p. 330.

NOTE

1. [Ed.] Gay's *Beggar's Opera* may well have grown out of this suggestion.

Anonymous   (1738)

As the *Guardian* has thought it necessary to give a Receipt to make an *Epick Poem*, without a Genius; I think 'tis no less reasonable to give one for making an *Elegy*, after the same Manner, that is, without the Assistance of natural Parts, but merely mechanically; particularly, since I'm inform'd a great many Noblemen and Gentlemen Commoners of both Universities, have been discourag'd from shewing their Loyalty on the late Occasion,[1] for want of such a *Recipe*.

For a *Pastoral Elegy*

Take *Damon* and *Thyrsis*, both which Virgil will lend you with all his Heart; put them in a *Cave* together; be sure it be garnish'd well with Cypress, and don't forget a murmuring Stream, which may help you to a Rhyme or Simile upon Occasion. Let them lament *Daphnis* or *Pastorella*; or take any other Name, which you think will run off smoothly in your Verse. One thing never forget in the Conclusion, which is, to comfort your Shepherds with a Trail of Light, from which they will conclude, and inform us, the Nymph is gone off to Heaven; or else perhaps some silly Reader might not suspect it. Blast an old Oak or two, wither your Flowers *secundum Artem*, season it with Prodigies *quantum sufficit*, and 'twill make an excellent *Elegy*. . . .

SOURCE: extract from an unsigned letter to the *London Magazine* (March 1738).

NOTE

1. [Ed.] Possibly a reference to the death of Queen Caroline in 1737.

Samuel Johnson (1750; 1780)

1 On Pastoral and Country Life (1750)

In writing or judging of pastoral poetry, neither the authors nor criticks of latter times seem to have paid sufficient regard to the originals left us by antiquity, but have entangled themselves with unnecessary difficulties, by advancing principles, which, having no foundation in the nature of things, are wholly to be rejected from a species of composition in which, above all others, mere nature is to be regarded.

It is, therefore, necessary to enquire after some more distinct and exact idea of this kind of writing. This may, I think, be easily found in the pastorals of Virgil, from whose opinion it will not appear very safe to depart, if we consider that every advantage of nature, and of fortune, concurred to complete his productions; that he was born with great accuracy and severity of judgment, enlightened with all the learning of one of the brightest ages, and embellished with the elegance of the Roman court; that he employed his powers rather in improving, than inventing, and therefore must have endeavoured to recompense the want of novelty by exactness; that taking Theocritus for his original, he found pastoral far advanced towards perfection, and that having so great a rival, he must have proceeded with uncommon caution.

If we search the writings of Virgil, for the true definition of a pastoral, it will be found 'a poem in which any action or passion is represented by its effects upon a country life'. Whatsoever therefore may, according to the common course of things, happen in the country, may afford a subject for a pastoral poet.

In this definition, it will immediately occur to those who are versed in the writings of the modern criticks, that there is no mention of the golden age. I cannot indeed easily discover why it is thought necessary to refer descriptions of a rural state to remote times, nor can I perceive that any writer has consistently preserved the Arcadian manners and sentiments. The only reason, that I have read, on which this rule has been founded, is, that, according to the customs of modern life, it is improbable that shepherds should be capable of harmonious numbers, or delicate sentiments; and therefore the reader must exalt his ideas of the pastoral character, by carrying his thoughts back to the age in which the care of herds and flocks was the employment of the wisest and greatest men.

These reasoners seem to have been led into their hypothesis, by considering pastoral, not in general, as a representation of rural nature, and consequently as exhibiting the ideas and sentiments of those, whoever they are, to whom the country affords pleasure or employment, but simply as a dialogue, or narrative of men actually tending sheep, and busied in the lowest and most laborious offices; from whence they very readily concluded, since characters must necessarily be preserved, that either the sentiments must sink to the level of the speakers, or the speakers must be raised to the height of the sentiments.

In consequence of these original errors, a thousand precepts have been given, which have only contributed to perplex and to confound. Some have thought it necessary that the imaginary manners of the golden age should be universally preserved, and have therefore believed, that nothing more could be admitted in pastoral, than lilies and roses, and rocks and streams, among which are heard the gentle whispers of chaste fondness, or the soft complaints of amorous impatience. In pastoral, as in other writings, chastity of sentiment ought doubtless to be observed, and purity of manners to be represented; not because the poet is confined to the images of the golden age, but because, having the subject in his own choice, he ought always to consult the interest of virtue.

These advocates for the golden age lay down other principles, not very consistent with their general plan; for they tell us, that, to support the character of the shepherd, it is proper that all refinement should be avoided, and that some slight instances of ignorance should be interspersed. Thus the shepherd in Virgil is supposed to have forgot the name of Anaximander, and in Pope the term Zodiack is too hard for a rustick apprehension. But if we place our shepherds in their primitive condition, we may give them learning among their other qualifications; and if we suffer them to allude at all to things of later existence, which, perhaps, cannot with any great propriety be allowed, there can be no danger of making them speak with too much accuracy, since they conversed with divinities, and transmitted to succeeding ages the arts of life.

Other writers, having the mean and despicable condition of a shepherd always before them, conceive it necessary to degrade the language of pastoral, by obsolete terms and rustick words, which they very learnedly call Dorick, without reflecting, that they thus become authors of a mingled dialect, which no human being ever could have spoken, that they may as well refine the speech as the sentiments of their personages, and that none of the inconsistencies which they endeavour to avoid, is greater than that of joining elegance of thought with coarseness of diction. Spenser begins one of his pastorals with studied barbarity;

> Diggon Davie, I bid her good-day;
> Or, Diggon her is, or I missay.
> *Dig.* Her was her while it was day-light,
> But now her is a most wretched wight.
>
> SHEPHERD'S CALENDAR, 'September', 1–14

What will the reader imagine to be the subject on which speakers like these exercise their eloquence? Will he not be somewhat disappointed, when he finds them met together to condemn the corruptions of the church of Rome? Surely, at the same time that a shepherd learns theology, he may gain some acquaintance with his native language.

Pastoral admits of all ranks of persons, because persons of all ranks inhabit the country. It excludes not, therefore, on account of the characters necessary to be introduced, any elevation or delicacy of sentiment; those ideas only are improper, which, not owing their original to rural objects, are not pastoral. Such is the exclamation in Virgil,

> *Nunc scio quid sit Amor, duris in cautibus illum*
> *Ismarus, aut Rhodope, aut extremi Garamantes,*
> *Nec generis nostri puerum nec sanguinis, edunt;*
>
> ECLOGUES, VIII 43–5

> I know thee, love, in desarts thou wert bred,
> And at the dugs of savage tygers fed:
> Alien of birth, usurper of the plains.
>
> Dryden

which Pope endeavouring to copy, was carried to still greater impropriety.

> I know thee, Love, wild as the raging main,
> More fierce than tigers on the Libyan plain;
> Thou wert from Ætna's burning entrails torn,
> Begot in tempests, and in thunders born!
>
> 'Autumn', 89–92

Sentiments like these, as they have no ground in nature, are indeed of little value in any poem, but in pastoral they are particularly liable to censure, because it wants that exaltation above common life, which in tragick or heroick writings often reconciles us to bold flights and daring figures.

Pastoral being the 'representation of an action or passion, by its effects upon a country life', has nothing peculiar but its confinement to rural imagery, without which it ceases to be pastoral. This is its true characteristick, and this it cannot lose by any dignity of sentiment, or beauty of diction. The Pollio of Virgil, with all its elevation, is a composition truly bucolic, though rejected by the criticks; for all the images are either taken from the country, or from the religion of the age common to all parts of the empire.

The Silenus is indeed of a more disputable kind, because though the scene lies in the country, the song being religious and historical, had been no less adapted to any other audience or place. Neither can it well be defended as a fiction, for the introduction of a god seems to imply the golden age, and yet he alludes to many subsequent transactions, and mentions Gallus, the poet's contemporary.

It seems necessary, to the perfection of this poem, that the occasion which is supposed to produce it, be at least not inconsistent with a country life, or less likely to interest those who have retired into places of solitude and quiet, than the more busy part of mankind. It is therefore improper to give the title of a pastoral to verses, in which the speakers, after the slight mention of their flocks, fall to complaints of errors in the church, and corruptions in the government, or to lamentations of the death of some illustrious person, whom when once the poet has called a shepherd, he has no longer any labour upon his hands, but can make the clouds weep, and lilies wither, and the sheep hang their heads, without art or learning, genius or study.

It is part of Claudian's character of his rustick, that he computes his time not by the succession of consuls, but of harvests. Those who pass their days in retreats distant from the theatres of business, are always least likely to hurry their imagination with publick affairs.

The facility of treating actions or events in the pastoral stile, has incited many writers, from whom more judgment might have been expected, to put the sorrow or the joy which the occasion required into the mouth of Daphne or of Thyrsis, and as one absurdity must naturally be expected to make way for another, they have written with an utter disregard both of life and nature, and filled their productions with mythological allusions, with incredible fictions, and with sentiments which neither passion nor reason could have dictated, since the change which religion has made in the whole system of the world.

SOURCE: essay in *The Rambler*, No. 37 (24 July 1750); reproduced in W. J. Bate and Albrecht B. Strauss (eds), *The Works of Samuel Johnson* (New Haven, 1969), III, pp. 200–5.

II   On Milton's *Lycidas* (1780)

. . . One of the poems on which much praise has been bestowed is Lycidas; of which the diction is harsh, the rhymes uncertain, and the numbers unpleasing. What beauty there is, we must therefore seek in the sentiments and images. It is not to be considered as the effusion of real passion; for passion runs not after remote allusions and obscure opinions. Passion plucks no berries from the myrtle and ivy, nor calls upon Arethuse and Mincius, nor tells of rough satyrs, and fauns with cloven heel. Where there is leisure for fiction, there is little grief.

In this poem there is no nature, for there is no truth; there is no art, for there is nothing new. Its form is that of a pastoral – easy, vulgar, and therefore disgusting; whatever images it can supply are long ago exhausted; and its inherent improbability always forces dissatisfaction on the mind. When Cowley tells of Hervey, that they studied together, it is easy to suppose how much he must miss the companion of his labours, and the partner of his discoveries; but what image of tenderness can be excited by these lines?

> We drove a field, and both together heard,
> What time the grey fly winds her sultry horn,
> Battening our flocks with the fresh dews of night.

We know that they never drove a field, and that they had no flocks to batten; and though it be allowed that the representation may be allegorical, the true meaning is so uncertain and remote, that it is never sought, because it cannot be known when it is found.

Among the flocks, and copses, and flowers, appear the heathen deities; Jove and Phœbus, Neptune and Æolus, with a long train of mythological imagery, such as a college easily supplies. Nothing can less display knowledge, or less exercise invention, than to tell how a shepherd has lost his companion, and must now feed his flocks alone, without any judge of his skill in piping; and how one god asks another god what is become of Lycidas, and how neither god can tell. He who thus grieves will excite no sympathy; he who thus praises will confer no honour.

This poem has yet a grosser fault. With these trifling fictions are mingled the most awful and sacred truths, such as ought never to be polluted with such irreverend combinations. The shepherd likewise is now a feeder of sheep, and afterwards an ecclesiastical pastor, a superintendant of a christian flock. Such equivocations are always unskilful; but here they are indecent, and at least approach to impiety; of which, however, I believe the writer not to have been conscious.

Such is the power of reputation justly acquired, that its blaze drives away the eye from nice examination. Surely no man could have fancied that he read Lycidas with pleasure, had he not known the author. . . .

SOURCE: extract from 'Milton' in *The Lives of the Poets* (London, 1779–81; new edn, Edinburgh, 1820), pp. 144–6.

William Wordsworth   (1800)

. . . The principal object then which I proposed to myself in these Poems [*Lyrical Ballads* – Ed.] was to make the incidents of common life interesting by tracing in them, truly though not ostentatiously, the primary laws of our nature: chiefly as far as regards the manner in which we associate ideas in a state of excitement. Low and rustic life was generally chosen because in that situation the essential passions of the heart find a better soil in which they can attain their maturity, are less under restraint, and speak a plainer and more emphatic language; because in that situation our elementary feelings exist in a state of greater simplicity and consequently may be more accurately contemplated and more forcibly communicated; because the manners of rural life germinate from those elementary feelings; and from the necessary character of rural occupations are more easily comprehended; and are more durable; and lastly, because in that situation the passions of men are incorporated with the beautiful and permanent forms of nature. The language too of these men is adopted (purified indeed from what appear to be its real defects, from all lasting and rational causes of dislike or disgust) because such men hourly communicate with the best objects from which the best part of language is originally derived: and because, from their rank in society and the sameness and narrow circle of their intercourse, being less under the action of social vanity they convey their feelings and notions in simple and unelaborated expressions. Accordingly such a language arising out of repeated experience and regular feelings is a more permanent and a far more philosophical language than that which is frequently substituted for it by Poets, who think that they are conferring honour upon themselves and their art in proportion as they separate themselves from the sympathies of men, and indulge in arbitrary and capricious habits of expression in order to furnish food for fickle tastes and fickle appetites of their own creation . . .

SOURCE: extract from the Preface to *Lyrical Ballads* (1800 edn); reproduced in W. J. B. Owen and Jane Worthington Smyser (eds), *The Prose Works of William Wordsworth* (Oxford, 1974), pp. 122–3.

William Hazlitt   (1818)

. . . We have few good pastorals in the language. Our manners are not Arcadian; our climate is not an eternal spring; our age is not the age of gold. We have no pastoral-writers equal to Theocritus, nor any landscapes like those of Claude Lorraine. The best parts of Spenser's Shepherd's Calendar are two fables, Mother Hubberd's Tale, and the Oak and the Briar; which last is as splendid a piece of oratory as any to be found in the records of the eloquence of the British senate! Browne, who came after Spenser, and Withers, have left some pleasing allegorical poems of this kind. Pope's are as full of senseless finery and trite affectation, as if a peer of the realm were to sit for his picture with a crook and cocked hat on, smiling with an insipid air of no-meaning, between nature and fashion. Sir Philip Sidney's Arcadia is a lasting monument of perverted power; where an image of extreme beauty, as that of 'the shepherd boy piping as though he should never be old', peeps out once in a hundred folio pages, amidst heaps of intricate sophistry and scholastic quaintness. It is not at all like Nicholas Poussin's picture, in which he represents some shepherds wandering out in a morning of the spring, and coming to a tomb with this inscription – 'I also was an Arcadian!' Perhaps the best pastoral in the language is that prose-poem, Walton's Complete Angler. That well-known work has a beauty and romantic interest equal to its simplicity, and arising out of it. In the description of a fishing-tackle, you perceive the piety and humanity of the author's mind. It is to be doubted whether Sannazarius's Piscatory Eclogues are equal to the scenes described by Walton on the banks of the river Lea. He gives the feeling of the open air; we walk with him along the dusty road-side, or repose on the banks of the river under a shady tree; and in watching for the finny prey, imbibe what he beautifully calls 'the patience and simplicity of poor honest fishermen'. We accompany them to their inn at night, and partake of their simple, but delicious fare; while Maud, the pretty milk-maid, at her mother's desire, sings the classical ditties of the poet Marlow; 'Come live with me, and be my love.' Good cheer is not neglected in this work, any more than in Homer, or any other history that sets a proper value on the good things of this life. The prints in the Complete Angler give an additional reality and interest to the scenes it describes. While Tottenham Cross shall stand, and longer, thy work, amiable and happy old man, shall last! . . .

SOURCE: extract from 'On Thomson and Cowper', in *Lectures on the English Poets* (London 1818); reproduced in P. P. Howe (ed.), *The Complete Works of William Hazlitt* (London, 1930), III, pp. 98–9.

PART TWO

Twentieth-Century Studies

1. DEFINITIONS OF PASTORAL

W. W. Greg 'Pastoral Poetry and the Pastoral Ideal' (1906)

In approaching a subject of literary inquiry we are often able to fix upon some essential feature or condition which may serve as an Ariadne's thread through the maze of historical and aesthetic development, or to distinguish some cardinal point affording a fixed centre from which to survey or in reference to which to order and dispose the phenomena that present themselves to us. It is the disadvantage of such an artificial form of literature as that which bears the name of pastoral that no such *a priori* guidance is available. To lay down at starting that the essential quality of pastoral is the realistic or at least recognisably 'natural' presentation of actual shepherd life would be to rule out of court nine-tenths of the work that comes traditionally under that head. Yet the great majority of critics, though they would not, of course, subscribe to the above definition, have yet constantly betrayed an inclination to censure individual works for not conforming to some such arbitrary canon. It is characteristic of the artificiality of pastoral as a literary form that the impulse which gave the first creative touch at seeding loses itself later and finds no place among the forces at work at blossom time; the methods adopted by the greatest masters of the form are inconsistent with the motives that impelled them to its use, and where these motives were followed to their logical conclusion, the result, both in literature and in life, became a byword for absurd unreality. To live at all the ideal appeared to require an atmosphere of paradox and incongruity: in its essence the most 'natural' of all poetic forms, pastoralism came to its fairest flower amid the artificiality of a decadent court or as the plaything of the leisure hours of a college of learning, and its insipid convention having become 'a literary plague in every European capital', it finally disappeared from view amid the fopperies of the Roman Arcadia and the puerile conceits of the Petit Trianon.

Wherein then, it may be wondered, does the pastoral's title to consideration lie. It does not lie primarily, or chiefly, in the fact that it is associated with names of the first rank in literature, with Theocritus and Vergil, with Petrarch, Politian, and Tasso, with Cervantes and Lope de Vega, with Ronsard and Marot, with Spenser, Ben Jonson, and Milton; nor yet that works such as the *Idyls*, the *Aminta*, the *Faithful Shepherdess*, and *Lycidas* contain some of the most graceful and perfect verse to be found in any language. Rather is its importance to be sought in the fact that the form is the expression of instincts and impulses deep-rooted in the nature of humanity, which, while affecting the whole course of literature, at times evince themselves most clearly and articulately here; that it plays a distinct and distinctive part in the history of human thought and the history of artistic expression. Moreover, it may be argued that, from this point of view, the very contradictions and inconsistencies to which I have alluded make it all the more important to discover wherein lay the strange vitality of the form and its power of influencing the current of European letters.

From what has already been said it will be apparent that little would be gained by attempting beforehand to give any strict account of what is meant by 'pastoral' in literature. Any definition sufficiently elastic to include the protean forms assumed by what we call the 'pastoral ideal' could hardly have sufficient intension to be of any real value. If after considering a number of literary phenomena which appear to be related among themselves in form, spirit and aim, we come at the end of our inquiry to any clearer appreciation of the term I shall so far have attained my object. I notice that I have used the expression 'pastoral ideal', and the phrase, which comes naturally to the mind in connexion with this form of literature, may supply us with a useful hint. It reminds us, namely, that the quality of pastoralism is not determined by the fortuitous occurrence of certain characters, but by the fact of the pieces in question being based more or less evidently upon a philosophical conception, which no doubt underwent modification through the ages, but yet bears evidence of organic continuity. Thus the shepherds of pastoral are primarily and distinctively shepherds; they are not mere rustics engaged in sheepcraft as one out of many of the employments of mankind. As soon as the natural shepherd-life had found an objective setting in conscious artistic literature, it was felt that there was after all a difference between hoeing turnips and pasturing sheep; that the one was capable of a particular literary treatment which the other was not. The Maid of Orleans might equally well have dug potatoes as tended a flock, and her place is not in pastoral song. Thus pastoral literature must not be confounded with that which has for its subject the lives, the ideas, and the emotions of simple and unsophisticated mankind, far from the centres of our complex civilisation. The two may be in their origin related, and they occasionally, as it were, stretch out feelers towards one another, but the pastoral of tradition lies in its essence as far from the human document of humble life as from a scientific treatise on agriculture or a volume of pastoral theology. Thus the tract which lies before us to explore is equally remote from the idyllic imagination of George Sand, the gross actuality of Zola, and the combination of simple charm with minute and essential realism of Mr Hardy's sketches in Wessex. Nor does the adoption of the pastoral label suffice to bring within the fold the fanciful animalism of Mr Hewlett. By far the most remarkable work of recent years to assume the title is Signor d'Annunzio's play *La Figlia di Iorio*, a work in which the author's powerful and delicate imagination and wealth of pure and expressive language appear in matchless perfection. It is perhaps scarcely necessary to add that there is nothing in common between the 'pastoral ideal' and the rugged strength and suppressed fire of the great modern Italian's portrait of his native land of the Abruzzi.

Some confusion of thought appears to have prevailed among writers as to the origin of pastoral. We are, for instance, often told that it is the earliest of all forms of poetry, that it characterises primitive peoples and permeates ancient literatures. Song is, indeed, as old as human language, and in a sense no doubt the poetry of the pastoral age may be said to have been pastoral. It does not, however, follow that it bears any essential resemblance to that which subsequent ages have designated by the name. All that we know concerning the songs of pastoral nations leads us to suppose that they bear a close resemblance to the type of popular verse current wherever poetry exists, folk-songs of broad humanity in which little stress is laid on the peculiar circumstances of shepherd life. An insistence upon the objective pastoral setting is of prime importance in understanding the real nature of pastoral poetry; it not only serves to distinguish the pastoral proper from the more vaguely idyllic forms of lyric verse, but helps us further to understand how it was that the outward features of the kind came to be preserved, even after the various necessities of sophisticated society had metamorphosed the content almost beyond recognition. No common feature of a kind to form the basis of a scientific classification can be traced in the spontaneous shepherd-songs and their literary counterpart. What does appear to be a constant element in the pastoral as known to literature is the recognition of a contrast, implicit or expressed, between pastoral life and some more complex type of civilisation. At no stage in its development does literature, or at any rate poetry, concern itself with the obvious, with the bare scaffolding of life: whenever we find an author interested in the circle of prime necessity we may be sure that he himself stands outside it. Thus the shepherd when he sang did not insist upon the conditions amid which his uneventful life was passed. It was left to a later, perhaps a wiser and a sadder, generation to gaze with fruitless and often only half sincere longing at the shepherd-boy asleep under the shadow of the thorn, lulled by the low monotonous rustle of the grazing flock. Only when the shepherd-songs ceased to be the outcome of unalloyed pastoral conditions did they become distinctively pastoral. It is therefore significant that the earliest pastoral poetry with which we are acquainted, whatever half articulate experiments may have preceded it, was itself directly born of the contrast between the recollections of a childhood spent among the Sicilian uplands and the crowded social and intellectual city-life of Alexandria.[1]

As the result of this contrast there arises an idea which comes perhaps as near being universal in pastoral as any – the idea, namely, of the 'golden age'. This embraces, indeed, a field not wholly coincident with that of pastoral, but the two are connected alike by a common spring in human emotion and constant literary association. The fiction of an age of simplicity and innocence found birth among the Augustan writers in the midst of the complex and luxurious civilisation of Rome, as an illustration of the principle enunciated by Professor Raleigh, that 'literature has constantly the double tendency to negative the life around it, as well as to reproduce it'. Having inspired Ovid and Vergil, and been recognised by Lucretius, it passed as a literary legacy to Boethius, Dante and Jean de Meung; it was incorporated by Frezzi in his strange allegorical composition the *Quadriregio*, and was thrice handled by Chaucer; it was dealt with humorously by Cervantes in *Don Quixote*, and became the prey of the satirist in the hands of Juvenal, Bertini and Hall. The association of this ideal world with the simplicity of pastoral life was effected by Vergil, and in this form it was treated with loving minuteness by Tasso in his *Aminta* and by [William] Browne in his *Britannia's Pastorals*. The fiction no doubt answered to some need in human nature, but in literature it soon came to be no more than a polite convention.

The conception of a golden age of rustic simplicity does not, indeed, involve the whole of pastoral literature. It does not account either for the allegorical pastoral, in which actual personages are introduced, in the guise of shepherds, to discuss contemporary affairs, or for the so-called realistic pastoral, in which the town looks on with amused envy at the rustic freedom of the country. What it does comprehend is that outburst of pastoral song which sprang from the yearning of the tired soul to escape, if it were but in imagination and for a moment, to a life of simplicity and innocence from the bitter luxury of the court and the menial bread of princes.[2]

And this, the reaction against the world that is too much with us, is, after all, the keynote of what is most intimately associated with the name of pastoral in literature – the note that is struck with idyllic sweetness in Theocritus, and, rising to its fullest pitch of lyrical intensity, lends a poignant charm to the work of Tasso and Guarini. For everywhere in these soft melodies of luscious beauty, even in the studied sketches of primitive innocence itself, there is an undercurrent of tender melancholy and pathos:

Il mondo invecchia
E invecchiando intristisce.[3]

I have said that a sense of the contrast between town and country was essential to the development of a distinctively pastoral literature. It would be an interesting task to trace how far this contrast is the source of the various subsidiary types – of the ideal where it breeds desire for a return to simplicity, of the realistic where the humour of it touches the imagination, and of the allegorical where it suggests satire on the corruption of an artificial civilisation. . . .

SOURCE: extract from ch. 1, 'Foreign Pastoral Poetry', in *Pastoral Poetry and Pastoral Drama* (London, 1906), pp. 1–7.

NOTES

[Abbreviated from the original – Ed.]

1. The often cited pastoralism of the *Song of Solomon* resolves itself on investigation into an occasional simile. . . . With regard to possible Greek predecessors of Theocritus, it must be borne in mind that there were singing contests between shepherds at the Sicilian festival of Artemis, and it is possible that the competitors may have been sufficiently influenced by other orders of civilisation to have given a definitely pastoral colouring to their songs. Little is known of their nature beyond the fact that they probably contained the motive of the lament for Daphnis, which appears to be as old as Stesichorus. They have perished, all but the two lines which are found prefixed by way of a motto to Theocritus's *Idyls*. . . . What I have wished to emphasise above is the fact that because shepherds sang songs we have no reason to assume that these were distinctively pastoral. . . .

2. The tendency to form an ideal picture of his own youth is common both to mankind and man. The romance of childhood is the dream with which age consoles itself for the disillusionments of life. . . .

3. [Ed.] 'The world grows old, and ageing makes it sad'.

William Empson   Proletarian and Pastoral Literature   (1935)

. . . Gray's *Elegy* is an odd case of poetry with latent political ideas:

> Full many a gem of purest ray serene
> The dark, unfathomed caves of ocean bear;
> Full many a flower is born to blush unseen
> And waste its sweetness on the desert air.

What this means, as the context makes clear, is that eighteenth-century England had no scholarship system or *carrière ouverte aux talents*. This is stated as pathetic, but the reader is put into a mood in which one would not try to alter it. (It is true that Gray's society, unlike a possible machine society, was necessarily based on manual labour, but it might have used a man of special ability wherever he was born.) By comparing the social arrangement to Nature he makes it seem inevitable, which it was not, and gives it a dignity which was undeserved. Furthermore, a gem does not mind being in a cave and a flower prefers not be picked; we feel that the man is like the flower, as short-lived, natural, and valuable, and this tricks us into feeling that he is better off without opportunities. The sexual suggestion of *blush* brings in the Christian idea that virginity is good in itself, and so that any renunciation is good; this may trick us into feeling it is lucky for the poor man that society keeps him unspotted from the World. The tone of melancholy claims that the poet understands the considerations opposed to aristocracy, though he judges against them; the truism of the reflections in the churchyard, the universality and impersonality this gives to the style, claim as if by comparison that we ought to accept the injustice of society as we do the inevitability of death.

Many people, without being communists, have been irritated by the complacence in the massive calm of the poem, and this seems partly because they feel there is a cheat in the implied politics; the 'bourgeois' themselves do not like literature to have too much 'bourgeois ideology'.

And yet what is said is one of the permanent truths; it is only in degree that any improvement of society could prevent wastage of human powers; the waste even in a fortunate life, the isolation even of a life rich in intimacy, cannot but be felt deeply, and is the central feeling of tragedy. And anything of value must accept this because it must not prostitute itself; its strength is to be prepared to waste itself, if it does not get its opportunity. A statement of this is certainly non-political because it is true in any society, and yet nearly all the great poetic statements of it are in a way 'bourgeois', like this one; they suggest to many readers, though they do not say, that for the poor man things cannot be improved even in degree. This at least shows that the distinction the communists try to draw is a puzzling one; two people may get very different experiences from the same work of art without either being definitely wrong. One is told that the Russians now disapprove of tragedy, and that there was a performance of *Hamlet* in the Turk-Sib region which the audience decided spontaneously was a farce. They may well hold out against the melancholy of old Russia, and for them there may be dangerous implications in any tragedy, which other people do not see. I am sure at any rate that one could not estimate the amount of bourgeois ideology 'really in' the verse from Gray.

The same difficulty arises in the other direction. Proletarian literature usually has a suggestion of pastoral, a puzzling form which looks proletarian but isn't. I must worry the meaning of the term for a moment. One might define proletarian art as the propaganda of a factory-working class which feels its interests opposed to the factory owners'; this narrow sense is perhaps what is usually meant but not very interesting. You couldn't have proletarian literature in this sense in a successful socialist state. The wider sense of the term includes such folk-literature as is by the people, for the people, and about the people. But most fairy stories and ballads, though 'by' and 'for', are not 'about'; whereas pastoral though 'about' is not 'by' or 'for'. The Border ballads assume a society of fighting clans who are protected by their leaders since leaders can afford expensive weapons; the aristocrat has an obvious function for the people, and they are pleased to describe his grandeur and fine clothes. (This pleasure in him as an object of fantasy is the normal thing, but usually there are forces the other way.) They were class-conscious all right, but not conscious of class war. Pastoral is a queerer business, but I think permanent and not dependent on a system of class exploitation. Any socialist state with an intelligentsia at the capital that felt itself more cultivated than the farmers (which it would do; the arts are produced by overcrowding) could produce it; it is common in present-day Russian films, and a great part of their beauty (for instance the one called *The General Line* when it came to England). My reason for dragging this old-fashioned form into the discussion is that I think good proletarian art is usually Covert Pastoral.

Before theorising about this I had best speak of some recent English artists. A book like Lionel Britton's *Hunger and Love*, one of the few ostensibly proletarian works of any energy that England has to show (I disliked it too much to finish it), is not at all pastoral; it is a passionate and feverish account of a man trying to break his way out of the proletariat into the intelligentsia, or rather the lower middle class into the upper. As such it may be good literature by sheer force, and useful propaganda if it is not out of date by the time it is written, but what the author wanted was the opportunity not to be proletarian; this is fine enough, but it doesn't make proletarian literature. On the other hand nobody would take the pastoral of T. F. Powys for proletarian, though it really is about workers; his object in writing about country people is to get a simple enough material for his purpose, which one might sum up as a play with Christian imagery backed only by a Buddhist union of God and death. No doubt he would say that country people really feel this, and are wiser about it than the cultivated, and that he is their spokesman, but the characters are firmly artificial and kept at a great distance from the author. W. W. Jacobs makes the argument amusingly clear; it is not obvious why he is not a proletarian author, and it would annoy a communist very much to admit that he was. Probably no one would deny that he writes a version of pastoral. The truth that supports his formula is that such men as his characters keep their souls alive by ironical humour, a subtle mode of thought which among other things makes you willing to be ruled by your betters; and this makes the bourgeois feel safe in Wapping. D. H. Lawrence's refusal to write proletarian literature was an important choice, but he was a complicated person; to see the general reasons for it one had best take a simpler example. George Bissill the painter, who worked from childhood in the mines and did some excellent woodcuts of them, refused to work for the *New Leader* (which wanted political cartoons) because he had rather be a Pavement Artist than a Proletarian one. As a person he is obviously not 'bourgeois', unless being determined not to go back to the mines makes you that. Such a man dislikes proletarian art because he feels that it is like pastoral, and that that is either patronising or 'romantic'. The Englishman who seems to me nearest to a proletarian artist (of those I know anything about) is Grierson the film producer; *Drifters* gave very vividly the feeling of actually living on a herring trawler and (by the beauty of shapes of water and net and fish, and subtleties of timing and so forth) what I should call a pastoral feeling about the dignity of that form of labour. It was very much under Russian influence. But herring fishermen are unlikely to see *Drifters*; for all its government-commercial claim to solid usefulness it is a 'high-brow' picture (that blasting word shows an involuntary falsity in the thing); Grierson's influence, strong and healthy as it is, has something skimpy about it. Of course there are plenty of skilled workers in England who are proud of their skill, and you can find men of middle age working on farms who say they prefer the country to the town, but anything like what I am trying to call pastoral is a shock to the Englishman who meets it on the Continent. My only personal memory of this sort is of watching Spaniards tread out sherry grapes and squeeze out the skins afterwards, which involves dance steps with a complicated rhythm. I said what was obvious, that this was like the Russian Ballet, and to my alarm the remark was translated; any English worker would take it as an insult, probably a sexual one. They were mildly pleased at so obvious a point being recognised, and showed us the other dance step used in a neighbouring district; both ways were pleasant in themselves and the efficient way to get the maximum juice. The point is not at all that they were living simple pretty lives by themselves; quite the contrary; some quality in their own very harsh lives made them feel at home with the rest of civilisation, not suspicious of it. This may well show the backwardness of the country; for that matter there were the same feelings in Russia for the Soviets to use if they could get at them. They seem able to bring off something like a pastoral feeling in Spain and Russia, but in an English artist, whatever his personal sincerity, it seems dogged by humbug, and has done now for a long time. This may well be a grave fault in the English social system, but it is not one an English artist can avoid by becoming a proletarian artist. . . .

. . . The essential trick of the old pastoral, which was felt to imply a beautiful relation between rich and poor, was to make simple people express strong feelings (felt as the most universal subject, something fundamentally true about everybody) in learned and fashionable language (so that you wrote about the best subject in the best way). From seeing the two sorts of people combined like this you thought better of both; the best parts of both were used. The effect was in some degree to combine in the reader or author the merits of the two sorts; he was made to mirror in himself more completely the effective elements of the society he lived in. This was not a process that you could explain in the course of writing pastoral; it was already shown by the clash between style and theme, and to make the clash work in the right way (not become funny) the writer must keep up a firm pretence that he was unconscious of it. Indeed the usual process for putting further meanings into the pastoral situation was to insist that the shepherds were rulers of sheep, and so compare them to politicians or bishops or what not; this piled the heroic convention onto the pastoral one, since the hero was another symbol of his whole society. Such a pretence no doubt makes the characters unreal, but not the feelings expressed or even the situation described; the same pretence is often valuable in real life. I should say that it was over this fence that pastoral came down in England after the Restoration. The arts, even music, came to depend more than before on knowing about foreign culture, and Puritanism, suspicious of the arts, was only not strong among the aristocracy. A feeling gradually got about that any one below the upper middles was making himself ridiculous, being above himself, if he showed any signs of keeping a sense of beauty at all, and this feeling was common to all classes. It takes a general belief as harsh and as unreal as this to make the polite pretence of pastoral seem necessarily absurd. Even so there was a successful school of mock-pastoral for so long as the upper and lower classes were consciously less Puritan than the middle. When that goes the pastoral tricks of thought take refuge in child-cult. . . .

. . . The convention was, of course, often absurdly artificial; the praise of simplicity usually went with extreme flattery of a patron (dignified as a symbol of the whole society, through the connection of pastoral with heroic), done so that the author could get some of the patron's luxuries; it allowed the flattery to be more extreme because it helped both author and patron to keep their self-respect. So it was much parodied, especially to make the poor man worthy but ridiculous, as often in Shakespeare; nor is this merely snobbish when in its full form. The simple man becomes a clumsy fool who yet has better 'sense' than his betters and can say things more fundamentally true; he is 'in contact with nature', which the complex man needs to be, so that Bottom is not afraid of the fairies; he is in contact with the mysterious forces of our own nature, so that the clown has the wit of the Unconscious; he can speak the truth because he has nothing to lose. Also the idea that he is in contact with nature, therefore 'one with the universe' like the Senecan man, brought in a suggestion of stoicism; this made the thing less unreal since the humorous poor man is more obviously stoical than profound. And there may be obscure feelings at work, which I am unable to list, like those about the earth-touching Buddha. . . .

Thus both versions, straight and comic, are based on a double attitude of the artist to the worker, of the complex man to the simple one ('I am in one way better, in another not so good'), and this may well recognise a permanent truth about the aesthetic situation. To produce pure proletarian art the artist must be at one with the worker; this is impossible, not for political reasons, but because the artist never is at one with any public. The grandest attempt at escape from this is provided by Gertrude Stein, who claims to be a direct expression of the Zeitgeist (the present stage of the dialectic process) and therefore to need no other relation to a public of any kind. She has in fact a very definite relation to her public, and I should call her work a version of child-cult, which is a version of pastoral; this does not by any means make it bad. The point is to this extent a merely philosophical one, that I am not concerned to deny any practical claim made for what is called proletarian literature so long as the artist had not been misled by its theory; I only call it a bogus concept. It may be that to produce any good art the artist must be somehow in contact with the worker, it may be that this is what is wrong with the arts in the West, it may be that Russia is soon going to produce a very good art, with all the vigour of a society which is a healthy and unified organism, but I am sure it will not be pure proletarian art and I think it will spoil itself if it tries to be. . . .

The realistic sort of pastoral (the sort touched by mock-pastoral) also gives a natural expression for a sense of social injustice. So far as the person described is outside society because too poor for its benefits he is independent, as the artist claims to be, and can be a critic of society; so far as he is forced by this into crime he is the judge of the society that judges him. This is a source of irony both against him and against the society, and if he is a sympathetic criminal he can be made to suggest both Christ as the scapegoat (so invoking Christian charity) and the sacrificial tragic hero, who was normally above society rather than below it, which is a further source of irony. Dostoevsky is always using these ideas; perhaps unhealthily, but as very strong propaganda. But I doubt whether they are allowed in pure proletarian literature; the communists do not approve of them, either as tragic or Christian, both because they glorify the independent man and because they could be used against any society, including a communist one. . . .

The poetic statements of human waste and limitation, whose function is to give strength to see life clearly and so to adopt a fuller attitude to it, usually bring in, or leave room for the reader to bring in, the whole set of pastoral ideas. For such crucial literary achievements are likely to attempt to reconcile some conflict between the parts of a society; literature is a social process, and also an attempt to reconcile the conflicts of an individual in whom those of society will be mirrored. (The belief that a man's ideas are wholly the product of his economic setting is of course as fatuous as the belief that they are wholly independent of it.) So 'fundamentally true' goes to 'true about people in all parts of society, even those you wouldn't expect', and this implies the tone of humility normal to pastoral. 'I now abandon my specialised feelings because I am trying to find better ones, so I must balance myself for the moment by imagining the feelings of the simple person. He may be in a better state than I am by luck, freshness, or divine grace; value is outside any scheme for the measurement of value because that too must be valued.' Various paradoxes may be thrown in here; 'I must imagine his way of feeling because the refined thing must be judged by the fundamental thing, because strength must be learnt in weakness and sociability in isolation, because the best manners are learnt in the simple life' (this last is the point of Spenser's paradox about 'courtly'; the Book of Courtesy takes the reader among Noble Savages). Now all these ideas are very well suited to a socialist society, and have been made to fit in very well with the dogma of the equality of man, but I do not see that they fit in with a rigid proletarian aesthetic. They assume that it is sometimes a good thing to stand apart from your society so far as you can. They assume that some people are more delicate and complex than others, and that if such people can keep this distinction from doing harm it is a good thing, though a small thing by comparison with our common humanity. Once you allow the arts to admit this you will get works of art which imply that the special man ought to be more specially treated, and that is not proletarian literature.

It is for reasons like these that the most valuable works of art so often have a political implication which can be pounced on and called bourgeois. They carry an implication about the society they were written for; the question is whether the same must not be true of any human society, even if it is much better than theirs. My own difficulty about proletarian literature is that when it comes off I find I am taking it as pastoral literature; I read into it, or find that the author has secretly put into it, these more subtle, more far-reaching, and I think more permanent, ideas.

It would be interesting to know how far the ideas of pastoral in this wide sense are universal, and I think that to attempt a rough world-view brings in another point about the communist aesthetic. With the partial exception of *Alice* they are all part of the normal European tradition, but they might seem dependent on that, especially as dependent on Christianity. In my account the ideas about the Sacrificial Hero as Dying God are mixed up in the brew, and these, whose supreme form is Christianity, mainly belong to Europe and the Mediterranean. *The Golden Bough* makes a clear distinction between this hero and the Sincere Man as One with Nature, who is also sacrificial so far as national calamity proves that the emperor is not sincere, but refuses to try to separate them; it seems clear that they are at home respectively in the West and the East. On the other hand interest in the problems of the One and the Many, especially their social aspects, is ancient and obvious in the East, and many of the versions of pastoral come out of that. The idea of everything being included in the humble thing, with mystical respect for poor men, fools, and children, and a contrasting idea of everything being included in the ruling hero, were a main strand of Chinese thought by the third century BC; before Buddhism and not limited to Taoism. In China the feeling that everything is everything so nothing is worth doing, natural to this mode of thought, was balanced by the Confucian stress on the exact performance of local duties and ceremonies. One can make a list of European ideas with the same purpose, of making the immediate thing real, all of which stress the individual more or less directly and are denied in the East. God is a person; each separate individual is immortal, with the character he has acquired in this life; so one must continually worry about whether he is free; and he is born in sin so that he must make efforts; and because of this only a God, individual like the rest of us, is worthy to be sacrificed to God. These ideas were knocking about Europe before they were Christian, and the rejection of Christ may well be a less dangerous element in the communist position than the acceptance of Hegel. Gorki said in the early days of the Soviets that the great danger for Russia is that she may 'go East', a pregnant remark even if the East itself is inoculated against this sort of philosophy. It may be said that men always go in droves, and that all versions of the claim to individualism are largely bogus; but that gives the reason why the prop of individualist theory is needed. Once you have said that everything is One it is obvious that literature is the same as propaganda; once you have said that no truth can be known beyond the immediate dialectical process of history it is obvious that all contemporary artists must prepare the same fashionplate. It is clear too that the One is limited in space as well as time, and the no less Hegelian Fascists are right in saying that all art is patriotic. And the dialectical process proceeds through conflicts, so we must be sure and have plenty of big wars. Of course to talk like this is to misunderstand the philosophy, but once the philosophy is made a public creed it is sure to be misunderstood in some such way. I do not mean to say that the philosophy is wrong; for that matter pastoral is worked from the same philosophical ideas as proletarian literature – the difference is that it brings in the absolute less prematurely. Nor am I trying to say anything about the politics and economics, only that they do not provide an aesthetic theory.

In the following essays I shall try to show, roughly in historical order, the ways in which the pastoral process of putting the complex into the simple (in itself a great help to the concentration needed for poetry) and the resulting social ideas have been used in English literature. One cannot separate it from the hero business or from the device of 'pantification' (treating the symbol as everything that it symbolises, which turns out to be everything). The book is very far from adequate to such a theme; taken widely the formula might include all literature, and taken narrowly much of the material is irrelevant. Probably the cases I take are the surprising rather than the normal ones, and once started on an example I follow it without regard to the unity of the book. Certainly it is not a solid piece of sociology; for that matter many of the important social feelings do not find their way into literature. But I should claim that the same trick of thought, taking very different forms, is followed through a historical series.

SOURCE: extracts from ch. 1 in *Some Versions of Pastoral* (London, 1935; revised edn, 1979), pp. 4–9, 11–13, 13–14, 14–15, 16–17, 19–23.

W. H. Auden   'Arcadia and Utopia'   (1948)

. . . However he accounts for it, every adult knows that he lives in a world where, though some are more fortunate than others, no one can escape physical and mental suffering, a world where everybody experiences some degree of contradiction between what he desires to do and what his conscience tells him he ought to do or others will allow him to do. Everybody wishes that this world were not like that, that he could live in a world where desires would conflict neither with each other nor with duties nor with the laws of nature, and a great number of us enjoy imagining what such a world would be like.

Our dream pictures of the Happy Place where suffering and evil are unknown are of two kinds, the Edens and the New Jerusalems. Though it is possible for the same individual to imagine both, it is unlikely that his interest in both will be equal and I suspect that between the Arcadian whose favourite daydream is of Eden, and the Utopian whose favourite daydream is of New Jerusalem there is a characterological gulf as unbridgeable as that between Blake's Prolifics and Devourers.

In their relation to the actual fallen world, the difference between Eden and New Jerusalem is a temporal one. Eden is a past world in which the contradictions of the present world have not yet arisen;

New Jerusalem is a future world in which they have at last been resolved. Eden is a place where its inhabitants may do whatever they like to do; the motto over its gate is, 'Do what thou wilt is here the Law'. New Jerusalem is a place where its inhabitants like to do whatever they ought to do, and its motto is, 'In His will is our peace'.

In neither place is the moral law felt as an imperative; in Eden because the notion of a universal law is unknown, in New Jerusalem because the law is no longer a law-for, commanding that we do this and abstain from doing that, but a law-of, like the laws of nature, which describes how, in fact, its inhabitants behave.

To be an inhabitant of Eden, it is absolutely required that one be happy and likable; to become an inhabitant of New Jerusalem it is absolutely required that one be happy and good. Eden cannot be entered; its inhabitants are born there. No unhappy or unlikable individual is ever born there and, should one of its inhabitants become unhappy or unlikable, he must leave. Nobody is born in New Jerusalem but, to enter it, one must, either through one's own acts or by Divine Grace, have become good. Nobody ever leaves New Jerusalem, but the evil or the unredeemed are forever excluded.

The psychological difference between the Arcadian dreamer and the Utopian dreamer is that the backward-looking Arcadian knows that his expulsion from Eden is an irrevocable fact and that his dream, therefore, is a wish-dream which cannot become real; in consequence, the actions which led to his expulsion are of no concern to his dream. The forward-looking Utopian, on the other hand, necessarily believes that his New Jerusalem is a dream which ought to be realised so that the actions by which it could be realised are a necessary element in his dream; it must include images, that is to say, not only of New Jerusalem itself but also images of the Day of Judgement.

Consequently, while neither Eden nor New Jerusalem are places where aggression can exist, the Utopian dream permits indulgence in aggressive fantasies in a way that the Arcadian dream does not. Even Hitler, I imagine, would have defined his New Jerusalem as a world where there are no Jews, not as a world where they are being gassed by the million day after day in ovens, but he was a Utopian, so the ovens had to come in.

How any individual envisages Eden is determined by his temperament, personal history and cultural milieu, but to all dream Edens the following axioms, I believe, apply.

1) Eden is a world of pure being and absolute uniqueness. Change can occur but as an instantaneous transformation, not through a process of becoming. Everyone is incomparable.

2) The self is satisfied whatever it demands; the ego is approved of whatever it chooses.

3) There is no distinction between the objective and the subjective. What a person appears to others to be is identical with what he is to himself. His name and his clothes are as much *his* as his body, so that, if he changes them, he turns into someone else.

4) Space is both safe and free. There are walled gardens but no dungeons, open roads in all directions but no wandering in the wilderness.

5) Temporal novelty is without anxiety, temporal repetition without boredom.

6) Whatever the social pattern, each member of society is satisfied according to his conception of his needs. If it is a hierarchical society, all masters are kind and generous, all servants faithful old retainers.

7) Whatever people do, whether alone or in company, is some kind of play. The only motive for an action is the pleasure it gives the actor and no deed has a goal or an effect beyond itself.

8) Three kinds of erotic life are possible, though any particular dream of Eden need contain only one. The polymorphous-perverse promiscuous sexuality of childhood, courting couples whose relation is potential, not actual, and the chastity of natural celibates who are without desire.

9) Though there can be no suffering or grief, there can be death. If a death occurs, it is not a cause for sorrow – the dead are not missed – but a social occasion for a lovely funeral.

10) The Serpent, acquaintance with whom results in immediate expulsion – any serious need or desire.

The four great English experts on Eden are Dickens, Oscar Wilde, Ronald Firbank and P. G. Wodehouse.[1]

SOURCE: extract from 'Dingley Dell and The Fleet' (essay first published in 1948); reproduced in Auden's *The Dyer's Hand and Other Essays* (New York, 1962; London, 1963), pp. 409–11.

NOTE

1. To my surprise, the only creators of Edens during the last three centuries I can think of have all been English. [See Laurence Lerner's discussion, below, of Auden's Eden / New Jerusalem and Arcadian / Utopian distinctions – Ed.]

Frank Kermode   'Nature versus Art'   (1952)

... When Marvell ... wrote about a mower's hatred of gardens, he was representing the world of Nature, the uncultivated, the pure, by the untamed, uncorrupted fields; and the world of Art, the civilised, the cultivated, the sphere in which men had meddled with Nature, by the garden. He was, of course, simplifying for his own purposes a difficult philosophical opposition between Art and Nature, but he is none the less putting, with considerable subtlety, a point of view which was frequently expressed in the Renaissance, and which recurs with some persistence in the history of our literature. Probably the contrast between town and country – the social aspect of the great Art-Nature antithesis which is philosophically the basis of pastoral literature – was more poignant at that time than it has been since. London was becoming a modern metropolis, with a distinctively metropolitan ethos, before the eyes of its citizens, who were by tradition and even by upbringing much more rural than any town-dweller can now be. The plays of Jonson, and some of Shakespeare's too, contain many references to the new morality, the new men, the new social standing of the commercial classes, the growth of wealth not based upon the soil; and the death of an old order which hated usury and did not imagine that cakes and ale were hostile to virtue. The great Astrophel himself, like many other courtiers, was deeply in debt, and consciously living the life of a dead and lamented epoch – a kind of golden age of chivalry – in the age which saw the inauguration of modern capitalist finance. Puritanism, at its best a way of life and worship worthy of fine minds, was legitimately associated, by Jonson and others, with a tendency to hypocritical self-aggrandisement and to a mean interference with the traditional pleasures and customs of others. Essentially an urban growth, it was suspicious of country matters, and its hatred for the maypole and its associated sports, which Puritans rightly conjectured to be descended from pagan religious rites, was logical in a religious attitude which also condemned the drama. The satirist looked about him in a town which was turning into a metropolis, and observed that its citizen body was stratifying into new classes, actively discontented with the old dispensation, and living under a municipal authority predominantly Puritan. The court was held to be corrupt and affected; the increase in luxury and artificiality visible in the lives of courtier and burgher alike deeply troubled Jonson, who found that the language was imitating 'the public riot'. When Jonson turned from

Satire to Pastoral, at the end of his career, he lamented the death of an order as old, he thought, as the countryside; a way of life in which generosity, in the fullest sense of that word, accompanied a purity of life and pleasure which the Juvenalian town had exchanged for disease, obscurantism, affectation and bigotry. The moving passage from his *Sad Shepherd* which I have included in this collection is one of the themes which occur frequently in Elizabethan Pastoral.[1]

The contrast between town and country is frequently expressed in the literature of the period. There was a tendency to laugh at country folk, and this was a traditional activity; but there was also a tendency to idealise them. Overbury writes of a milkmaid:

The golden ears of corn fall and kiss her feet when she reaps them, as if they wished to be bound and led prisoners by the same hand that felled them. Her breath is her own, which scents all the year long of June, like a new made haycock. She makes her hands hard with labour, and her heart soft with pity: and when winter evenings fall early (sitting at her merry wheel) she sings a defiance to the giddy wheel of fortune. . . . The garden and bee-hive are all her physic and chirurgery, and she lives the longer for it. . . . Thus lives she, and all her care is she may die in the spring-time, to have store of flowers stuck upon her winding-sheet.[2]

Something of the Elizabethan sense of the urgent beauty of the country life emerges in Nicholas Breton's dialogue, 'The Courtier and the Countryman'. The Countryman speaks:

Now for the delight of our eyes, we have the May – painting of the earth, with flowers of dainty colours, and delicate sweets: we have the berries, the cherries, the peas and the beans, the plums and the codlings, in the month of June: in July the pears and the apples, the wheat, the rye, the barley and the oats, the beauty of the wide fields, and the labours with delight and mirth, and merry cheer at the coming home of the harvest cart. We have, again, in our woods the birds singing: in the pastures the cow lowing, the ewe bleating, the foal neighing, which profit and pleasure makes us better music than an idle note and a worse ditty, though I highly do commend music, when it is in the right key. Again, we have young rabbits that in a sunny morning sit washing their faces, while as I have heard there are certain old conies that in their beds sit painting of their faces. . . .

To all this, the worsted Courtier replies, 'I can the better bear with your humour because it is more natural than artificial, yet could I wish you would not so clownify your wit, as to bury your understanding under a clod of earth.' Which earns him the reproof, 'Now for your Nature and Art, I think better of a natural Art than an artificial Nature'; for this is a pastoral countryman, who understands the terms of the town. We might note what he has to say about love, the passion which occupies so much space in Elizabethan pastoral poetry:

And for love, if it be in the world, I think it is in the country, for where envy, pride, and malice and jealousy makes buzzes in men's brains, what love can be in their hearts, howsoever it slip from their tongues? No, no, our turtles ever fly together, our swans ever swim together, and our loves live and die together. Now if such love be among you, it is worthy to be made much of, but if you like today and loathe tomorrow, if all your love be to laugh and lie down, or to hope of gain or reward, that is none of our love. . . .

Here is the Golden Age envisaged in the countryside, all the more poignantly because the countryside is still very near one's own doorstep. This tension between town and country seems to be productive of the special kind of literature we call Pastoral. Poets were interested in the contrast between the wild and the cultivated. But their interest was not dependent entirely upon social changes and the discovery of ancient Pastoral; the interest of Renaissance poets in Nature was stimulated by the discovery of countries in which men were living in a state of nature, unaffected by Art, and outside the scope of Grace. Anyone who turns to Montaigne's essay *Of Cannibals* may read an account of one sensitive and subtle reaction to the news from the New World. The travellers came back with their accounts of the natives, or even brought the savages back with them – Montaigne conversed with some. But, because there were two opinions about natural men, one holding that they were virtuous because unspoilt, and the other that they were vicious because they belonged to what the theologians called the state of nature as opposed to the state of grace, the travellers emphasised the evidence which suited the theory they favoured; some reported the New World savages to live in perfect concord and happiness (as Montaigne says they did), but others found them treacherous and devil-worshipping. Both these views fell in neatly with preconceptions already held and already expressed in literature and philosophy. On the one hand there is the classic expression of Golden Age happiness in the much-imitated chorus of Tasso's *Aminta*; this could easily be extended to the 'naturalist' libertine poetry of Donne and Carew and Randolph, which Marvell subtly countered in his poetry. On the other hand there is the deeper examination of Nature and its true relationship to Art and Grace which Spenser in *The Faerie Queene*, Shakespeare in his last comedies, and Milton in *Comus* undertook. Each of these poets sometimes presents Nature for what it is – that state from which men, by nurture and grace, have been led away. The generous 'salvage man' in Spenser is so by reason of the cultivated stock from which he sprang; his nature is improved by the action of grace. The King's sons in *Cymbeline* cannot suppress their nobility, and Caliban is natural and vile in contrast with Miranda, who has the virtues of nobility; *nobile*, it was believed, was a contraction of *non vile*. Comus rules over the realm of Nature, and attempts to deprave the lady, who is clad in the magical armour of nobility and chastity, by using the very arguments of the 'naturalist'.

This is only a very hurried glimpse of the serious philosophic element which penetrates the English Pastoral of the Renaissance. In the longer poems, and in the plays, it is rarely far from the surface – as, for example, in Fletcher's *The Faithful Shepherdess*. It mingles with serious attempts to reproduce the ancient tradition in the modern Eclogue by inventing a native Doric and adapting the equipment of the Sicilian shepherd to his English equivalent; with studious adaptations and translations of modern authors like Mantuan, Sannazaro, Marot, Ronsard, Montemayor, Tasso and Guarini. Every device of literary Pastoral is found in some form or other in the poetry of this period; every use to which the kind can be put is exploited, from the ecclesiastical allegory which Googe derived from Mantuan to the elegies which Bryskett and Milton derived from Moschus. All the moral and scientific interests of the time found expression in the form, and the age's passion for allegory found the Pastoral a particularly congenial form of expression. In Spenser alone one may study almost every aspect of Renaissance Pastoral. It is generally acknowledged that the publication of *The Shepheardes Calender*, in 1579, was one of the most important events in the history of English poetry, and not only in the history of Pastoral. In this work Spenser, while not ignoring the charms of the English pastoral scene, which often gave the work of his contemporaries a fresh, unstudied charm, brought into the tradition of English poetry the influence of every great pastoral poet of the past, from Theocritus to the modern French poets. As E.K. says, after a roll-call of the bucolic poets of the past, Spenser follows their 'footing' everywhere, 'yet so as few, but they be wel sented, can trace him out'. [See excerpt in Part One, above – Ed.] Spenser's imagination worked freely within the classical tradition, which he explored in depth, but he was also capable of sustained efforts in heroic Pastoral of a sort not contemplated by the ancient poets. In the Sixth Book of the *Faerie Queene*, which is the Legend of Courtesy, we have the richest and most impressive example of a distinctively English development of the pastoral tradition, which was later imitated by Shakespeare and Milton.

But it is not only the great who engage us. Hundreds of poets wrote Pastoral in one form or another, and the general level of achievement was almost incredibly high; never had Pastoral seemed a more natural mode of song. And when its summer had passed, and poets had for a while contented themselves with re-examining the formal

Eclogue, there came Herrick, who seemed to look back on all the richness of the Elizabethan Pastoral and distil from it a nostalgic essence, and Marvell, whose handful of poems seem to sum up the whole story of the English Pastoral, inexhaustibly rich in their solemn undertones.

With Marvell the story really ends, for the later Pastoral lived in a quite different atmosphere, and in a quite different relationship to its readers. Marvell's lyrics, whenever they were written, were not published until the tradition in which they existed was already being forgotten. Dryden's translations of Theocritus are pert, as Theocritus never was; the true impulse of rustic Pastoral petered out; it was something the Giant Race had understood. The Pastorals of Pope show how much and how little the new poetry could do in this kind; in Pope there is a union, impossible a century earlier, between the practice and the academic theory of Pastoral. The eighteeenth century excelled in the mock-Pastoral, which is a kind of pantomime following the great play. The Augustans were often conscious of their defects, and Pope understood the significance of his addiction to mock-Epic; the *Dunciad*, he said, was a kind of satyr-play appended to the great trilogy of Homer, Virgil and Milton. It is not too difficult to see an analogy with mock-Pastoral. Human needs had, perhaps, not changed; but certain things of importance had reduced the relevance of the old Pastoral. London had lost the country; its maypole, as Pope observed, had been taken down. The literary and philosophical preoccupations of the Renaissance poets had largely given way to a new, or newly expressed, set of problems. The old poetry, and everything that gave it its peculiar richness, had been largely forgotten by the time Johnson expressed his rational objections to *Lycidas*. . . .

SOURCE: extract from the Introduction to *English Pastoral Poetry, from the Beginnings to Marvell* (London, 1952), pp. 37–42.

NOTES

1. Characteristically, Jonson chose the Robin Hood legend as the theme of his *Sad Shepherd*. This hero of the dead golden world of England echoes throughout Elizabethan Pastoral.

2. This Character, with others of the same kind, may be found in J. Dover Wilson, *Life in Shakespeare's England* (Cambridge, 1925).

Renato Poggioli 'Pastorals of Innocence and Happiness' (1957)

I

The psychological root of the pastoral is a double longing after innocence and happiness, to be recovered not through conversion or regeneration but merely through a retreat. By withdrawing, not from the world, but from 'the world', pastoral man tries to achieve a new life in imitation of the good shepherds of herds, rather than of the Good Shepherd of the Soul. The bucolic ideal stands at the opposite pole from the Christian one, even if it believes with the latter that the lowly will be exalted and that the only bad shepherds are shepherds of men. The bucolic invitation, to be like shepherds, although seemingly easier to follow than the Christian summons to self-sacrifice, has always remained a voice crying in the wilderness. Man has walked farther under the burden of Christ's cross than with the help of the shepherd's rod. Faith moves mountains, while a sentimental or aesthetic illusion is hardly able to force man to cross the short distance that separates town and country, or plowlands from woodlands. Christ kept his promise to his faithful, who found redemption and bliss through renunciation and martyrdom, while the few men who earnestly heeded the pastoral call found in no time that country life is at best a purgatory, and that real shepherds are even less innocent and happy than city-dwellers and courtiers.

If the Christian view rests on the cornerstone of creed, the pastoral ideal shifts on the quicksands of wishful thought. Wishful thinking is the weakest of all moral and religious resorts; but it is the stuff dreams, especially daydreams, are made of. Mankind had not to wait for Freud to learn that poetry itself is made of that stuff. The bucolic dream has no other reality than that of imagination and art. This is why it has been so often accused of insincerity by those wondering, with Raleigh, what kind of truth may be found 'in every shepherd's tongue'. Jacopo Sannazaro did not lie when he named Sincero the hero of his *Arcadia*, the earliest of all modern pastoral romances. Samuel Johnson may have been right in affirming in his *Life of Pope* that pastorals, 'not professing to imitate real life, require no experience'; yet his statement must be qualified by saying that they *are* a kind of experience. Although not a 'martyr' in the Christian sense, the literary shepherd may still be a 'witness', in the ancient meaning of that term. The testimony he bears is simply that it is easier to reach moral truth and peace of mind (in other terms, innocence and happiness) by abandoning the strife of civil and social living and the ordeal of human fellowship for a solitary existence, in communion with nature and with the company of one's musings and thoughts.

The ancient writers of Greece, when dealing with the contrast between town and country, never turned it to the advantage of the latter. All classical Greek poets, on the contrary, including the devotees of the lyric muse in its monodic as well as in its choral forms, expressed and celebrated the city-state, the *polis*, or at least the civic community. This remains true later even for the philosophers, whose peripatetic dialogues took place along the streets of Athens or under the porches of the Academy. Socrates speaks for all Greek culture when he says in the *Phaedrus* that he is looking for knowledge not in the woods and among trees, but within the city walls and among his fellow men. The contrast between town and country is equally alien to the Christian vision. In reply to a question from Charles Martel, Dante affirms (*Par.* viii) that for man on earth it would be worse if he were not civilised ('sarebbe il peggio / per l'omo in terra, se non fosse cive'). The Church itself is an *ecclesia*, or community of the faithful, and the Christian is a citizen of both Rome and the City of God. As Beatrice tells Dante (*Purg.* xxxii), the Earthly Paradise, that Arcadia of the spirit, is but a resting place during the soul's pilgrimage from the worldly to the heavenly city:

> Qui sarai tu poco tempo silvano;
> e sarai meco sanza fine cive
> di quella Roma onde Cristo è romano.

Here you will be for a while a denizen of the woods, and then you will dwell forever with me a citizen in that Rome of which Christ is a Roman.

In brief, the pastoral dispensation and its cultural fruits are neither Christian nor classical in essence. They are not a Hellenic but a Hellenistic product, which Roman literature inherited, and which each neo-classical age has reshaped in its own fashion after the Vergilian pattern or, less frequently, from Theocritus's original model. Theocritus himself was born in a great city, Syracuse, and lived in Alexandria, an even greater one. Thus the birth of the pastoral coincided with the decline of the ancient *polis* or city-state and with the appearance of a quasi-modern metropolis, which, as Rutilius Namatianus later said of imperial Rome, was more an *orbis* than an *urbs*. Yet, perhaps because of its complexity, the new urban center seems to reveal, besides the public and civic, the private and bourgeois side of life. Unlike Vergil's *Eclogues* (Excerpts, in the original sense), not all of Theocritus's *Idylls* (Little Pictures) are bucolic in form and content; several present mimetic scenes, depicting, in the fashion of the comedy of manners or of genre painting, the lives and mores of the little people of the great city. But most are the earliest pastorals we know, establishing for all time the pattern of the bucolic (from βουκόλος, guardian of cattle). They express a genuine love of the countryside, as well as the citydweller's yearning for greener pastures.

Vergil and after him many others have followed Theocritus's example in the pastoral, not only in conformity with the tradition of literary imitation, but also as a means to moral relaxation and emotional release. For pastoral poetry appears whenever the hustle and bustle of metropolitan life grows hard to bear and man tries to evade its pressures at least in thought. As civilisation becomes more complex and sophisticated, it tires man's heart, although it sharpens his wit. In the process the artistic and literary mind is made aware of cultural demands and psychological needs hardly felt before. Art and poetry tend to become more realistic and elegant, more ideal and passionate, more subjective and personal. From the very beginning pastoral poets seem to anticipate modern attitudes; to speak in Schillerian terms, they replace the 'naive' with the 'sentimental', looking with more irony at life and recoiling from the tragic and heroic sides of human experience. (Theocritus's *epyllia* are not miniature epic poems but semi-fabulous idylls.) Pastoral poets leave the theater and the agora, to cultivate, like Candide, their own garden, where they grow other flowers than those of communal myth and public belief.

II

As with all ways or visions of life, the pastoral implies a new ethos, which, however, is primarily negative. Its code prescribes few virtues, but proscribes many vices. Foremost among the passions that the pastoral opposes and exposes are those related to the misuse, or merely to the possession, of worldly goods. They are the passions of greed: cupidity and avarice, the yearning after property and prosperity, the desire for affluence and opulence, for money and precious things. The bucolic considers the pursuit of wealth – *auri sacra fames* – as an error as well as a crime, since it makes impossible 'the pursuit of happiness'. An acquisitive society, however, holds those two pursuits to be different aspects of the same virtue and views *enrichissez-vous* as a moral as well as an economic command. Thus the shepherd is the opposite of the *homo oeconomicus* on both ethical and practical grounds. Yet even the pastoral presupposes an economy of its own, which is home economics in the literal sense of the term. Pastoral economy seems to realise the contained self-sufficiency that is the ideal of the tribe, of the clan, of the family. The pastoral community produces all it needs, but nothing more, except for a small margin of security. It equates its desires with its needs; it ignores industry and trade; even its barter with the outside world is more an exchange of gifts than of commodities. Money, credit and debt have no place in an economy of this kind. By a strange and yet natural miracle, the system seems to avoid any disproportion between production and consumption, despite its lack of planning and foresight. The pastoral family head is never a provider in the bourgeois sense. Thrift is in him an almost mystical trait, even more than a necessary virtue; he never saves for a 'rainy day' that supposedly will never come. The shepherd of poetry finds his emblem not in the wise and prudent ant of the fable, who works all year round to be ready to face the challenge of winter, but in the carefree grasshopper, who spends all summer in song and dance.

Such a state of things presupposes a new Garden of Eden, where nature is a fertile mother and generous giver. All shepherds could tell their visitors what Vergil tells Dante when showing him the bounties of the Earthly Paradise (*Purg.* xxvii):

> Vedi l' erbette, i fiori e li arbuscelli,
> che qui la terra sol da sè produce.

Look at the grass, the flowers, and the little trees that earth grows here by itself.

Yet the spontaneous generation of the staples of life does not change the pastoral countryside into a Land of Cockaigne, where sausages hang on the trees and people indulge in a perpetual kermess. Manna does not fall on pastoral soil, and the shepherd neither fasts nor feasts but satisfies his thirst and hunger with earth's simplest gifts, such as fruit and water, or with the milk and cheese he gets from tending his sheep, which provide also the wool for his rustic garments. The shepherd does not need to grow wheat like the farmer, or prey on wildlife like the hunter. He is a vegetarian on moral as well as on utilitarian grounds, choosing to live on a lean diet rather than on the fat of the land. This is why only a few poets, and generally modern ones, describe their favorite pastoral country as a horn of plenty, overflowing with inexhaustible abundance. In his *Fábula de Polifemo y Galatea*, Góngora evokes fabulous Sicily, the historic breadbasket of the Roman Empire, as 'Bacchus's goblet and Pomona's orchard' ('copa es de Baco, huerto de Pomona'). Goethe, in the second part of *Faust*, paints his Arcadia as a land of milk and honey in so literal and exuberant terms as to change it into a wonderland or fairyland (III 9546–9):

Und mütterlich im stillen Schattenkreise
Quillt laue Milch bereit für Kind und Lamm;
Obst ist nicht weit, der Ebnen reife Speise,
Und Honig trieft vom ausgehöhlten Stamm.

And motherlike, within a quiet circle of shadows, warm milk flows for child and lamb; fruit is at hand, the ripe food of the meadow, and honey drips from the hollowed trunk.

Flowing happily and quietly under the protection of both Ceres and Flora, pastoral life is an economic idyll, made possible not only by nature's generosity but also by its mercy. The shepherd's existence is spared not only thirst and hunger, but also 'the penalty of Adam, / The seasons' difference' (*As You Like It*, II i): in brief, the inclemency of the weather. Thus all true pastoral lands are blessed with the pleasant mildness of an unchanging climate.

By picking berries and gathering straw the shepherd may fill his bowl and build a roof over his head. This redeems him from the curse of work, which is part of man's estate and the specific lot of the peasant, who earns his daily bread by the sweat of his brow. It is this triumph of the 'days' over the 'works', rather than the mere replacement of a rural with a pastoral setting, that marks the difference between the bucolic and the georgic. The shepherd enjoys the blessings of idleness even more than the rich man, whose servants hardly lighten his burdens and whose cares never allow him to rest. Thus literary shepherds form an ideal kind of leisure class, free from the compulsions of conspicuous consumption and ostentatious waste. Gratuitous interests, including such leisurely activities as hobbies and pastimes, but excluding such strenuous exercises as sports, are the main endeavor of the pastoral world. 'Deus nobis haec otia fecit' (I owe this happy leisure to a god), says Vergil's Tityrus (*Ecl.* i), who calls divine the donor of his farm for granting him, along with freedom from want, the freedom of his own time, or an exemption from occupations as well as from preoccupations. While for all other people time is money, the shepherd always has time to waste or to spare; and this enables him to put fun before duty and pleasure before business; or to follow no other will than his caprice.

This contrasts the shepherd with the merchant, the man who prefers *negotium* to *otium* and whose business is business; and also with the sailor, who ventures his life for adventure and profit. The shepherd of fiction is likewise neither a pioneer nor a settler but rather a homesteader or, better, a stay-at-home; he is never a nomad, as real shepherds are often forced to be. He lives a sedentary life even in the open, since he prefers to linger in a grove's shade rather than to wander in the woods. He never confronts the true wild, and this is why he never becomes even a part-time hunter. Venatical attitudes consistently oppose the pastoral: on one side they resemble too closely martial exploits; on the other, they are connected with Diana, the goddess of chastity, whom shepherds, unlike the hunter Hippolytus, neglect in favor of Venus. Pastoral life may reserve instead a small place for the fisherman, if he does not risk his life on the high seas, but throws his net not too far from shore or sinks his line into a nearby pond or brook. Such a fisherman is twin brother to the shepherd, and the congeniality, already discovered by Theocritus, was reasserted by Sannazaro, the first to write piscatory eclogues in Latin, followed by Bernardino Rota, who transplanted them into the vulgar tongue. Izaak Walton's view of amateur fishing as a quasi-pastoral calling is shown by his description in *The Compleat Angler* of its patient and leisurely practitioners as 'men of mild, and sweet, and peaceable spirits', far more philosophical and pious than hunters and falconers. Those words of praise may be applied to the literary shepherd himself, an old Adam who returns to the Garden of Eden, a stranded traveler who finds his island on terra firma, to prosper there without labors and hardships, a happy and indolent Robinson Crusoe.

III

The ideal of the perfect shepherd or, for that matter, of the complete angler is then based, like the Christian one, on the practice of poverty or, at least, on its praise. Both Christian theologians and pastoral poets see in that condition both a sign of humility and a token of grace. The former, however, exalt the pauper's estate because it teaches self-resignation; the latter, because it teaches self-contentment. The first alternative connects poverty with self-mortification and self-abasement; the second, with a self-gratification that finds its check in self-control. In brief, Christian poverty is a quest after innocence; pastoral poverty, after happiness as well. The truth of this may be seen in the very paradox of the main pastoral myth, which calls golden the times when there was no gold. The Golden Age, unlike Eldorado and the Gilded Age, is a dream of happiness without being a dream of wealth.

The logic of renunciation and sacrifice leads the Christian to become an anchorite, and to build the Thebais in the desert. Yet, even when it cloisters itself, a pastoral community cannot choose any hermitage other than the Abbaye de Thélème, where *Fay ce que vouldras* is the golden rule. The shepherd, unlike the saint or the monk, is obsessed by neither temptation nor guilt, and is free from the sense of sin. Being quiet and passive, he is rarely driven to sins of commission; as for sins of omission, he is inclined to treat them as virtues. Poverty teaches him practical rather than mystical lessons, and helps him to avoid the dangers of exaggeration and excess. He easily extends the theory and practice of moderation from the material to the moral field, from the sphere of property to that of power, and rejects ambition as well as greed. If there is a domain where he shows less self-restraint, up to the point of confusing liberty and licence, that is only in the realm of sex.

As a conscious or unconscious philosopher, the shepherd is neither a stoic nor a cynic, but rather an epicurean and observes with natural spontaneity the ethics of that school. His eudaemonism is not only spiritual but physical as well, and includes the practice of hedonism. The shepherd, rejecting sybaritic pleasure as spoiled by its extreme refinement and complexity, finds gratification not in the breach but in the observance of his ethos, based on the virtues of sobriety, frugality and simplicity. Like the aged Leo Tolstoy, the converted shepherd may find sensual delight, as well as moral contentment, by merely satisfying his needs; by discarding the obsessive luxury and the laborious comfort of 'high life' for simple living, with its homespun clothes, homely furnishings and unseasoned meals.

This enlightened hedonism, as well as the fact that vine growing and wine making are hard agricultural tasks, may easily explain why Bacchus, unlike Venus, plays a negligible role in the pastoral world. The drinking habits of shepherds, unlike those of peasants, are exemplary: pastoral mores have no place for intoxication and alcoholism. Only old satyrs, like Silenus, may indulge in that vice. Taking a leaf from the anacreontic, the pastoral allows that weakness as a compensation for the loss of youth, which puts the fruit of love out of man's reach. Age may well take everything away ('Omnia fert aetas'), as Vergil says (*Ecl.* ix), and yet it spares from its heavy toll the consoling oblivion provided, if fleetingly, by strong drink.

IV

Man may linger in the pastoral dreamworld a short while or a whole lifetime. Pastoral poetry makes more poignant and real the dream it wishes to convey when the retreat is not a lasting but a passing experience, acting as a pause in the process of living, as a breathing spell from the fever and anguish of being. Then it fixes the pastoral moment, within the category of space as well as of time, as an interval to be chosen at both the proper hour and the right point. The right point at which to stop and rest from a journey is a secluded spot, appealing to the traveller through the charm of its quiet and shade. Hence the topos of the *locus amoenus*, the 'lovely place' or ideal landscape, which, according to E. R. Curtius, medieval Latin literature received from Vergil and bequeathed to vernacular writing.

Curtius maintains that the commonplace is directly related to pastoral poetry, although it occurs elsewhere. Its presence in an epic or a chivalric poem, in a romance or a tragicomedy, foretells the unexpected apparition of a bucolic episode, which breaks the main action or pattern, suspending for a while the heroic, romantic or pathetic mood of the whole. Accordingly the topos itself is but an idyllic prelude to a bucolic interlude, where the characters rest from their adventures or passions. Since the pause normally occurs in an obscure and faraway place, the intermezzo itself should be termed the 'pastoral oasis'. Such 'oases' appear in the *Aeneid*, the *Commedia*, the *Furioso*, the *Lusíadas*, *Don Quixote*, and *As You Like It*. One of the most beautiful, and the most typical of them, is in Tasso's *Gerusalemme liberata* (vii). The episode, known as 'Erminia's stay among the shepherds', deserves analysis, since it is a complete summary of all the pastoral motifs emphasised up to this point.

The pagan maid Erminia dons the armor of the heroine Clorinda in order to save the wounded Tancredi, a Christian knight whom she loves in secret and without hope. A band of Crusaders pursues her by mistake, and she flees for her life. When night comes, she finds shelter in a wood. At dawn, she is wakened by birdsong, and grieves again about her plight. While weeping, she finds that her refuge is a *locus amoenus*, with lonely pastoral abodes ('alberghi solitarii de' pastori') nearby. Her plaint is suddenly interrupted by a mixed music of human songs ('pastorali accenti') and of rude woodpipes ('boscareccie inculte avene'). She moves forward and suddenly discovers in a shady grove an old man, who sits weaving baskets while watching his herd and listening to the song of three boys. The scene is a vision of perfect pastoral innocence, the more so since women are seemingly absent. The youths are frightened by the maiden's warlike attire, but Erminia takes off her helmet and shows herself to be but a damsel in distress. The situation is symbolic of the pastoral fear of even the signs of might and power. Erminia disclaims any intent to harm or disturb human beings who appear to her the favorites of God and fortune (VII vii):

> – Seguite, – dice – avventurosa gente
> al Ciel diletta, il bel vostro lavoro:
> ché non portano già guerra quest' armi
> a l'opre vostre, a i vostri dolci carmi.

Continue your lovely work, lucky folk beloved by Heaven; these weapons bring no war to your occupations, nor to your sweet songs.

Erminia then wonders why the security of these people seems not to be threatened by the war raging all over the countryside. The old man explains that they owe the exceptional peace they are enjoying to the obscurity of their dwelling place, to the mercy of the gods, who spare from cruelty and injustice the guiltless and the meek, and, above all, to a poverty that tempts nobody with promises of booty. The old man values highly the condition of poverty, while most men hold it in scorn, as worthless and despicable ('altrui vile e negletta; a me sì cara'); he considers it the pledge of a life untroubled by envy, either given or received. Thus, to its moral advantages, poverty adds practical ones. It guarantees the conservation of life, through a modicum of security. Poverty saves man from the blight of fear: no shepherd will ever think that the spring water he drinks may be poisoned by a rival or an enemy. But, above all, poverty emancipates man from the slavery of desire (VII ix) –

> Ché poco è il desiderio, e poco è il nostro
> bisogno onde la vita si conservi

Since we desire and need very little to conserve our life

– and relieves man from the burdens of wealth, the chief of which is having charge of a host of servants. The old shepherd is the patriarch but not the master of his clan, and this is why he lives in peace, without the responsibilities and worries of a taskmaster. He is the more conscious of the happy innocence of his way of life, since once he lost it and recovered it only through the ordeal of experience. In his youth he had been tempted into leaving the country for the city, and settled in the center of all splendor and power, the court. Although he served there only as a gardener, he soon realised that he had fallen into a den of iniquity, and returned without regret to his lonely and lovely place.

Erminia addresses the old shepherd with words recalling Vergil's 'fortunate senex' (*Ecl.* i), and asks him to grant her hospitality, in the hope that a stay among the shepherds will heal the wounds of her soul. Her sorrowful tale moves the tender heart of the old man, who welcomes and consoles her. He brings her to his wife, who helps her to don a shepherdess's garb. By doing so, Erminia perfectly observes the conventions of the pastoral oasis, which treats the bucolic experience as a temporary retirement to the periphery of life, as an attempt to charm away the cares of the world through the sympathetic magic of a rustic disguise. Yet the episode represents the pastoral ideal not in Erminia's reflected role but in the exemplary images of the old man and his wife 'che di conforme cor gli ha data il Cielo' (whom Heaven gave him, endowed with a heart like his).

This means that the natural outcome of the pastoral of innocence is the family situation, or the domestic idyll. As Tasso's episode shows, pastoral poetry prefers generally to present that idyll in terms of old age, rather than of youth. Some modern poets have changed the pattern: so, for instance, Goethe's *Hermann und Dorothea* is a bourgeois pastoral where all promise of domestic happiness is contained in a young couple's troth. Aware of his deviation, Goethe claimed to have followed a Homeric rather than a Vergilian example: to have written an *epyllion* rather than an *eidyllion*. Tasso's episode follows, however, the traditional scheme and portrays its old couple after an ancient and perfect archetype, Ovid's fable of Philemon and Baucis (*Met.* viii). In that fable sexual and parental love play no part and are replaced by the tender affections of the decline of life. It is not only their hospitality but the very purity of their souls that earns for Philemon and Baucis the grace of the gods. Jupiter and Mercury will grant them their wish, which is to die at the same time, and will change them into two trees, with mutually supporting trunks and interwoven branches.

V

If Erminia's stay among the shepherds, or the pastoral oasis of the *Gerusalemme*, mirrors the pastoral of innocence, Tasso's minor masterpiece, the pastoral drama *Aminta*, reflects with equal significance the other side of the picture, or the pastoral of happiness. The bucolic imagination equates happiness with the fulfillment of the passion of love, with the consummation of man's erotic wishes, and identifies unhappiness with the rejection or denial of one's heart's desire, in brief, with unrequited love. The second alternative may recur more frequently than the first, which is why pastoral poetry remodulates constantly in its saddest tunes what one might call after Apollinaire 'la chanson du mal aimé'. Love, however, may remain unsatisfied even when it is returned: when it is public morality, or the ties of honor and duty, rather than the heart's inconstancy or indifference that prevents the beloved one from heeding the entreaties of her lover. Love was born free, but family and society hold that winged creature in a gilded cage. Often pastoral poetry is but a voice of protest against society's power to replace the fruitions with the frustrations of love. When pastoral man becomes aware of the impossibility of realising here and now his ideal of an absolute erotic anarchism, his protest has no outlet but the very dream on which his heart feeds. Thus he projects his yearning after free love, his longing for sexual freedom and even licence, into a state of nature that exists nowhere, or only in the realm of myth.

The theme of *Aminta's* first chorus is a praise of free love or, rather, of the only time when Eros was really free. That was the Golden Age, which Tasso now lauds for that reason alone. 'O bella età de l'oro' (O beauteous Golden Age), exclaims the poet, not for being blessed by the spontaneous fertility of the earth and the everlasting clemency of the weather, nor for being spared the curses of war, trade and work (1 ii),

> Ma sol perché quel vano
> nome senza soggetto,
> quell'idolo d'errori, idol d'inganno,
> quel che da 'l volgo insano
> Onor poscia fu detto,
> che di nostra natura il feo tiranno,
> non mischiava il suo affanno
> fra le liete dolcezze
> de l'amoroso gregge;
> né fu sua dura legge
> nota a quell'alme in libertate avvezze;
> ma legge aurea e felice
> che Natura scolpì: *S'ei piace, ei lice.*

But only because that vain and hollow name, that idol of error and deceit, which the insane crowd later called honor, thus making it our nature's tyrant, had not yet mixed its worries among the merry delights of the amorous throng; nor was its harsh law known to those souls accustomed to freedom, but rather the happy and golden rule that nature engraved: *What delights, is lawful.*

It is noteworthy that in the closing sentence Tasso uses as a term of praise almost the same words Dante had employed (*Inf.* v) to suggest one of the worst transgressions of the sexual instinct, and to indict that Semiramis who by legalising incest 'libito fé licito in sua legge' (made a law of her pleasure). In Tasso's version, 'S'ei piace, ei lice', the formula seems to anticipate the Freudian view, with its acceptance of the libido and the pleasure principle.

The pastoral longing is but the wishful dream of a happiness to be gained without effort, of an erotic bliss made absolute by its own irresponsibility. This, rather than a sense of decency, is the very reason why the pastoral often limits the sexual embrace to mere kissing, so as to escape the danger of parenthood and the nuisance of birth control. (In this connection, nothing is more typical in a pastoral sense than the episode of Rousseau's *Confessions* that goes under the name of 'l'idylle des cérises'.) Yet in its extreme form pastoral happiness is conceived as an absolute acceptance of the law of instinct, with no sense of guilt or any regard for its consequences. This was well understood by Thomas Mann when he described in *The Magic Mountain* . . . the feelings suggested by Debussy's *L'Après-midi d'un faune:* . . .

The youthful faun was very happy in his flowery meadow. Here there was no

'Justify yourself!', no responsibility. . . . Here reigned oblivion itself, the blissful arrest of very motion, the innocence of timelessness. It was licentiousness in quiet conscience, the daydreamlike apotheosis of each and every denial of the Western imperative of action.

All this means that the task of the pastoral imagination is to overcome the conflict between passion and remorse, to reconcile innocence and happiness, to exalt the pleasure principle at the expense of the reality principle. No one prized the pleasure principle more highly than those eighteenth-century representatives of libertine thought whose literary education had been conditioned by pastoral poetry. Even the greatest among the *philosophes* used the bucolic convention in their protest against authority and conformism in matters of sexual morality. In this field, Diderot was a greater emancipator than even Voltaire or Rousseau. His most extreme affirmation of the legitimacy of free love is the *Supplément au voyage de Bougainville*, which inaugurates the modern attempt to replace the Arcadias of old with the islands of the South Seas, where the white man lives merrily and happily with many female companions, rather than with a single masculine slave or helpmate, as Robinson Crusoe with his man Friday. Diderot stated his message in the subtitle summing up the theme of the *Supplément* as 'l'inconvénient d'attacher des idées morales à certaines actions physiques qui n'en comportent pas' (the inconvenience of applying moral standards to certain physical acts for which they have no relevance).

It is the reality principle which, by proving that erotic happiness cannot be fully attained in our civilisation, has forced the modern pastoral imagination to find other havens beyond the Western world. Yet the pleasure principle has reasserted itself even within the boundaries of our culture, pushing the moral limits of passion even further than pagan licence would have done. Thus many writers of our time have used the pastoral dispensation to justify the claims of homosexual love. André Gide dared to protest against the exclusion of that forbidden territory from love's realm in a book that he named after Vergil's Corydon, disregarding the fact that the original Corydon is a half-comic, half-pathetic character, doomed to a hopeless infatuation for a boy. That the dark region of that unnatural passion is still envisaged in pastoral images may be proved by the title *Arcadie* given by a group of Parisian writers to a new little review pleading and preaching the cause of sexual perversion.

The pastoral is aristocratic in temper, yet the operation of the pleasure principle prevents it from falling into the pitfalls of romantic love. A shepherd may love a duchess; but what he loves is the woman in her. Bucolic Eros cares more for *amour-passion* than for *amour-vanité*, for freshness and youth rather than for glamour and charm. Pastoral love is unromantic in the sense that it looks down rather than up, that it prefers a simple and rustic loveliness to the elegant beauty of a fashionable paramour. George Santayana felt this truth when in his *Three Philosophical Poets* he reproached Goethe for having made Helena the queen of Arcadia, during Faust's brief sojourn in that land: 'But to live within Arcadia Helen was not needed; any Phyllis would have served.' This implies that the pastoral is a private, masculine world, where woman is not a person but a sexual archetype, the eternal Eve.

That world is but a utopian projection of the hedonistic instinct, the demands of which may be stated in Goethe's exhortation in the same Arcadian episode: 'Arkadisch frei sei unser Glück!' (Let our bliss be arcadically free!). This obsession with an unrestrained erotic happiness makes a modest pastoral almost impossible. In such a context there is no 'cold pastoral' in the Keatsian sense of the term. Yet a 'warm pastoral' is equally rare, since the fire of love cannot burn continuously without fuel, and passion's devouring flame is reduced to a flicker under the ashes. It is more human and natural to treat of love in elegiac than in idyllic terms. Hence the most poignant of all pastoral love motifs seem to be, to use the formula by which George Orwell defined Housman's poetry in his essay *Inside the Whale*, nothing more than 'hedonism disappointed'. When he warns his reader with such words as Vergil's 'Nunc scio, quid sit Amor' (Now I know what Love is; *Ecl.* viii), the pastoral poet is about to bare the emptiness, rather than the fullness, of a frustrated heart. . . .

SOURCE: extract from 'The Oaten Flute', in *Harvard Library Bulletin*, XI, no. 2 (Spring 1957); reproduced in *The Oaten Flute: Essays on Pastoral Poetry and the Pastoral Ideal* (Cambridge, Mass., 1975), pp. 1–16.

T. G. Rosenmeyer   'Pastoral and the Theocritean Tradition'   (1969)

At the end of the first book of Plato's *Republic*, Socrates confesses to Thrasymachus that there has been something restless and greedy about his search. 'For instead of finding out what justice is, I moved on to the next question and the one after that, asking whether justice is good or bad, or whether it is profitable.' Discussions of the pastoral lyric often suffer from a similar lack of frugality. We are ready to assume that we are dealing with a pastoral whenever a poem shows an interest in the countryside, no matter whether the subject is cattle or olive groves, highland rocks or greensward; or whether the mood is lyrical or anthropological.[1] Even what I shall call the 'Hesiodic' world, the arena of sweat and labor and farmers' almanacs, is often included in the general scope of what is understood by pastoral. The poets themselves, by certain willful or perhaps malicious titlings, have added to the lavishness. Tennyson's 'Dora', a ballad in the spare biblical style without a trace of feeling for nature, prompted Wordsworth's admiration: 'I have been endeavouring all my life to write a pastoral like your "Dora" and have not succeeded.'[2]

It is important to listen to the poets. In all probability a tidy definition of what is pastoral about the pastoral tradition is beyond our reach. The tradition is extraordinarily rich and flexible. And yet, at first glance, definers may take courage from the presence of certain features which have always struck the critics of the genre, and prompted the charge that pastoral cramps originality. Johnson's notorious snort, 'easy, vulgar, and therefore disgusting',[3] derives from his judgement that the genre is inherently imitative. It was, he felt, classical, and had changed little since the days of Theocritus and Virgil. [See first Johnson excerpt in Part One, above – Ed.] . . .

Tradition, imitation, continuity of artistic purpose: these were the auspices under which the pastoral lyric was transmitted to the modern world. More than most literary forms its familiar patterns appealed to those who thought of the whole field of literature as compartmentalised, and who drew confidence from what they regarded a natural articulation of its parts. No wonder that Renaissance critics were surprised to find that Aristotle had not included the genre in his discussion. Antonio Sebastiano Minturno, one of their leaders, decided that Aristotle's omission could be accounted for on the assumption that Aristotle considered pastoral a subspecies of epic.[4] Aristotle would, of course, have had to be clairvoyant to include the pastoral in his treatment, seeing that the genre did not come into being until two generations after his death.[5] But even after the advent of Theocritus, Hellenistic and Roman critics appear to have made no room for a separate pastoral genre. Longinus, for instance, compares Homer favorably with Apollonius and Theocritus (*On the Sublime*, ch. 33). When, in speaking of Theocritus, he refers to his *Bucolica*, the term is parallel to the title of Apollonius's poem, *Argonautica*, hence not a genre designation. One is intrigued to note that, once again, Theocritus appears to be thought of as a writer of epic; and this is paralleled in Quintilian (10.1.55), though he describes the *musa rustica et pastoralis* as a special type of epic. We may assume that Proclus and other Byzantine scholars, as well as other medieval critics who failed to recognise a separate pastoral genre, were guided by this ancient classification of Theocritus and Virgil as writers of epic. In imitation of Quintilian, Minturno divided epic verse into *heroici* (*summi*), *epici* (*mediocres*), and *bucolici* (*infimi*), though most of his immediate predecessors, presumably catching fire from the contemporary stirrings which were to lead to Tasso's *Aminta*, designated pastoral a *genus dramaticum*. Another classification, which goes back to the first century AD and Manilius's *Astronomy* (2.39 ff.), counts Theocritus among the didactic poets, along with Homer and Hesiod.

The scholars, it appears, found it rather difficult to identify the special characteristics of pastoral, more difficult, in fact, than Johnson's gibe would have led us to expect. We shall return to the pastoral as epic, which has much to be said in its favor. When the Renaissance finally came round to the view that pastoral was a genre in its own right, the identification was achieved at an unacceptable cost. The critics proceeded to argue for certain canons of theme, form, and mood which held out little hope for the inclusion of much of Theocritus or Virgil. This is especially true of the narrow definitions offered by J. C. Scaliger, with their stress on decorum and instruction.[6] Such exclusiveness was not destined to last. The quarrel between neo-classicists and the supporters of *le bon sens* – that is, in Britain, the quarrel between the camps of Rapin and Fontenelle – helped to relax the canon.[7] [See excerpts in Part One, above – Ed.]

In our day the pendulum may be said to have swung too far in the opposite direction. William Empson's conception of the pastoral is so general that it accommodates an ample spectrum of experiences and styles.[8] The same latitude characterises the treatment of pastoral in the essays of Renato Poggioli, the one modern critic whose pronouncements on the pastoral rival Empson's in influence.[9] The importance of the story of Ahab and Naboth in Poggioli's thinking indicates that he, like Empson, regards social criticism, whether overt or hidden, as an important element in the pastoral convention. Pastoral, on this assumption, is a kind of anatomy. ... [For statements by Empson and by Poggioli, see previous material in this section of Part Two – Ed.] How uninformative the term 'pastoral' has become, perhaps as a reaction to Renaissance constraints, is shown in the *Pastorals* of Graham Hough, a collection of poems which convey, above all, emptiness and horror.[10] ...

Throughout the history of the genre, therefore, both critics and poets have on occasion permitted themselves a wide margin in their

interpretation of what a pastoral is. A definition of the genre and its
limits is likely to run counter to much accumulated experience. We
are reminded of Coleridge's 'Do not let us introduce an Act of
Uniformity against poets'.[11] Nevertheless it will be useful, if only for
the establishing of first guidelines, to tabulate what earlier generations have found fit to include under the heading of the term. We need
not indulge in the frenzy of division which mars some of the
classifications of the Renaissance, particularly Scaliger's whose
categories merrily scramble formal and substantive criteria: Quarrels, Rejoicings, Thanksgivings, Loves, Entreaties, Complaints, Love
Songs, Monodies, Vows, Recitals of Happenings, Rustic Festivities,
Encomia, Conversations, Dialogues between a Suitor and a Maiden,
and so forth.[12] But we must recognise that this divisionary ardor,
operating by the principle of 'divide and conquer', is a critical
response to the feeling that pastoral is full and expansionist.

The French *Eclogues of State*, headed by Ronsard's 'Chant Pastoral',[13] owed their thematic variety to the view that public as well as
private matters could be taken up in pastoral form. But along with
this pride in diversity went an important caveat. The apparatus, that
is, the characters and the setting, were felt to be subject to restriction.
Guillaume Colletet, for instance, a seventeenth-century successor of
Scaliger, allows goatherds, shepherds, and cowherds; he disallows
herders of pigs or horses, hunters, fishermen, laborers and sailors.[14]
The reasons Colletet gives for his exclusions are interesting, and bear
on some of the matters which will be discussed in the body of this
study. Pigs are dirty; horses are not essential to the economy; hunters
are never still enough; fishermen may not talk; and laborers and
sailors work too hard. The exclusions are, it appears, based on specific
assumptions about the kind of people and activities that best
represent the ethos to be associated with the pastoral. These
assumptions may of course vary. Pope wishes to exclude Virgil's first
Eclogue because its herdsmen are ex-soldiers; Chatterton's eclogues
give soldiers a prominent place, as does Coleridge's 'Fire, Famine,
and Slaughter: A War Eclogue'.[15] But these, along with the town
eclogue (Swift), the native eclogue (Ramsay), and the exotic eclogue
(Collins), are virtuoso attempts to conquer new territory. Their
authors are conscious of the innovatory character of their undertakings. For our discussion they will prove to be of little use. . . .

There is another factor complicating matters. In antiquity the
pastoral lyric is usually self-sufficient. Later its patterns and its moods
become ingredients in other genres, especially drama and romance.
Dio Chrysostom's *The Hunters of Euboea*[16] and Longus's *Daphnis and
Chloe* provide our earliest hints of the new mixture. The pure pastoral

lyric, on the order of Marlowe's 'Passionate Shepherd to his Love', is rarely found among the more significant products of the European pastoral tradition. By comparison with the pastoral romance and pastoral drama, not to mention opera, the pastoral lyric is often the preserve of lesser poets, as if a serious poet could not properly concern himself with a type of literature that lacked complexity and weight. To compensate for this lack Thomas Purney, chaplain at Newgate Prison and one of the more interesting eighteenth-century critics of the pastoral, demanded that the pastoral have a plot and a certain length and a moral result. His insistence on what he calls the *implex fable*, corresponding roughly to Aristotle's complex plot, marks the impatience with which intelligent men regarded the slightness and the lack of Aristotelian virtues in the conventional pastoral lyric.[17]

This impatience, which is also at the root of Johnson's acerbity, has always been particularly pronounced in England. As a result of it, we may speak of two pastoral traditions in English literature. To quote E. K. Chambers:

On the one hand, there is a body of poetry, transparent, sensuous, melodious, dealing with all the fresh and simple elements of life, fond of the picture and the story, rejoicing in love and youth, in the morning and the spring; on the other, a more complex note, a deeper thrill of passion, an affection for the sombre, the obscure, the intricate, alike in rhythm and in thought, a verse frequent with reflections on birth and death, and their philosophies, a humour often cynical or pessimistic. . . . Donne and his fellows write pastorals, but the shepherd's smock sits awkwardly upon them. They twist the bucolic theme and imagery to the expression of alien emotions and alien ideas, . . . 'the hands are the hands of Esau, but the voice is the voice of Jacob'.[18]

Much English criticism has, because of its attraction to complexity and ferment, encouraged the notion that the best pastoral is the least traditional. Chambers's first type is frequently referred to as merely decorative.[19] Dissatisfaction, even embarrassment, with the 'thinness' of the Theocritean model has led to the conclusion that the value of a pastoral poem is proportionate to its distance from the ancient simplicities, and its convergence with the more complex structures of romance and drama. If a pastoral lyric cannot be used within the economy of a larger pattern, as in Sidney's *Arcadia* or a Shakespearean comedy, then it should itself exhibit some of the richer harmonies.[20]

The relation between pastoral and drama is of much interest. . . . Now it is undeniable that the pastoral lyric requires a sense of drama, even if there is no formal contest or confrontation between two characters. That is one of the reasons why Horace, Tibullus, and even Ovid are not lightly to be associated with the pastoral tradition. But it is important that the dramatic element in pastoral be distinguished from drama proper, the art of the theater. Pastoral does not make for a movement toward explosion or reconciliation, death or resolution, as tragedy and comedy do. If we take Theocritus as our norm, a pastoral lyric involves little action, no development, no dramatic peripety, and in fact only so much drama as is needed to show that men must love and hate to be men; which is to say that there are characters, and the natural friction between characters, but no plot.

There is another way of putting this. Let me, in anticipation of a later theme, distinguish between a Stoic and an Epicurean use of character. The Stoic, in his actions, seeks conformity with the natural patterns and tensions of his world. His behavior is founded on an insight into his standing within a larger whole. His conduct is, as it were, syllogistic; it answers to a continuous barrage of questions which he must ask himself as he goes along. That is why drama, and the autobiographical essay, are appropriate vehicles for Stoic thought. The Senecan character and the Elizabethan soliloquiser know that they are, in Epictetus's well-known phrase, players with an assigned role (*Enchiridion*, section 17). The Stoic strikes a pose because that pose is a token of his mission to fulfill his promise as a man.

The Epicurean, on the other hand, attempts to live a life determined by pleasure, and pleasure is unreflected. He is at his best, at his most enjoyably human, when he comes closest to the unposed simplicity of the animal, or, if the accent is on intellectual joy, when he achieves a simplicity that is analogous to the spontaneity of the animal. The herdsmen of Theocritus are, obviously, of the Epicurean rather than of the Stoic type. They rarely strike a pose; they never point beyond themselves. Their careers within the poetry are self-terminating; they do not invite us to meet them halfway on some common or uncommon ground of opinion. A Daphnis, in spite of his laments, is a part of the scenery; a Thyestes or an Oedipus – or, for that matter, a Colin Clout – tries to gauge his distance from the environment, or to grow into it.

The affinity between Theocritean pastoralism and Epicurean hedonism will continue to interest us in subsequent sections of this study. What matters here is the incommensurability of early pastoral, on the one hand, and dramatic tension, on the other. It follows that in a consideration of the classical forms of pastoral, the 'pastoral' epigrams of Theocritus and the poets of the *Greek Anthology* should be disregarded. They exhibit the dramatic structure which Emil Staiger and others have analysed. They build to a climax, and a resolution, and they usually make a point. All this is quite the reverse of what is found in the pastoral idylls. There are modern examples of pastoral poetry that show a kinship with the pastoral epigram. Mallarmé's 'L'Après-midi d'un Faune' and Verlaine's *Fêtes galantes* are cases in point, the former exemplifying the dramatic structure and the intellectual brilliance, the latter exhibiting the mordancy and the minute compass of the epigram. Even some of the more traditional bucolics, such as Pope's fourth *Pastoral* ('Winter') and Ambrose Philips's fifth *Pastoral*, possess a degree of sophistication, a certain unquiet exoticism, that brings to mind the epigrammatic branch of the larger tradition of the idyll. But in the present study the pastoral epigram will be regarded as lying beyond the confines of the material in which we shall interest ourselves.

We conclude that drama plays only a very limited role in the pastoral of Chambers's first type. If we adopt the distinction proposed by Chambers and others, we must ask at what point a poem that contains pastoral elements ceases being a traditional or decorative pastoral. Once more, by a different route, we have returned to the principal issue: the nature of the pastoral; and once more the road appears to be blocked. It should not surprise anyone that the difficulties encountered in the criticism of any genre – the confluence and interdependence of romance, anatomy, apologue, and so forth – lie in wait also for the critic of the pastoral. The definition of a genre works by a process of abstraction. The vast majority of compositions must be triangulated from more than one fix. But pastoral has one advantage over the novel: it got its start in antiquity. If one looks for works that, given certain premises furnished by a succession of uneccentric critics, require a minimum of triangulation, the search leads us back into time, to pieces that stand at the beginning. Homer is likely to satisfy the demand for a test-case epic; Sophocles is looked to for supplying some of the important canons of tragedy; Heliodorus's *Ethiopian Tales* is generally accepted as the paradigm of romance. Just so it is easier to generate the criteria for an understanding of pastoral poetry from Theocritus rather than from Donne, and from Virgil rather than from Marino. . . .

. . . [It] is, I think, possible to differentiate the pastoral, and not only the ancient pastoral, from other kinds of poetry, and to define a unique pastoral mood which prevails when tempers clash, or when sadness jostles joy. The key word here is: detachment. About this I propose to speak at length [in a later chapter]. Here I can only suggest that the pastoral of Theocritus and his successors tends to achieve its successes by showing rather than telling. It presents a bird's-eye view of characters in action rather than an intimate exploration of motives and impulses. Virgil stands somewhat apart from the norm, and so do many of the metaphysicals. In our day Frost's regionalism recovers the impersonality, the mental distance, that is the hallmark of Theocritus's vignettes.[21] John Crowe Ransom connects Milton's choice of the pastoral form of 'Lycidas' with his 'intention to be always anonymous as a poet'.[22] It is probable that the pastoral was popular in the Renaissance because the rules of the genre permitted the poet to disregard, or virtually to refashion, his own feelings, and to disappear as a person behind the artifact of the poem. This provides an additional reason why Horace's references to the country, and their echoes in later European literature, should not be counted examples of pastoral writing. They are part of his spiritual and aesthetic autobiography. Horace felt happy and comfortable on his farm, away from the city. The emphasis is on his own sensations, not on the responses of a small set of characters unrelated to himself. It does not matter that, as in *Epistles* 1.16, he can draw a rustic landscape better than anybody else in the Augustan age. On the contrary, this is further proof of the same non-pastoral perception; alone with his satisfactions and his genial ease, Horace can fix his eyes on the color and the contours of the setting. The pastoral lyric . . . eschews descriptions of nature. . . .

. . . I suspect that Poggioli's 'pastoral of the self' is really the adaptation, and in effect the distortion, of pastoral toward confession and anatomy, purposes which are originally foreign to the mood of the pastoral.[23] Cervantes's Marcela, who, in Poggioli's opinion, paves the way for the pastoral of the self, is not a pastoral singer at all, but a tragic heroine who happens to choose the trappings of the pastoral life in order to make an impression on her fellows, while rejecting the advances of her lover. She is the enemy of the pastoral ideal; she is the coy lady from the cup of Theocritus's *Idyll* 1.

I dwell on Poggioli's treatment because his essays are among the few really interesting modern discussions of the pastoral, but also because in their way they represent a typical trend. As his remarks on Marcela, on Shakespeare's Jaques, and on Rousseau and Goethe show, he looks at pastoral largely from the vantage point of one interested in the European scene during the sixteenth, seventeenth and eighteenth centuries. When he coins the terms 'pastoral of solitude', 'pastoral of self', and the like, he appears to be committing himself to a teleological view: that pastoral started in a certain smallish way and developed to greater and greater heights, which were reached when the British and the Spanish poets created the pastoral of melancholy. Clearly, in Poggioli's mind, the poems of Donne and Marvell and the plays of Shakespeare and Goethe are more valuable and worthier of discussion than the rather bland structures which initiated the line.

A similar judgement is implied in the choices of William Empson. His speculations about the genre, like Poggioli's, are drawn from the most developed and the most differentiated products of the tradition. Like Poggioli also, Empson assumes that the pastoral must serve an openly moral purpose. With Scaliger and other Renaissance critics, Empson regards any literary piece, and especially the pastoral, as designed to impart instruction in a pleasurable form and to impel toward action. We can enjoy pastoral because it enables us to live, on our terms, with a nature we have abandoned; pastoral relieves our sense of loss without forcing us to give up our new gains as beneficiaries of the industrial age. This comes remarkably close to an old theory of the origins of pastoral as therapy, a theory invented by the Peripatos to supply a history where none existed. According to it, pastoral was designed as an instrument for salvation in a time of stress. Few ancient readers, one assumes, were fooled by this hypothesis. Plutarch's syllabus of reading matter for the young, *A Young Man's Guide to the Poets*, does not mention a single pastoral writer. Plutarch evidently did not believe that Theocritus would improve an adolescent mind or promote the integration of a youth in society. True, moral purpose in Plutarch is something quite different from social adjustment in Empson; but the two meet on the common ground of improvement.

If we look at the Theocritean pastoral, we find that it is neither an instrument for action or reconciliation, nor the vehicle of a program, nor is it philosophical in the sense in which, say, the romantic lyric is. It does not body forth a view of the world, except by accident and implication. It presents a picture of human intercourse that has philosophical analogues, ... But it does not attempt to place man in his environment in conformity to a metaphysical or ideological scheme. This is to the advantage of the pastoral, for it escapes the need to confront what romantics discovered to be the chief difficulty, how man could be conceived both as a product of nature and as an autonomous being. . . .

SOURCE: extracts from *The Green Cabinet: Theocritus and the European Pastoral Lyric* (Berkeley, Cal., 1969), pp. 3–4, 4–6, 6–8, 9–10, 11–13, 15–16, 16–18.

NOTES

[Reorganised and renumbered from the original – Ed.]

1. For a recent example, see D. J. Gillis, 'Pastoral Poetry in Lucretius', *Latomus*, 26 (1967), pp. 339–62.

2. Hallam Tennyson, *Tennyson: A Memoir* (London, 1897), I, p. 265.

3. Samuel Johnson's comments on pastoral are to be found in his *Rambler* essays, nos. 36 and 37; in his 'Milton' 'Pope' and 'Philips' (*Lives of the Poets*); in *Rasselas*, ch. 19; and in the *Adventurer*, no. 92.

4. Cited by René Rapin in his *Dissertatio de Carmine Pastorali* (1659), translated by Thomas Creech and prefixed to the latter's translation of the Idylls of Theocritus (Oxford, 1684), pp. 18–19.

5. Some modern critics, also, refuse to grant pastoral an independent standing.

6. J. C. Scaliger, *Poetices libri septem* (1561). Pastoral is discussed in Bk I, ch. 4, and Bk 5, ch. 5.

7. For details of the quarrel, see Thomas Purney, *A Full Enquiry into the True Nature of Pastoral* (London, 1717); critical edn, ed. Earl Wasserman (Berkeley, Cal., 1948).

8. W. Empson, *Some Versions of Pastoral* (London, 1935; rev. edn, 1979).

9. [Ed.] Renato Poggioli's essays were collected posthumously in *The Oaten Flute* (Cambridge, Mass., 1975). The story of Ahab and Naboth is discussed in ch. 10, 'Naboth's Vineyard: The Pastoral View of the Social Order'.

10. Graham Hough, *Legends and Pastorals* (London, 1961).

11. Cited by I. A. Richards, in T. A. Sebeok, (ed.) *Style in Language* (Bloomington, Ind., 1960), p. 9.

12. See A. Hulubei, *L'Eglogue en France au XVIe Siècle* (Paris, 1938), p. 18.

13. An elegiac amœbean commentary on the marriage of Ronsard's protectress, Marguerite of Savoy (1559).

14. J. E. Congleton, *Theories of Pastoral Poetry in England, 1684–1798* (Gainesville, Fl., 1952), p. 198.

15. R. F. Jones, 'Eclogue Types in English Poetry of the Eighteenth Century', *Journal of English and Germanic Philology*, 24 (1925), pp. 33–60.

16. The title is Moses Hadas's, in his translation of Dio's seventh oration in his *Three Greek Romances* (New York, 1953).

17. Thomas Purney, *A Full Inquiry into the True Nature of Pastoral* (1717), pp. 6ff.

18. E. K. Chambers (ed.), *English Pastorals* (London, 1895), pp. *xvii–xviii*.

19. See, e.g., E. W. Tayler, *Nature and Art in Renaissance Literature* (New York, 1964).

20. See W. W. Greg, *Pastoral Poetry and Pastoral Drama* (London, 1906), pp. 416ff.

21. See John F. Lynen, *The Pastoral Art of Robert Frost* (New Haven, Conn., 1960).

22. J. C. Ransom, 'A Poem Nearly Anonymous', *American Review*, 4 (1933).

23. R. Poggioli, 'The Pastoral of the Self', in *The Oaten Flute* (op. cit.).

Harry Levin   'The Golden Age'   (1970)

... We cannot look back to an age which did not look back toward *illud tempus*, time immemorial, half-forgotten days of yore, melted snows of yesteryear, *antan*. That ultimate recollection has always been sealed and separated from its commemorators by a cataclysm of some kind. Such was the giant race before the flood; such was life in the garden before the fall; such was the *douceur de vivre* before the revolution. After so many aeons of more or less painful vicissitude, man instinctively longs to reestablish contact with what he has never ceased to regard as his aboriginal situation. The elder statesman, Nestor, may shake his head, recalling his grandsires and reminding his juniors that they are lesser men than their fabulous forebears. But the old Yankee farmer is more realistic when he remarks, 'Things ain't so good as they used to be, and they never were'. Their memory keeps receding like a mirage; yet it remains, as Sir Kenneth Clark has stated, 'the most enchanting dream which has ever consoled mankind, the myth of a golden age in which man lived on the fruits of the earth, peacefully, piously, and with primitive simplicity'.[1] Consoled – the formulation is apt in suggesting the wastelands of actuality that loom behind this vision of well-being. The dream might be described by folklorists as an etiological fable, explaining how men came to be alienated from nature and why they have lived too seldom in peace and plenty, justice and freedom, leisure and love.

The consequence is their desire to recapture that primal freshness, to restore that innocence which later ages have blemished. The earliest age of mankind is associated with the verdure of springtime, with the spontaneity of childhood, and often with the awakening of love. Long before and long after Petrarch, poets have been chanting variations on the theme: 'Nel dolce tempo della prima etade ...'.[2] Novelists, discovering for themselves the principle that ontogeny recapitulates phylogeny, have concentrated more and more intensively on the joys and pangs of adolescence. In his book of reminiscent sketches, *The Golden Age*, Kenneth Grahame refers to his adults as the Olympians, with the implication that children are the true Saturnians, reliving the infantile fantasies of the race. 'Wo Kinder sind', said Novalis, 'da ist ein Goldnes Zeitalter' [Where children are, there is a Golden Age].[3] Nostalgia for a happier day would be a sterile emotion, if it merely sighed for what was not; encouraged by the rotation of the seasons, it is transfigured into a hope for recurrence. The Judeo-Christian tradition moves from paradise lost to paradise regained, from Eden through the wilderness to Canaan, the land flowing with milk and honey, and hence from retrospection to prophecy. It looks forward from the peaceable kingdom of Isaiah, where swords are beaten into plowshares while the wolf dwells with the lamb, toward the Apocalypse, with its city of resplendent gold, the New Jerusalem. And when these visions shift from the past to the future, they harbor terrors as well as hopes; Antichrist must battle with the Messiah, and Doomsday precede the kingdom of God on earth.

Our primary concern, however, is not millennial but primitivistic. Not only must we begin at the very beginning, but we shall be repeatedly coming back to it. Now cultural primitivism – which we need not distinguish here from chronological primitivism, since we shall be involved with chronology soon enough – has been paradoxically defined by its most authoritative students, Arthur Lovejoy and George Boas, as 'the discontent of the civilised with civilisation'.[4] Its exemplar is the queen who plays milkmaid or the artist who goes native on a South Sea isle. As the definition should imply, the positive thrust of this attitude has been provoked by a negativistic recoil: that is to say, the praise of times past, its *laus temporis acti*, is an implicit critique of nowadays. Moreover, the predilection for what it fancies to be primitive is essentially a sophisticated, not to say a sentimental, state of mind. That man is happy, it asserts, who lives far from affairs, like the pristine race of mortals.

> Beatus ille qui procul negotiis,
>   ut prisca gens mortalium,   [5]
>   . . .

And, having distinguished sharply between the alternatives of business and leisure, *negotium* and *otium*, Horace continues with a townsman's nostalgic description of the countryside and concludes by revealing that his spokesman is a money-lender, who will be back at his counter after a short vacation. Those sentiments have been emulated by weekenders and exurbanites ever since. The way of rural life especially envied by the city-dwelling poet is the leisure he imagines the shepherd to enjoy, fondly imagining – if we may judge from the immense accumulation of poems devoted to this notion – that shepherds spend more of their efforts in chasing shepherdesses than sheep. It is not for nothing that the homely word for herdsman, *swain*, has become synonymous with lover. Other humble outdoor occupations, such as fishing, have occasionally vied with the tending of sheep or of goats as subjects for poetic idealisation; the Renaissance produced a few piscatories along with its innumerable pastorals. But the classic ideal of pastoralism, refining upon the folkways of a sheep-grazing culture, would be hallowed by its coalescence with the Christian symbolism of the pastor and his flock. The emblem of Jesus, the lamb, tinges Chaucer's picture of 'The Former Age', when he commemorates 'The lambish peple, voyd of alle vyce.'[6] The pasture is the playground of Spenser's spokesman, Colin Clout, in *The Shepheardes Calender:*

> O happy *Hobbinoll*, I blesse thy state,
> That Paradise hast found, which *Adam* lost.

The pastoral, as a literary form, was primitivistic rather than primitive: sentimental rather than naive, in Schiller's terms, since the poet employed such conscious artifice to signalise his relationship with nature. The bucolic — to give the genre its Hellenistic title — was an Alexandrian invention, practised with particular elegance and elaboration by the cosmopolitan Theocritus, who set his rustic scenes on his native island of Sicily. In Latinising such idylls, it was Vergil who transplanted their setting to an isolated locality which, from a Roman vantage-point, would seem more remote and rugged. Arcadia, the mountainous hinterland of the Peloponnesian Peninsula, is celebrated in the Homeric hymn to Pan, the tutelary god of its singing herdsmen, as a land of many springs and the mother of flocks. Yet the shadow of Rome falls directly on Vergil's first eclogue, when his spokesman Tityrus voices his thanks to Octavius for having intervened to save his farm from confiscation. And with the poet's farewell, in the tenth and last eclogue, he detaches himself from his Arcadian companions and wistfully identifies himself with the departing onlooker: 'utinam ex vobis unus . . . fuissem'.[8] There, as at other moments, the Vergilian heartcry seems to sound like the voice of the modern artist, with his elegiac tone, his backward glance, and his innate self-consciousness. 'Would that I were truly one of you!' he exclaims in effect. Would that we might somehow close that rift between the isolated self and its natural environment!

The pastoral mode has been discussed by criticism and scholarship on a scale commensurate with the role it has played in the history of western literature. For so limited and so limiting a medium, its fortunes have been spectacular, and indeed could not be comprehended except through the emotional charge that it has single-mindedly and repetitively conveyed. 'Pastoral is an image of what they call the Golden Age',[9] wrote Alexander Pope at the age of sixteen. [See Pope's 1704 essay in Part One, above – Ed.] Following a neo-classical precept, he was starting his own poetic career by composing a series of pastorals. The eighteenth century had its urbanised critics who would disagree with his dictum, and who would uncritically believe in the genuine rusticity of a Theocritus. Doubtless there have been exceptions to Pope's rule; more logically he might have turned it around, and noted that the idea of the golden age was a pastoral image. But he made an important point by formulating a connection between the spatial and the temporal concepts, between the great good place and the good old days, between the ideal landscape – Arcady, Sicily, or wherever else – and the ideal epoch, whenever that may have been or might be. *Utopia*, our name for the best-known model of all model commonwealths, means nowhere. Its namer, Sir Thomas More, intended a pun in Greek on *Eutopia*, the good place, that happy realm which never existed on land or sea or in the air. In much the same fashion, taking up a hint from Charles Renouvier, we might speak of *Uchronia* or *Euchronia* to signify either never or the good time.[10]

The Ciceronian lament over modern manners, 'O tempora! O mores!',[11] has its sequel in the wish of Boethius that modernity might go back to the ways of antiquity:

> Utinam modo nostra redirent
> In mores tempora priscos!

Undetachably our lives stand rooted in the firm realities of here and now. Restlessness may project our thoughts in unspecified directions: 'Anywhere out of the world',[13] to echo the phrase that Baudelaire echoed from Thomas Hood. But if our longing to escape – or, more positively, to better our condition – has any goal, however dimly envisioned, it must be located elsewhere or otherwhile. Standing here and wishing to be there, we are given a choice, at least by imagination; we may opt for some distant part of the world, a terrestrial paradise, or for an otherworld, a celestial paradise. Living now and preferring to live then, we are not likely to get beyond an imaginative exercise; but again we are faced with a double option. If we reject the present, we must choose between the past and the future, between an Arcadian retrospect and a Utopian prospect. The spatial and the temporal distances may prolong one another, as they do in exotic imaginings that took place far away and long ago. Both of them fall within the orbit of primitivism. On the other hand, both the expectation of an afterlife and, on a more worldly plane, the resolve to build a heaven on earth through social planning share a common expectancy, which might be viewed as chiliasm or millennialism. . . . [Levin schematises his argument here in a diagram: see p. 10 in his original publication – Ed.] These are the possibilities that lie open to the visionary, whose area of speculation is bounded only by what a

German scholar calls wish-space (*Wunschraum*) and wish-time (*Wunschzeit*).[14]

SOURCE: extract from ch. 1, 'Prehistory', in *The Myth of the Golden Age in the Renaissance* (Bloomington, Ind., 1969; London, 1970), pp. 4–9.

NOTES

[Reorganised and renumbered from the original – Ed.]

1. Kenneth Clark, *Landscape into Art* (Boston, Mass., and London, 1961), p. 54.

2. Petrarch, *Le Rime*, Canzone XXIII, 1.

3. Novalis, *Gesammelte Werke*, ed. Carl Seelig (Zürich, 1945), II, 35 (*Fragmente*, 97). See also George Boas, *The Cult of Childhood* (London, 1966).

4. Arthur Lovejoy and George Boas, *A Documentary History of Primitivism and Related Ideas in Classical Antiquity* (Baltimore, Md., 1935), p. 7.

5. Horace, *Epodes*, II, 1–2. See M. S. Rœstvig, *The Happy Man: Studies in the Metamorphosis of a Classical Idea* (Oslo, 1954).

6. 'The Former Age', in *The Complete Works of Geoffrey Chaucer*, ed. F. N. Robinson (Boston, Mass., and London, 1933), p. 629, line 50.

7. Edmund Spenser, *The Shepheardes Calender*, VII, 9–10.

8. Vergil, *Eclogues*, X, 35.

9. Alexander Pope, 'A Discourse on Pastoral Poetry' (1717) – said by Pope to have been written in 1704.

10. Charles Renouvier, *Uchronie: L'Utopie dans l'histoire* (Paris, 1901).

11. Cicero, *In Catilinam*, I, 1, 2.

12. Boethius, *Philosophiae Consolatio*, II: Metrum V, 23–4.

13. Charles Baudelaire, *Le Spleen de Paris*, XVIII; Thomas Hood, 'The Bridge of Sighs'.

14. Alfred Doren, 'Wunschräume und Wunschzeiten', *Vorträge der Bibliothek Warburg* (1924–25), pp. 158–205.

Harold E. Toliver   Pastoral Contrasts   (1971)

The specific critical tasks that follow may come into focus more easily if we begin with some of the broader implications of the idyllic element of pastoral – usually imagined as a paradisal place where 's'ei piace, ei lice', or where 'if you like it you may have it' – which habitually calls forth an opposite and promotes a variety of 'perspective by incongruity'. Whether the scene is an explicit Arcadian society or some place or enclosed quiet, it is likely to be exposed to such things as industrialisation, death, unrequited love, unjust property division, or merely an opposing idea of perfection.[1] D. H. Lawrence touches upon a typical pastoral contrast when he remarks that 'a conquered universe, a dead Pan, leaves us nothing to live with. . . . And whether we are a store-clerk or a bus-conductor, we can still choose between the living universe of Pan, and the mechanical conquered universe of modern humanity' ('Pan in America', *Phoenix*). Traditionally, such contrasts not only vary a good deal from one period to another but tend to elicit different potentials from the pastoral setting according to how it is opposed. When 'society' and 'nature' are juxtaposed, for instance, such characteristics as the following emerge:

NATURE	SOCIETY
freedom	constriction
organicism	mechanical formality
democracy	hierarchy
plainness and honesty	masked artificiality
innocence, simplicity	experience, complexity
barbaric violence	cultured order

When opposed to art, nature becomes something quite different:

NATURE	ART
rough, inchoate	ordered, ornate
open, indefinite	timeless, permanent, enclosed
existential, immediate	artificial, imitative

Divided against itself, it becomes:

IDYLLIC NATURE	ANTI-PASTORAL NATURE
vernal or cyclical	wintry
humanised	indifferent or cruel
place of love and renewal	place of unrequited love, age

Or finally, if divided into levels:

NATURE	CELESTIAL PARADISE
temporal garden or Golden Age	apocalyptic sacred place
lesser gods (Venus, Pan, Cupid)	Hebraic or Christian God
shepherds and rustics	angels
mechanical or botanical nature	sublime nature

Such contrasts permeate the pastoral tradition from Theocritus to the eighteenth century and create similar tensive structures in pastorals with less definite conventions thereafter.

Not all pastoral makes explicit or full use of them, however. At one extreme, in the pure idyll, the poet leaves it largely to the reader to remember whatever contrasts the normative world affords – as Marlowe's passionate shepherd ignores the harsher realities that occur to Raleigh, Donne and C. Day Lewis in their answers to him. At the opposite extreme, forms of realism and naturalism concentrate on what *is* rather than what *might be* or what *ought to be*, even when the setting seems designed to capitalise on pastoral contrasts. Robinson Crusoe on his semi-paradisal island, for instance, is absorbed almost completely in material goods that can be arranged, labelled, traded for other goods, consumed, or wielded against those who would subtract from the total – with provender and produce, with seeds, slaves, goats, waterholes, linens, and other aspects of a pragmatic life. His basic impulses are closer to georgic than to pastoral in that he watches over the processes of fertility and renewal by which nature, through timely and efficient labor, is coaxed from a dormant period, brought to fruition, and prepared for harvest. Pastoral nature is more ceremonial than useful; it has no need of planting, cultivation or harvest, and its periodic renewal is less economic than symbolic or miraculous. Crusoe begins where the pastoral phase of Milton's Adam ends, as he is exiled to a landscape that requires management and contains dangers. Crusoe progresses from that primitive georgic occupation to the more complex economy of the market-place and toward the social relations of the more typical documentary novel whose society belongs to the drawing room and city.

Such enterprising programs of accretion as Crusoe's assume the importance of possession and property distinctions – which as a French anarchist once insisted, cause one to be inspected, directed, docketed, indoctrinated, assessed, taxed, valued, admonished, extorted, squeezed, hoaxed and betrayed, among other things unknown to Adam. A pastoral society, in contrast, is non-competitive or else converts a limited competition into such games and ceremonies as the friendly exchanges of rival singers. To the winner, the society of shepherds offers humble gifts more ornamental than practical. A pastoralist writing in this tradition might not have given Crusoe's island greater abundance than Defoe does, but the scene would have yielded its gifts much more easily, and if capital expansion had proved unavoidable, every increase would have brought a corresponding loss in simplicity and quiet. That Defoe is not concerned with such pastoral devices and themes is of course no criticism of *Robinson Crusoe* as a novel: the point here is a limited one, that where the potential contrasts between a golden age and the normative world are not exploited, we do not have the dialectical, tensive structure characteristic of all worthwhile pastoral.

Such a structure is not in itself difficult to isolate as an abiding feature of pastoral, but it operates on many levels and changes significantly in the evolution of pastoral forms. One of the tasks of a theory of pastoral is to explain the interaction of these levels and to use them to gauge the influence of the social and intellectual context on variations of pastoral form. Obviously lyrics, odes, elegies, romances, and novels and epics with pastoral elements handle that tension quite differently, and every period interprets and reconstitutes them in its own ways. . . .

THE POEM AS PASTORAL ENCLOSURE

A related theme in many pastorals is the contrast between reality and the poem itself, as a fictional construction – as its own kind of transforming locality capable of reshaping nature in art (to make 'poetic' is in part to 'pastoralise'), and one of the important threads in the evolution of pastoral is the shifting relationship between the poetic enclosure and the exterior world. Poggioli writes of the conventional shepherd figure that he 'represents man neither as *homo sapiens* nor as *homo faber*, but only as *homo artifex*: or more simply, as a musician and a poet'.[2] This association of the poet with the shepherd and of the poem with Arcadia comes about partly because when shepherds retreat to an enclosed and harbored world of song they are in a privileged position to indicate the nature of aesthetic distance and poetic transformations of reality. The force of the analogy between the poem and paradise is evident when whole books of verse in the Renaissance are taken to be bowers of bliss in which a reader can browse for idyllic or erotic pleasure. [For other aspects of Poggioli's conception of Pastoral, see above in this section of Part Two – Ed.]

An Arcadian retreat is not necessarily a lyric sublimation of unpleasantries, however (as Poggioli suggests); it is an image of nature so clearly artful as to suggest openly the poet's inevitable improvements on it. (If the poet assumes that reality is badly arranged or scattered, he may imagine its possible reconstruction in the order of words as perhaps the only reconstruction it is likely to receive.) The analogy between a poem and a perfect landscape holds to some extent even when the poet makes no explicit claim for it. Consider Emily Dickinson's description of a storm:

> The leaves unhooked themselves from trees
> And started all abroad;
> The dust did scoop itself like hands
> And threw away the road.

The storm is scarcely gentle, but the stanza cannot help taming its violence and suggesting a *locus amoenus* or pleasant place in spite of itself. It humanises the leaves and the dust and appeases our desire to find correspondences between the human and the natural world. (The two sentences develop in units of eight and six syllables in almost identical metrical arrangements, syntax and grammar: the twenty-eight syllables move in exact formation, commanding the event to take part in their poetic ritual.) Though these elements do not make the stanza explicitly pastoral, they do in a sense quiet discord and produce a pastoral harmony and transformation. With its 'rhyme' of daily and seasonal recurrence, its songs, and its graciously integral harmony, paradise often converges aesthetic ideal and scene in this way. That literary shepherds should spend more time singing than tending sheep is entirely in keeping with the impulse that a pastoral place indulges to celebrate nature rather than improve it with the georgic arts of the gardener or the home economist.

Rather than imposing a total harmony on nature, however, pastoralists in the main tradition usually suggest that paradise is beyond the reach even of poetry. It stands apart as the poet tries to imagine it, so that his description of it becomes a self-conscious artifice. Arcadia's dreamlike quality is especially marked from the romantics onward, as poets find it difficult to reconcile the harbored bowers of pastoral with a world given over increasingly to industry and social strife. The poet must come forth from his dreams, Moneta tells the Keatsian dreamer in *The Fall of Hyperion*, and speak directly to the social problems of the times: he must put his pastoral vision to use as social therapy. At the same time, the poet cannot claim too much for whatever therapy poetry and its idyllic dreams may work on its subject or on the minds it touches, since it is after all merely verbal. 'Every good poem is very nearly a Utopia', W. H. Auden writes, an idyllic 'community of substances forced to yield their disagreements for the sake of the poem', and therefore 'an attempt to present an analogy to that paradisal state in which Freedom and Law, System and Order are united in harmony'.[3] But its harmony 'is possible and verbal only'. When it issues forth to do its work in society it may accomplish very little, and it may itself be changed in the minds of hearers – the only place where it really exists. The words 'of a dead man' (Yeats specifically) 'are modified in the guts of the living'. Ireland's madness and her weather remain as they always have been, her madness as far beyond cure as her thunderstorms:

> Poetry makes nothing happen: it survives
> In the valley of its saying where executives
> Would never want to tamper; it flows south
> From ranches of isolation and the busy griefs,

Raw towns that we believe and die in; it survives
A way of happening, a mouth.

[W. H. Auden, 'In Memory of W. B. Yeats']

Since poems cannot pull the real world all the way into their paradisal orders, 'Ariel', the spirit of beauty, must learn to live with 'Prospero', who demands exacting truth:

The effect [of a poem's] beauty . . . is good to the degree that, through its analogies, the goodness of created existence, the historical fall into unfreedom and disorder, and the possibility of regaining paradise through repentance and forgiveness are recognised. Its effect is evil to the degree that beauty is taken, not as analogous to, but identical with goodness, so that the artist regards himself or is regarded by others as God, the pleasure of beauty taken for the joy of Paradise, and the conclusion drawn that, since all is well in the work of art, all is well in history. But all is not well there.[4]

[For Auden's specific discussion of pastoral, see above in this section of Part Two – Ed]

Thus modern versions of pastoral often suggest that the distance between fictional idylls and the daily world precludes any genuine transformation of reality except an imagined one. Aware of pastoral's artifice and of the contrast between fiction and reality, the modern pastoralist is likely to take a sceptical view of the pastoral tradition and use it primarily as a device for gaining perspective on the nature of the imagination itself. . . .

SOURCE: extracts from ch. 1, 'Pastoral Contrasts', in *Pastoral Forms and Attitudes* (Berkeley, Cal., 1971), pp. 1–5, 11–14.

NOTES

[Reorganised and renumbered from the original – Ed.]

1. Virgil's eclogues employ a number of dialectical pairings. In the first eclogue, for example, Meliboeus and Tityrus, having fallen into entirely opposite fortunes, 'match' them in dialogue. . . .

2. R. Poggioli, 'The Oaten Flute', *Harvard Library Bulletin*, XI (1957), p. 157; reproduced in the collected essays of the same title (Cambridge, Mass., 1975).

3. W. H. Auden, in *The Dyer's Hand* (New York, 1962; London, 1963), p. 71.

4. Auden, loc. cit.

Peter V. Marinelli   The Retreat into Childhood
(1971)

It has been some time since the pastoral was the province of knights and shepherds, and we should . . . glance briefly at the child, the figure who, more than any other, has taken their place . . . .[1] The pastoral of childhood in the form of the novel is the bequest to us, like the eclogue and the elegy, of antiquity. The association of childhood and pastoral is implicit from the first in the *Idylls* of Theocritus, but the author whom we know by the name of Longus was the first freely and thoroughly to explore the vein of supposed innocence in young people. His romance, *Daphnis and Chloe*, the earliest form of the pastoral novel, had little effect on the great chivalric-pastoral romances of the sixteenth century, largely because they were the result of the fusion of various other literary traditions, but also because the exploration of childhood sensibilities seem to have been of no particular interest to our forebears. Though the décor and cast of the chivalric-pastoral romances is sometimes like that of this earlier purely pastoral romance – pastoralism, foundlings, pirates, providential restorations to wealthy parents – the suggestion might be made that its true descendant is the modern novel of childhood and abolescence. There is no direct influence whatever, and yet the presence in both of certain motifs, especially that of incipient sexuality and of the pleasures it generates, is very striking.

Practically the entire subject of *Daphnis and Chloe* is the awakening of the passion of love in the two foundlings who give their names to the tale. Their ignorance, first of its name and nature, and then of the ways by which it may be consummated, provides the work with its subtle and charming ironies. In many ways, Longus is very like Theocritus in portraying a golden world of youth and beauty, but by the gesture of irony implicit in the complex simplicity of his language, revealing that it is a world that has never been and will never be except in the imagination of an older and wiser human being. Daphnis and Chloe are too simple, too naïvely libertine to be real. Longus paints a world of nature, but it is a world governed at every point by the processes of art. The constant self-awareness of the author extends even to the droll mockery of his own narrative tricks, and his treatment of his hero and heroine maintains an enchanting balance between lyricism and humour. They might have been mere libertines or they might have been mere rustics, but in Longus the two are one. Both the humour and the irony of the work stem from the fact that the unlucky pair of neophytes in sensuality can learn nothing from nature about relief for their predicament, even though they live in surroundings where the natural process is visible at every moment. Even from the mating of goats they can learn nothing, and their awkward attempts at fruition in imitation of those lecherous animals result, curiously, in an augmented sense of their innocence and simplicity. It is a line both dangerous and daring, and it is oddly successful.

The vulnerability of their world is many times asserted. It succumbs to attack from without, as in the invasion of a band of city-gallants who piratically carry Chloe away for a while, and to attack from within: the repellent Gnathon forces his attentions upon Daphnis, and Chloe is attacked by the lustful Dorcon dressed in animal skins. Neither town nor country is awarded the palm, but perhaps the former derives a slight advantage from the fact that when the lovers are able to be so in fact, it is because Daphnis has finally been initiated into the mysteries of sexual pairing by a townswoman – of course it would be a townswoman. It is Longus's humorous way of saying that there is an art even in 'natural' functions and that nature, though she gives much, does not give all. The novel is astonishing for the equilibrium it maintains between the freshness and beauty of the pastoral world and the sense of its fragility and finally of its insufficiency. Nostalgia and wisdom go hand in hand, and the fusion of the two produces a marvellous good humour that lightens from every page.

Like the pastoral of rural life, whose essential characteristic is that it is written at a distance from the country and from a sophisticated point of view, the pastoral of childhood requires the adult perspective. Where poets in the early tradition generally initiated their careers with a set of Arcadian pastorals, the novelist who has succeeded him is generally wont to initiate his career with a story, either openly autobiographical or very thinly fictionalised, of childhood. Distant time has succeeded distant place as the great focus of pastoral interest, and the golden pastures of Arcadia have yielded to the golden time of childhood.

This emphasis on childhood and adolescence in our literature is sometimes not recognised, especially by the young, as the comparative novelty it is. Before Rousseau and the Romantic poets, only Henry Vaughan (and then in another context entirely) appears to be at all aware of the child as other than an embryonic adult. Ambrose Philips, of course, won a reputation from Pope as a fool for his pastorals, but he had won it earlier by his sentimental poems on childhood, along with the epithet 'Namby-Pamby'. The emphasis on childhood is essentially a Romantic innovation based on the notion that the clear natural vision of the child is somehow superior to that of the man. It is an endearing idea, but we must take it on faith that it is truly so, for the innocence attributed to the child may be only the projection of the author's imaginings about that earlier state of life, and they are bound to be coloured by his experience and by his nostalgia. As shepherds do not write pastoral poetry, children do not write in praise of childhood. When we are presented with this wonderful phenomenon of the child wiser and more innocent than the man – we may use Wordsworth's *Prelude* as an example that unites the pastoral of rural life with the pastoral of childhood – it becomes a matter of real difficulty to disentangle the art of the adult author from the supposed naturalness of the child of whom he writes. In a very real sense, the Romantics discovered, not really the child himself, but a way of writing about him. Previous to Wordsworth the accepted way to write about children was to treat them with a kind of gentle irony, a way that captured their fresh innocence, but also captured its fragility. One thinks immediately of Longus's novel, and in poetry, of Herrick, of Marvell and Matthew Prior. The Romantic innovation consisted in treating them with a sublimity of feeling that reflected the sublimity of their being: the same thing, it seems clear, occurred in the treatment of the shepherd.

Our novelists appear to have developed both ways of writing about children, lessening the sense of sublimity but preserving the sense of relative innocence in the one case, and preserving the sense of vulnerability and extending it into a real capacity for evil in the other case. There is a kind of Pelagian or Rousseauistic vision in the one, an Augustinian vision in the other. The two main forms our modern pastorals of innocence take, city and country pastorals of childhood, result in either naturalistic idylls in a rural setting or memoirs of a terrifying urban development of which the discovery of a sense of evil is the central focus. The field is vast, and we can choose only a few illustrative instances.

Thomas Wolfe's *Look Homeward, Angel*, Richard Llewellyn's *How Green Was My Valley*, Laurie Lee's *Cider with Rosie* may all stand as examples of the country pastoral of childhood. Here the life of the child, lived in some idyllic setting in the proximate past – South Carolina, Wales, the Cotswold Hills – is a generally ecstatic one of golden visions; it is not perfect, certainly, but it preserves some distant gleams of the golden age that irradiate their surroundings. What sexuality there is in these novels – and it is a ground-note in all of them as setting the boundary between childhood and maturity – is customarily voluptuous and pagan. The image that comes to mind for all of them is of a discovery of love on an idle summer afternoon in which all the blind strivings of youth to secret knowledge appear in sharper focus. The thirtieth chapter in the novels of both Wolfe and Llewellyn might have been headed as Laurie Lee headed his chapter on the entrance into sexual experience, 'First Bite at the Apple'. The Fall in the garden is repeated in all three, and the picture that springs to mind for all of them is that of the sensual Rosie stuffing her young swain's shoes with flowers as they lie for a long moment afterwards under the hay-rick in the summer heat. All the myths of hedonistic and wanton innocence in the golden age have been transferred from the shepherd to the child or young adolescent. Yet the entrance into sexual life represents a move into a world of experience, and sometimes there is a vivid sense of the awakening of a sense of sin as old as man, though it is merely glanced at and drowned in the rapture of the moment. This is Wolfe, aware of a disappointment to come and of the fact that he has snatched an apple from a Hesperian garden guarded by a dragon:

They clung together in the bright moment of wonder, there on the magic island, where the world was quiet, believing all they said. And who shall say – whatever disenchantment follows – that we ever forget magic, or that we can ever betray, on this leaden earth, the apple-tree, the singing, and the gold?

And this is Llewellyn, as explicit as Lee in his recall of an old Fall and as uncaring:

Then the tight-drawn branch is weak, for the string has sung its song, and breath comes back to empty lungs and a trembling to the limbs. Your eyes see plainly. The trees are green, just the same as they were. No change has come. No bolts of fire. No angels with a flaming sword. Yet this it was that left the Garden to weeds. I had eaten of the Tree. Eve was still warm under me. Yet still no bolt, no fire, no swords. Only the song of a thrush, and the smell of green, and the peace of the mountain-side.

The experience of sex separates the child from the man; Lee's terse 'I was never the same again' might be a general motto for all.

The naturalness with which these boys enter upon their sexual lives reflects the naturalness of their surroundings: the natural world is the scene and the benign witness of their rapture. The torment of childhood plays little part in these naturalistic idylls, but it is in the foreground of the city pastorals, which more often than not portray the child as the victim of the adult world of experience whose innocence is asserted even as he struggles blindly to enter that world. One thinks immediately of the Stephen Dedalus of Joyce and his innocent quest for Dublin whores, of J. D. Salinger's innocent sophisticate Holden Caulfield in his amusing encounters with New York prostitutes in shady hotels, of the immigrant child David Schearl's desperate fumblings towards a forbidden knowledge in tenement rooms in Henry Roth's grim and horrific but tremendously powerful *Call It Sleep*. And one thinks too, inevitably, of Philip Roth's most recent novel, *Portnoy's Complaint*, where the sexual instinct turns in upon itself and achieves a comic explosion of desperately innocent wantonness. As I write, I notice that there has just been published a book entitled *The True Adventures of Huckleberry Finn*, by John Seelye, which is a rewriting of Mark Twain's classic pastoral of youth, and which apparently manages to infuse into it all those things which the modern view of childhood conceives to be missing in its pages, notably sex and the repeal of illusions about limitless horizons: there is no 'lighting out' for the Territory here. The city pastoral is extending a long reach.

Whether modern psychology or simple experience has taught us better, we are no longer accustomed to see childhood as a rapturous and lyrical existence, and we are probably in a post-Arcadian phase of the pastoral of childhood. In certain contemporary novels we find prevailing not only an unsentimental but a distinctly Augustinian view of human nature that sees the child as quite literally the father of the man in respect of his tendency to evil. These novels put no emphasis on sexuality whatever; the inclination to evil is demonstrated through a propensity to violence and cunning and secretiveness. Richard Hughes's *A High Wind in Jamaica* is an example. Two others are Ferenc Molnar's *The Boys on Paul Street* and William Golding's *Lord of the Flies*. With these, of course, we have passed into allegory: in Molnar, the street-games of a group of boys become a projection of the territorial ambitions leading to war which have immemorially racked the progress of the race; in Golding, the crash of a plane deposits a group of boys upon an island of primitive beauty which becomes the scene of primitive blood-lust on one hand and of primitive innocence on the other. The novel shatters all the romantic conceptions about childhood and natural goodness and the holiness of the heart's affections. Nor is it a paean to the world of Art, for the youths who revert to savagery are themselves the inheritors of all of the gains that mankind has made so painfully after the first expulsion from the garden. In its refusal to find an easy solution in either Nature or Art, its attribution of evil to the individual and not to surroundings, the novel is truly and seriously pastoral in its movement.

What will succeed to child-cult as a version of pastoral, no one has yet told us, but the pace of modern life is accelerating so greatly that the pace of literature is bound to be affected as well. If the child has half as long a literary life as the shepherd, he will be remarkable. Publishers continue, however, almost daily to announce new novels, new memoirs of childhood, and there is no fear that the fashion will end, or that one version of pastoral at least will not be with us for some time to come. Considering the spoliation of nature which our age is accomplishing to such an extent that the capacity of the life processes to continue in our time are daily being questioned, it is fortunate, perhaps, that the child has taken over the role of the shepherd. Residing in a definite landscape, the shepherd needed an external world of lovely fresh nature in which to appear; residing only in time, the child can survive as an emblem of innocence without it. As the evidence of a deep-rooted instinct for perfection, pastoral will survive even in this age of unthought-of horrors, perhaps flourish because of it. The descent to an age of plastic was something not contemplated by the ancients, who stopped at iron.

SOURCE: ch. 5, 'The Retreat into Childhood', in *Pastoral* ('Critical Idiom' series, London, 1971), pp. 75–82.

NOTE

1. [Ed.] For an interesting earlier discussion on pastoral aspects of 'the cult of the child', see the inimitable chapter, 'Alice in Wonderland', in William Empson's *Some Versions of Pastoral* (London, 1935; rev. edn, 1975).

Laurence Lerner   The Pastoral World: Arcadia and the Golden Age   (1972)

Every culture has one or more centres of social, artistic and moral standards, a place where the educated people live, where the King's English, or its equivalent, is spoken, where the theatres perform and the political decisions are taken. In the sixteenth and seventeenth centuries this centre was the court; by the nineteenth it was the city; in modern America it is becoming the university. Most literature is written from and for this centre; but there are always corners of society, rural or provincial pockets, lower social levels, with their own less articulate, less sophisticated traditions, sometimes imprinted by old-fashioned court mores, sometimes seeming to live an older, more unchanging life of their own. It used to be true that the literature of the centre was written, that of the corners oral, but literacy and radio have changed that.

To describe this contrast, we can speak of court, or metropolitan or (more generally) centric literature, and set it against unsophisticated, rural, popular or (more generally) provincial literature. To this can be added another contrast, concerning the way in which a poem sees the world it describes. It may present that world as it is, through the eyes of a familiar and an expert, subjecting it to none of the distracting expectations of the outsider. This I will call the direct vision. Or it may deliberately see its world as answering to the illusions or discontents of an outsider, as a projection rather than as the object of the matter-of-fact gaze of the inmate; this I will call the mediated vision. Now, by using these two pair of contrasts, we arrive at a fourfold scheme of classification.

The first class – centric and direct – will contain most of the great literature of Europe, which has naturally emerged from, and deals with, the court or the city. Tragedy belongs here (Hamlet's Denmark and Thésée's Athens are part of Renaissance court culture, wherever they are ostensibly situated), and so do most novels. It would be odd if this were not the area in which greatness harboured.

In the second class – provincial-direct – we must put the ballads, which emerge from, and belong to, regional pockets of our culture: the narrative poems of Wordsworth, proudly proclaiming their setting in humble and rustic life; the regional novel; dialect poetry.

The third class – centric-mediated – can take two forms, positive and negative. If positive, then the view of court or city is mediated by longing and respect; it is seen from far as the desirable top where, if we are lucky, there may be room. The archetype of such writing is the Dick Whittington story. If it is negative, we get pastoral satire: denunciation of court by contrasting it with Arcadian simplicity.

Finally, there is provincial-mediated, which is pastoral. This too can be positive or negative. If the poet's need is to escape from the sophisticated corruption of court life into the freshness, simplicity and honesty of an unspoiled countryside, the result is pastoral properly speaking. If, however, he looks at the country, not through the eyes of his wishes, but through those of fear or dislike, if he believes in courtly grace and subtlety and is simply pausing to laugh at rustic boors, we can call the result anti-pastoral.

What would a poem be like which did not strive towards the matter-of-fact gaze of the expert, but deliberately saw nature in terms of an outsider's expectations? – which brought to the countryside emotions and expectations which were not rejected, but which determined the way the poem was written? Would it not be like this? –

> O sweet woods, the delight of solitariness!
> O how much I do like your solitariness!
> Here nor treason is hid, veiled in innocence,
> Nor envy's snaky eye finds any harbour here,
> Nor flatterer's venomous insinuations,
> Nor cunning humourist's puddled opinions,
> Nor courteous ruins of preferred usury,
> Nor time prattled away, cradle of ignorance,
> Nor causeless duty, nor cumber of arrogance,
> Nor trifling title of vanity dazzleth us,
> Nor golden manacles stand for a paradise.
> Here wrong's name is unheard, slander a monster is.
> Keep they spright from abuse; here no abuse doth haunt:
> What man grafts in a tree dissimulation?
>
> [Sidney, song from *Arcadia* (1598)]

No poem could have a simpler structure than this. It is a plain insistent assertion that the country is free from certain evils. This negative point is the only one it makes. Almost every detail mentioned is a detail, not about the country, but about the court – it is a poem about what the country is *not* like. This gives it a curious kind of strength, a kind that is incompatible with subtlety: a growing passion of indignation and need mounts in its cumulative rhetoric, and its very formality adds to its power, in a way that is only possible in Elizabethan poetry, when men sometimes (especially for emotions like hate and indignation) seem to have thought, and felt, in rhetorical patterns.

Sidney shows us the poetic mechanism we are looking for so clearly that his poem consists entirely of an announcement of what kind of poem he is writing. Let us turn to someone who has the same point to make, but spent rather longer in the woods:

> Now my co-mates, and brothers in exile,
> Hath not old custom made this life more sweet
> Than that of painted pomp? Are not these woods
> More free from peril than the envious court?
> Here feel we but the penalty of Adam,
> The season's difference, as the icy fang
> And churlish chiding of the winter's wind,
> Which when it bites, and blows upon my body
> Even till I shrink with cold, I smile, and say
> This is no flattery: these are counsellors
> That feelingly persuade me what I am:
> Sweet are the uses of adversity
> Which like the toad, ugly and venomous,

> Wears yet a precious jewel in his head:
> And this our life, exempt from public haunt,
> Finds tongues in trees, books in the running brooks,
> Sermons in stones, and good in everything.
> I would not change it.

> [*As You Like It* (1599), II i 1–18]

Nothing in this passage is an attempt to see the countryside as it is. One point runs through it all, that the country is not the court. The contrast with 'painted pomp', with 'flattery', with 'public haunt', determines everything. Real toads are not venomous, and carry no jewels, but to the exiled Duke this does not matter, for the toads of Arden are not real.

The next example is also highly conventional: but it is non-dramatic, and of greater verbal complexity than the Duke's lines. It is by the most sophisticated and, probably, the most pastoral of seventeenth-century poets:

> Ametas and Thestylis Making Hay-ropes

> A. Thinkst thou this love can stand,
>   Whilst thou still dost say me nay?
>   Love unpaid does soon disband:
>   Love binds love as hay binds hay.

> Th. Thinkst thou that this rope would twine
>   If we both should turn one way?
>   Where both parties so combine,
>   Neither love will twist nor hay.

> A. Thus you vain excuses find,
>   Which yourselve and us delay:
>   And love ties a woman's mind
>   Looser than with ropes of hay.

> Th. What you cannot constant hope
>   Must be taken as you say.

> A. Then let's both lay by our rope,
>   And go kiss within the hay.

> [Marvell (c. 1650)][1]

Marvell is a poet of paradox: not flagrantly, like Donne and Crashaw, but delicately and deeply. The deepest paradox in this poem is both hidden and obvious: it is the contrast between its rustic image and its verbal sophistication. The poem depends utterly on the figure of the hay-ropes, as if the two lovers had no other way of expressing themselves: their dialectic consists in modifying the analogies that can be drawn from this one vehicle. Yet it is not as if they think in images: for the comparison is regularly deployed as a formal simile, and at least in a technical sense the thought exists independently of it. It is a poem in which we can see the rhetorical art, and admire the poet's skill.

Yet as long as we admire the skill, the lovers stay apart: the better they express their feelings, the less they love. This is the paradox, too, of Marvell's 'The Definition of Love', that perfection and fulfilment are incompatible:

> My love is of a birth as rare
> As 'tis for object strange and high;
> It was begotten of Despair
> Upon Impossibility.

The perfect love, that poem says, does not exist: 'Ametas and Thestylis' moves in exactly the opposite direction. Here is a perfect image for love, it says; look how much can be expressed through it. But its lovers, rejecting despair and impossibility, must reject the attempt to express their love. They must lay aside the rope and go kiss within the hay. The poem is over, and the rest is silence.

The sophistication of this poem completely prevents us from seeing haymaking as it really is, and country life is shamelessly subordinated to the poet's wish to turn a polished analogy. And then, in the end, the poem gaily rejects everything it has done. The country folk, showing more good sense than the poem, are going to stop talking about love, and get on with it.

The Renaissance poets were, of course, well aware that their version of the countryside was an illusion. To show this, we can turn to the first and most famous of all, Jacopo Sannazaro, whose *Arcadia*, published in 1502, began a vast literary fashion. In the Epilogue to this work, Sannazaro defends himself for writing pastoral. Addressing his pipe ('sampogna'), he says: 'Do not mind if someone, accustomed perhaps to more exquisite sounds, rebukes your baseness or considers you rude'; nor (the opposite criticism) if they say that you have not followed the laws of shepherds properly, and 'that it is not fitting for anyone to pass further than what belongs to him' ('passar più avanti, che a lui si appartiene'): which seems to refer both to social and stylistic climbing. To this latter criticism Sannazaro replies that he has been the first in this age to

awaken the sleeping woods, and teach shepherds to sing the songs they had forgotten. All the more since he who made you out of these reeds came to Arcadia not as a rustic shepherd but as a most cultured youth, although unknown and a pilgrim of love.

Pastoral poetry, in other words, is the work of courtiers: for that reason, it would be inappropriate to censure it for baseness (it isn't really) or for presumption (why shouldn't he 'passare più avanti', considering who he really is?). Sannazaro is having his oatcake and eating it. Not surprising, then, that when Selvaggio meets Montano (*Prosa Secunda*) and asks him to sing, he addresses him 'con voce assai umana'. This 'humanist voice' (a modern translation renders it 'in a most courteous phrase') is no doubt a deliberate slip of the tongue, a quiet reminder of how educated these shepherds naturally are.

There is a formal device that corresponds to the fact that the version of the countryside is mediated. The song which Montano sings in reply to Selvaggio's request tells how he found Uranio stretched out sleeping, and woke him, and they then discussed whether to sing. In *Prosa Terzia*, the shepherds go to the feast of Pales, and as they enter the holy temple they see various scenes painted on the gate – nymphs, Apollo guarding Admetus's cattle, Endymion, and so on. When we hear the priest's prayer in the temple, we realise that we are in the same world as these mythological paintings: he prays not to see Diana bathing, or the vengeful nymphs.

What we have in these two examples is the obliqueness of presentation so common in pastoral. The shepherd poet sings only after announcing he is going to sing, or discussing what, or taking part in a contest. Rural or mythological scenes are not described direct, but paintings of them are described. The method is old, and goes back to Virgil, to Theocritus even; and some scholars tell us that it has its origin in the actual shepherd contests of rural Sicily. Whether that is true or not, its place in Renaissance pastoral is surely the opposite – not as a sign of realism, but as a sign of sophistication, a way of removing us from the immediacy of real rustics in real fields.

PASTORAL AND ANTI-PASTORAL: 'AS YOU LIKE IT'

Of course, the same work may hover between positive and negative – as for instance *As You Like It* does. The Duke, we have seen, is a poet of simple pastoral enthusiasm; but the play as a whole sets pastoral and anti-pastoral constantly against each other, and does not encourage us to form a clear preference.

They are set against each other most directly in III ii: the conversation between Corin and Touchstone on the shepherd's life. Each speaks unequivocally for one of the attitudes: courtly trickery against the good sense of Arden, or courtly polish against the slow-witted rustic chewing his straw. It is an old argument, going back at least to the twentieth idyll of Theocritus, in which Eunica despises the neatherd for his coarse smell, and he tells himself indignantly about the neatherds who have been loved by goddesses. Who wins that argument? And who wins this one?

TOUCH. Hast any philosophy in thee, shepherd?

CORIN. No more, but that I know the more one sickens, the worse at ease he is; and that he that wants money, means and contentment is without three good friends. That the property of rain is to wet, and fire to burn. That a good pasture makes fat sheep; and that a great cause of the night is lack of the sun. That he that hath learned no wit by nature, nor art, may complain of good breeding, or comes of a very dull kindred.

TOUCH. Such a one is a natural philosopher.   [III ii 21 ff.]

It is quite wrong to play this scene (as I have seen it done) with a sly Corin winking at the audience, and smiling to see whether Touchstone will take him seriously. If Touchstone believes in courtly wit, as he clearly does, then Corin must be allowed to believe in rustic sense, and not turn into a secondary Touchstone. It is easy to say what each stands for; but it is not so easy to say who has the better of it.

A natural philosopher has no need of artificialities or rhetoric, for he goes directly to what is really important; a 'natural' who philosophises will produce nothing but empty platitudes like these. Touchstone is consciously punning, but which meaning of 'natural' more truly describes Corin? 'The property of rain is to wet', he says – just like the Bachelierus of Molière, who has been taught in medical school the reason why opium makes us sleep:

> A quoi respondeo
> Quia est in eo
> Virtus dormitiva,
> Cuius est natura
> Sensus assoupire.

Chorus: Bene, bene, bene respondere
        . . .   [*Le Malade Imaginaire*, 3me Intermède]

Isn't Corin, too, offering a tautology as if it were a substantive point? That's what rain is. Or is he? Shakespeare is at his most elusive here. These are the things that a countryman needs to know – not how to kiss hands, but how to look after his sheep, who have to be protected from the elements. In a world of servants, coaches and umbrellas, rain doesn't wet any more.

Of course, it would be wrong for either of them to win clearly in the third act. The balance must continue to the end: a balance between the play's official self and its undercurrents – for, of course, it is officially pastoral, and on the deepest level, I believe, it stays so. Act I is certainly pastoral in its preference. The court is corrupt, as Le Beau

admits with a sad gesture towards a happiness that he can locate only
by saying it is not to be found here:

> ...   Sir, fare you well
> Hereinafter in a better world than this,
> I shall desire more love and knowledge of you.   [I ii 272–5]

We have already been told where this better world is. In (surely) one
of the most haunting sentences in English – given, with an irony the
play can easily handle, to Charles the thug – we have been told of the
Duke's banishment:

> They say he is already in the Forest of Arden, and a many merry men with
> him; and there they live like the old Robin Hood of England: they say many
> young gentlemen flock to him every day, and fleet the time carelessly as they
> did in the golden world.
>
> [I ii 108 ff.]

England and France are casually mixed up because we are in neither
England nor France: this Arden is out of space and time. C. S. Lewis
has described very well where it is, in his defence of Spenser's
shepherds:

> Some readers cannot enjoy the shepherds because they know (or say they
> know) that real country people are not more happy or more virtuous than
> anyone else; but it would be tedious to explain to them the many causes
> (reasons too) that have led humanity to symbolise by rural scenes and
> occupations a region in the mind which does exist and which should be visited
> often.[2]

Arden is the world that Le Beau was longing for (though he, alas,
never gets there). The visitors to Arden sing its praises in much the
same terms as the Duke's simple solemn eulogy:

> Blow, blow, thou winter wind,
> Thou art not so unkind
> As man's ingratitude.
> ...   [II vii 175–8]

What little action there is mostly confirms this idyllic view. Orlando
'thought that all things had been savage here', but he finds only
hospitality and friendship. Above all, Arden is the place of happy
lovers: there they find what they could not find at court – leaving, if
necessary, their wickedness behind them. To dress Corin up as
Hymen is an ingenious way of relating the happy love-stories to the
pastoral element – though at a price, since it destroys the atmosphere
of mystery, even magic, that seems to be growing at the end.

All this, then, makes *As You Like It* a pure pastoral . . . but: inevitably, there are buts. First, the action. However much the Duke may like Arden, the moment he is offered his kingdom back he forgets the sermons in stones and takes it. He was speaking as exiled dukes no doubt should in Arden; but he did not actually *mean* it.

As we look carefully at them, all the pastoral points grow slightly dubious. Orlando finds kindness in the forest, but at the hands of courtiers, not countrymen. The lovers marry, but then they leave Arden: it is the place for love but not for marriage. And, most important of all, there are Touchstone and Jaques.

The task of these two choric characters is to comment and to mock: to remind us of what the others forgot. Touchstone, as we have already seen, is explicitly anti-pastoral, mocking the Arcadian life as he mocks romantic love – and often both at once:

> . . . I remember when I was in love I broke my sword upon a stone, and bid him take that for coming a-night to Jane Smile, and I remember the kissing of her batlet, and the cow's dugs that her pretty chopped hands had milked; . . .
>
> [II iv 42 ff.]

Jaques is a more complicated character, and his relation to the pastoral theme is less obvious. He mocks at romantic love more churlishly than Touchstone ('Rosalind is your love's name?': we can hear the sneer); at poetry ('call you 'em stanzas?'); and at the pastoral life:

> If it do come to pass
> That any man turn ass,
> Leaving his wealth and ease
> A stubborn will to please,
> . . .
>
> [II v 47–50]

He is anti-pastoral from the moment he appears – indeed, before he appears, for the corollary of telling the Duke that he usurps more than his brother (Jaques's first, reported opinion) is that there should not be any people in Arden – or, at any rate, no courtiers. Jaques welcomes Touchstone into the forest along with that un-Arcadian property, a watch; he thinks marriage should obey the proper rules and not be carried out under a bush, like a beggar. In this his morality is centric; and, most interesting of all, he refuses to go along with the others at the end of the play.

Most interesting: for what he is refusing is to go back to court yet this does not make him a pastoral character. He is not staying in Arden either, not even for the rest of the dance. During the brief time remaining to the play, he would rather stay at the abandoned cave, a forest without pastoralists. After that, he will go where he really belongs: to a monastery or hermitage. There his sneers can be sublimated into *contemptus mundi*; in Arden they are merely kill-joy. Pastoral and monasticism are both retreats from the world, but quite different from each other. A monastery is an act of pure withdrawal, and because of this it can be accepted by the community it withdraws from. Retreat is a human need, and the occasional or partial retreats everyone needs are symbolised and reinforced by the existence of groups who have retreated totally. The countryside, however, is accepted by the court, not psychologically, but economically: it represents, not withdrawal, but simply farming. The pastoral poet is therefore exploiting his medium as the hermit is not, turning country life, which is community life, into an occasion for withdrawal from the community. Out of this exploitation can come a fruitful artistic tension, but this tension will be destroyed by anyone who has no interest whatever in the medium, only in withdrawal. That is why Jaques never felt at home in Arden. Touchstone disliked it because it was not the court. Jaques discovers only at the end that his true vocation is that of an old religious man.

Touchstone and Jaques were added by Shakespeare to Lodge's story.[3] This makes it obvious that he has changed his source by complicating the simple pastoralism into something more ambivalent, where the choruses undermine the official message. It is not surprising that a few other changes mock the pastoral world, or stand tiptoe on the edge of mockery. Thus Shakespeare removed the violence. Lodge's wrestler kills the franklin's sons and is killed by Rosader; Charles breaks their ribs ('that there is little hope of life in them'), and when he is thrown by Orlando, Le Beau reports, 'He cannot speak, my lord' (the line usually gets a laugh), and Charles is then carried out. No actual deaths, but very nearly. Lodge's usurper is killed in battle; but Shakespeare's, though he raises an army, turns out at the last minute to be harmless:

> . . .
> And to the skirts of this wild wood he came;
> Where meeting with an old religious man,
> After some question with him, was converted
> Both from his enterprise and from the world,
> His crown bequeathing to his banished brother
> And all their lands restored to them again
> That were with him exiled. This to be true
> I do engage my life.   [v iv 164–71]

He needs to engage it, the whole story is so gloriously improbable. The outcome reeks gaily of fairy-tale. Having removed the battle, Shakespeare makes fun of what he has done, as if all you have to do, to get rid of the violence, is to wave a happy ending at your story.

The one touch of violence that remains is the wounding of Orlando, which is brought right on stage in the form of the bloody napkin – at sight of which Rosalind forgets her shepherd's role and almost puts an end to the game she has been playing. This is Shakespeare's comment on the tone of his play. 'Look', he has already said, 'no blood.' Now he says, 'See what blood would do to my pastoral; it would spoil everything'.

ARCADIA AND UTOPIA

'First of all', Hesiod tells us, 'the deathless Gods who dwell on Olympus made a golden race of mortal men who lived in the time of Cronos when he was reigning in heaven. And they lived like Gods without sorrow of heart, remote and free from toil and grief; miserable age rested not on them; but with legs and arms never failing they made merry with feasting beyond the reach of all evils. When they died, it was as though they were overcome with sleep, and they had all good times; for the fruitful earth unforced bore them fruit abundantly and without stint.'[4]

This Golden Age ended, and it was succeeded by a silver, then a bronze, then a fourth, and now at last a fifth age, when 'men never rest from labour and sorrow by day, and from perishing by night'. Every age runs its course, and perishes: 'Zeus will destroy this race of mortal men also', says Hesiod in a wonderful image, 'when they come to have grey hairs on the temples at their birth.'

Hesiod's account of the Golden Age is the first version of a long series in ancient literature. Plato has various modified versions of it. The poet Aratus, of the third century BC, has a version that introduces the virgin Astraea, who represents Justice, and thus gives a moral as well as a physical superiority to the first age:

Not yet did men understand hateful war or vituperative disputes or din of battle, but they lived simply . . . and Justice herself, mistress of the people, giver of just things, furnished all things a thousand-fold.[5]

But the most familiar version of the Golden Age does not, of course, come from classical literature at all. 'Men never rest from labour', says Hesiod: 'In the sweat of thy face thou shalt eat bread', said the Lord God to Adam, 'till thou return into the ground.' The biblical story of the Garden of Eden is a version of the same myth, and phrases like these show how it must have originated – as an attempt to explain why life is so hard. In Eden, as in the Golden Age, the fruitful earth unforced bore fruit.

It is not simply a modern quirk to compare the Christian and pagan versions of this story. From patristic times to at least the seventeenth century there was a tradition that pagan mythology was really about the same things as Christianity. It underlies the whole medieval tradition of 'moralising' or allegorising the classical authors. For a sixteenth-century example, here is part of the prefatory Epistle to Arthur Golding's translation of the *Metamorphoses*:

> Moreover by the Golden Age what other thing is meant,
> Than Adam's time in Paradise, who being innocent
> Did lead a blest and happy life until that thorough sin
> He fell from God? From which time forth all sorrow did begin.[6]

In one respect, Golding is certainly wrong: he has compared not only Eden itself, but also its loss, to the classical story. Now Eden and the Golden Age are the same while we still have them; but they do not come to an end in the same way.

We all know how Eden was lost; but Hesiod's golden race perished through the whim of Zeus. There is nothing you can do about the arbitrariness of the gods except lament and submit; and the implications of the Golden Age story are therefore quietist. But Adam fell: there is a moral dimension in his story. And a moral decision can be discussed, defended, protested against, and perhaps, eventually, reversed. History now becomes a long effort to make ourselves worthy of Paradise again; the story that starts with Eden will culminate in the New Jerusalem.

> Behold, a king shall reign in righteousness, and princes
>   shall rule in judgement.
>   . . .
> And the eyes of them that see shall not be dim, and the
>   ears of them that hear shall hearken.
>   . . .
> Then judgement shall dwell in the wilderness, and righteousness
>   remain in the fruitful field.
>
> They shall not build and another inhabit; they shall not plant
>   and another eat: for as the days of a tree are the days of
>   my people, and mine elect shall long enjoy the work of their
>   hands.
>   . . .
> The wolf and the lamb shall feed together, and the lion shall
>   eat straw like the bullock: and dust shall be the serpent's
>   meat. They shall not hurt nor destroy in all my holy
>   mountain, saith the Lord.
>   [*Isaiah*, ch. 32 (1, 3, 16); ch. 65 (22, 25)]

Isaiah's Paradise is different from Hesiod's. It belongs not at the beginning of time but at the end. It is ruled, not by magic, but by justice. It is not amiable but fiercely moral. The good are to be rewarded, and perhaps their reward is sharpened by the punishment of the wicked: 'dust shall be the serpent's meat'. In the Golden Age there was no agriculture; but in Isaiah's New Jerusalem everyone will work, and distribution will be just.

The Christian version of lost paradise is Eden; the pastoral version is Arcadia (if one is thinking of the place) or the Golden Age (if of the time). Paradise to come is, to the Christian, Heaven (if in another world) or the New Jerusalem (if in this). The secular term is Utopia – or the withering away of the state.

It is true that Arcadia is an actual region of Greece, but as the setting for pastoral poetry it is a land entirely of the fancy. This transformation goes right back to the ancient world: Bruno Snell claims it was due to Virgil.[7] And it is true, too, that the relation between Heaven and the New Jerusalem is sometimes more complicated. In the Book of Revelation there is a period of a thousand years when Satan will be bound and the martyrs will reign with Christ; then the loosing of Satan and a final battle; then the new heaven and the new earth, and 'the holy city, new Jerusalem, coming down from God out of heaven, prepared as a bride for her husband'. All this can be variously interpreted, according as the thousand-year binding of Satan is placed in the past or the future. After the Reformation, when apocalyptic ideas surged into European thought, it was often held that the thousand years were just over. But if they were yet to come, then there were two millennia ahead, and the first or earthly one might well (though this is not John's terminology) be called the New Jerusalem. Yet it does not really matter if the millennium is simple or compound, for in both cases it offers an abolition of history by violent divine intervention, and a kingdom of justice in the end. All this is utterly different from Arcadia and the Golden Age. The one structures our experience with sadness, the other with fierce hope. One speaks an elegy, the other a call to action.

In Christian mouths this call has often had a note of sharp paradox. Though the Fall introduces a moral dimension into history, one prominent strand of Christianity (justification by faith alone) contains a deep rejection of morality. To the Calvinist, we do not make ourselves worthy of Heaven: we are permitted by grace to enter into it. One might have expected this to lead to quietism – the Calvinist, like Hesiod, sadly shrugging his shoulders and waiting for what God is pleased to give him. It has, of course, been one of the great paradoxes of Calvinism that this has not happened: a paradox it shares with Marxism, the great secularised belief in the New Jerusalem. In both cases we have an all-embracing theory that claims understanding of first causes; in both cases the first cause is beyond the control of the individual; and both systems therefore contain a strong potential quietism that has never emerged, for they are both deeply moral. With often astonishing subtlety, both systems tell you that the coming of Jerusalem does not depend on you, and urge you to strive for it.

The most brilliant description I know of the difference between Eden and Utopia is by W. H. Auden.[8] [See the third paragraph in the Auden excerpt in this section of Part Two, above – Ed.] . . .

Auden's poem 'Vespers' describes an encounter between himself and his anti-type: 'I am an Arcadian, he is a Utopian.' The Arcadian's reactions to the world are aesthetic, the Utopian's are political:

Glancing at a lampshade in a store window, I observe it is too
hideous for anyone in their senses to buy: He observes that
it is too expensive for a peasant to buy.

Each has his own dishonesty:

Passing a slum child with rickets, I look the other way: He
looks the other way if he passes a chubby one.

And each has his own kind of religion, the Arcadian's ritualistic, the Utopian's reduced to mere morality:

In my Eden each observes his compulsive rituals and superstitious
tabus but we have no morals: In his New Jerusalem the temples
will be empty but all will practise the rational virtues.

Eden is amiably inaccurate, New Jerusalem is planned:

In my Eden our only source of political news is gossip: In his
New Jerusalem there will be a special daily in simplified
spelling for non-verbal types.

['Vespers', in *The Shield of Achilles* (1955)]

Auden's preference is clear: the resigned preference of the conservative. The Arcadian, having retreated into memory, will not change the world; but at least this means that he will not hurt anybody. People with superstitions instead of morals get nothing done, but they are nice to know. Auden is afraid of zeal, because it can be an outlet for aggression.

The Golden Age belongs to the past; and to put it in the future is likely to change it into Utopia. The restoring of the Golden Age was a commonplace of Renaissance panegyric; but if it is to be restored by the prowess of a prince, it is difficult for it to keep its primitive innocence. I take as an example an inoffensive work by Ben Jonson, his masque on *The Golden Age Restored* (1615). Jonson uses a good deal of traditional Golden Age imagery and did not, I am sure, intend to write an unconventional work. But simply because the Iron Age, as anti-masque, appears at the beginning, it must in some way be defeated. This means that there must be a struggle, and a victory: Pallas shows her shield, and the evils are returned to statues:

> So change and perish scarcely knowing how
> That 'gainst the gods do take so vain a vow.
>   . . .
> Twas time t'appear, and let their folly see
> 'Gainst whom they fought, and with what destiny
> Die all that can remain of you but stone.
>
> [l. 68 ff.]

The return of Astraea is meant to restore harmony, but it is accompanied with fierceness:

> Let narrow natures how they will mistake,
> The great should still be good for their own sake.

'Narrow natures': the intensity of this moral vocabulary destroys the Arcadian spirit. Flattery and Politics have no place in the true primitive ideal.

Yet the most famous of all versions of the Golden Age, and the one that introduced it into the pastoral tradition, is set in the future; somehow carefully preserving its true nature. This is the fourth of Virgil's *Eclogues*, probably the most famous short poem ever written. From the first, it stood out among the *Eclogues*; it is the only one which is neither in dialogue nor about named pastoral figures, and it announces in its opening lines that it is to be read with special awe:

> Sicelides Musae, paulo maiora canamus   [IV 1]

Sicilian Muses, let us sing of something rather greater.

What made the poem so celebrated in the Middle Ages was, of course, its announcement of the birth of a child who would rejuvenate the world; and to the natural interpretations (that the child is the son of Pollio or the son of Octavianus – neither quite fits) was added a supernatural one: that Virgil the magus was foretelling the birth of Christ forty years later. This goes, of course, with the *sortes virgilianae* and with his selection as Dante's guide through Hell and Purgatory.

So far we seem to be dealing with New Jerusalem; and it has even been suggested that Virgil knew a Greek version of Isaiah. But when we look at what this promised new age is going to be like, we can see that it is purely Arcadian. The earth will yield gifts without cultivation. Goats will run around oozing milk. The sheep will grow coloured wool, so that we shan't need dyes. No one will sail on the sea; or rather, they will at first, because of 'vestigia priscae fraudis', but once the child has grown up

> cedet et ipse mari vector, nec nautica pinus
> mutabit merces. [IV 38–9]

The voyager will abandon the sea, and no tall-masted ship will carry goods from one place to another.

It is a bad mistake to render 'priscae fraudis' (as one translator does) by 'primal error', or indeed by any phrase that suggests sin or the Fall. It simply means 'the way we live now'. What will impede our regeneration is not human wickedness but the slow revolving of the spindles of Fate. The Parcae have already given the command:

> 'Talia saecla' suis dixerunt 'currite' fusis
> concordes stabili fatorum numine Parcae. [IV 46–7]

The Fates, in accordance with the unalterable will of destiny, said to their spindles, 'Run through these new ages'.

The whole thing is to happen without human action: there is no Day of Judgement. For, though a day of Judgement is God's work, not man's, its purpose is to *judge*, to separate sheep from goats; and what happens will therefore in some degree depend on man. Even the fierce arbitrariness of the Calvinist God is presented as if it was moral, not as the waywardness of a world of natural magic, whereas Virgil's new age is quite unselective: it is simply what's going to happen to the world, and it is for the just and unjust alike.

The stages of the new Golden Age are marked in the poem by the growth of the child. At first he is an infant, then he has learned to read, then fully-grown age has made him a man. But these steps in his growth simply accompany the unfolding of the new age, they do not cause it. 'When he can read' – what follows is not what he will now be able to do for mankind, but simply what the spindles of the Parcae bring next:

> molli paulatim flavescet campus arista,
> incultisque rubens pendebit sentibus uva,
> et durae quercus sudabunt roscida mella. [IV 28–30]

Gradually the plain will grow yellow with supple corn, without cultivation the grape will hang ruddy on the brambles, and tough oaks will ooze honey-dew.

I can find only one truly Utopian touch in this Arcadian idyll; that is line 17:

> pacatumque reget patriis virtutibus orbem.

The child will rule over a world pacified by 'patriis virtutibus'.

Now here is an ambiguity. If it means 'by the prowess of his father', then there is going to be some political cleaning-up by the child's father – Octavianus, or Pollio, or whoever it is – to make things ready. Such cleaning-up, as Auden brilliantly reminds us, is Utopian, not Arcadian:

> . . .   when lights burn late in the Citadel,
>
> I (who have never seen the inside of a police station) am
>   shocked and think: 'Were the city as free as they say, after
>   sundown all her bureaus would be huge black stone':
>
> He (who has been beaten up several times) is not shocked at all
>   but thinks: 'One fine night our boys will be working up there.'

But if 'patriis virtutibus' means 'by our ancestral virtues', then Octavianus's boys are not going to be working late in the citadel, for the line is about the past only.

Certainly this is the only political line in the poem, the only line that looks forward to the fearful virtue of the *Aeneid*. It is a line which Pope leaned on very heavily for his free rendering of the Eclogue:

> No more shall nation against nation rise,
> Nor ardent warriors meet with hateful eyes,
> Nor fields with gleaming steel be cover'd o'er;
> The brazen trumpets kindle rage no more.   [*Messiah: A*
> *Sacred Eclogue in Imitation of Virgil's Pollio* (1712), 57–60]

All that is squeezed out of 'pacatum'. Pope set out to rewrite Virgil in the light of Isaiah, and to show 'how far the images and descriptions of the Prophet are superior to those of the Poet'. This meant turning Arcadia into Utopia, and he even called his version *Messiah*.

Virgil, however, has not left the Arcadian world: his first line was at least partly misleading. If he is writing prophecy, it is not Messianic prophecy; looking into the future he sees the original Golden Age. The Virgil of the *Aeneid* is a long way off: even the Virgil of the *Georgics* is not yet present.

The *Georgics* are nature poems. They tell of crops and weather, of the planting of trees and vines, of the raising of cattle and bees. They are almost a practical handbook, by a poet who prided himself on his knowledge of the countryside. They also contain a long praise of rural content, contrasted with the restless life of soldier or merchant, and seen as a thing of the past:

> Hanc olim veteres vitam coluere Sabini,
> hanc Remus et frater . . .   [*Georgics*, II 572–3]

This was the life which the ancient Sabines led, or Remus and his brother.

So the Golden Age is naturally mentioned; but when Virgil speaks of it at length, he speaks of its end:

> Ille malum virus serpentibus addidit atris
> praedarique lupos iussit pontumque moveri   [I 129–30]

He – Juppiter – gave deadly poison to the black snakes, and ordered wolves to pillage and the sea to rage in storms.

Not the Golden Age itself, but the evils that have followed it, is the theme of the *Georgics*; not Saturn's earth that yielded crops 'nullo culto', but the details of husbandry rendered necessary by the reign of Jove; not pastoral but nature.

Each of Virgil's three poems has its version of the Golden Age; and that in the *Aeneid* is different again. They had no agriculture, not because their life was easy, but because it was hard. They were not able to lay up stores,

> sed rami atque asper victu venatus alebat [*Aeneid*, VIII 318]

But lived off the hard fare of hunting and fruit from the bough.

This stern existence no doubt fits the epic spirit; and it puts Virgil (for the moment) among the hard primitives. I take the term from Lovejoy and Boas's useful contrast between soft primitivism, which delights in the freedom of primitive man to do as he pleases, in the dream 'of a life with little or no toil or strain of body or mind'; and hard primitivism, which praises the austerity and stern character training of primitive society.[9] The finest example of hard primitivism in English poetry is the eighth book of *The Prelude*, in which Wordsworth contrasts the life of classical or Mediterranean shepherds with those of Cumberland:

> Smooth life had flock and shepherd in old time,
> Long springs and tepid winters, on the banks
> Of delicate Galesus.   · · ·   [*Prelude*, VIII 173–5]

But the bleak life of the Lake District produces 'a free man, wedded to his life of hope and hazard' – austere, difficult, and imaginatively far richer:

> · · ·   The lingering dews of morn
> Smoke round him, as from hill to hill he hies,
> His staff pretending like a hunter's spear.   [VIII 244–6]

Hard primitivism is unpastoral – goes, even, with its explicit rejection. The shepherds of the Golden Age leapt from no rocks, battled through no mists, but spent their hours

> In unlaborious pleasure, with no task
> More toilsome than to carve a beechen bowl.   [VIII 205–6]

Wordsworth is the great unpastoral poet in English: not anti-pastoral in the sense of Touchstone and Sidney, rejecting country life for court, but unpastoral in his concern with incidents and situations from common life – a poet of the direct, not the mediated, provincial. So it is appropriate that he finds soft primitivism slightly unreal and not altogether admirable.

CONCLUSION

'Pastoral', says Pope, reproducing a commonplace of literary theory, 'is an image of what they call the Golden age. . . . we are not to describe our shepherds as shepherds at this day really are, but as they may be conceiv'd then to have been; when . . . the best of men follow'd the employment' ('A Discourse on Pastoral Poetry'). Samuel Johnson found this difficult to understand: 'I cannot understand easily discover why it is thought necessary to refer descriptions of a rural state to remote times . . . .' (*Rambler*, No. 37). [See the Pope and Johnson essays in Part One, above – Ed.] Nor does he make much effort to discover it, for with his usual sturdy empiricism Johnson deduces the qualities of pastoral, not from a conception of the genre, but from what he finds in pastoral poems – i.e. (since he is an equally sturdy defender of the Ancients), in Theocritus and Virgil. Surprisingly, he does not notice the Golden Age in the fourth Eclogue in which, he tells us, 'all the images are either taken from the country or from the religion of the age common to all parts of the Empire'. This is certainly untrue: neither the Italian countryside nor the religion of the age produces rams which

> . . .   iam suave rubenti
> murice, iam croceo mutabit vellera luto   [*Ec.*, IV 33–4]

will change their fleece, now to a pleasant purple colour, now to the yellow of the crocus.

There are two answers to Johnson. The first (from literary history) is that Renaissance pastoral is not really the work of Theocritus and Virgil but of Sannazaro, Tasso and Marot. The second (more far-reaching) is that we should wonder why a court poet would want to write about the country; and if I am right in suggesting that his interest is mediated, not direct, then it is not enough to refer his work to the natural countryside. 'We must . . . use some illusion', said Pope, 'to render a Pastoral delightful . . . in exposing the best side only of a shepherd's life, and in concealing its miseries.'

'Illusion': the term is Pope's, but as it happens the meaning corresponds to the Freudian use:

An illusion is not the same as an error, it is indeed not necessarily an error. Aristotle's belief that vermin are evolved out of dung . . . was an error. . . . On the other hand, it was an illusion on the part of Columbus that he had discovered a new sea-route to India. The part played by his wish in this error is very clear.[10]

An illusion, Freud concludes, is a belief in which 'wish-fulfilment is a prominent factor in its motivation'. The wish to find in country life a relief from the problems of a sophisticated society formed itself, in Renaissance times, into a set of poetic conventions. These are the conventions of pastoral. Pastoral is the poetry of illusion: the Golden Age is the historiography of wish-fulfilment.

SOURCE: adapted by the author, for this Casebook, from *The Uses of Nostalgia* (London, 1972).

NOTES

1. Marvell's 'Ametas and Thestylis Making Hay-ropes' was published in *Poems* (1681), but written c. 1650.

2. C. S. Lewis, *The Allegory of Love* (London, 1936), ch. 7.

3. Thomas Lodge, *Rosalynde* (1590) is the source of *As You Like It*.

4. Hesiod, *Works and Days* (8th century BC).

5. Aratus, *Phaenomena* (3rd century BC). See Harry Levin, *The Myth of the Golden Age in the Renaissance* (Bloomington, Ind., 1969; London, 1970), ch. 1.

6. Arthur Golding, *The XV Books of P. Ovidius Naso entitled Metamorphosis* (1567): the Epistle, 469–72.

7. Bruno Snell, *The Discovery of the Mind*, trans. T. G. Rosenmeyer (Cambridge, Mass., 1953), ch. 13.

8. W. H. Auden, 'Dingley Dell and The Fleet' (1948): in *The Dyer's Hand and Other Essays* (New York, 1962; London, 1963), p. 409.

9. Arthur Lovejoy and George Boas, *A Documentary History of Primitivism and Related Ideas in Antiquity* (Baltimore, Md., 1935).

10. Sigmund Freud, 'The Future of an Illusion' (1927); in James Strachey (ed.), *The Complete Psychological Works of Sigmund Freud* (London, 1961), XXI, p. 30.

Raymond Williams   Pastoral and Counter-
Pastoral   (1973)

> No longer truth, though shown in verse, disdain,
> But own the Village Life a life of pain.

This couplet of Crabbe's, which opens the second book of *The Village*,
is a significant introduction to the character of the general problem.
Where did it come from, that tone of apology about verse? Who was it
aimed at, that insistence on the truth? Crabbe's poem, *The Village*,
needs to be read between these questions.

> By such examples taught, I paint the Cot,
> As Truth will paint it, and as Bards will not.

Truth again, and against poetry. Whatever we may later ask about
Crabbe's England, it is clear that the contrast in his mind is not
between rural England past and present, but between true and false
ways of writing. More generally, the contrast he is forcing is between a
tradition of pastoral poetry and his own intention of realism. He
assumes, certainly, that there was once a basis for what he knew as
pastoral, but in classical times, not in his own or recent England:

> Fled are those times, when in harmonious strains
> The rustic poet praised his native plains:
> No shepherds now, in smooth alternate verse,
> Their country's beauty or their nymphs' rehearse.

It is a literary tradition, that of neo-classic pastoral, that is being
formally rejected: 'mechanick echoes of the Mantuan song'. Or, as
Crabbe originally wrote, before Johnson's amendment of his lines:

> In fairer scenes, where peaceful pleasures spring,
> Tityrus the pride of Mantuan swains might sing;
> But, charmed by him, or smitten with his views,
> Shall modern poets court the Mantuan muse?
> From Truth and Nature shall we widely stray,
> Where Fancy leads, or Virgil led the way.

Johnson weakened this by amending the last lines to 'where Virgil,
not where Fancy, leads the way'.[1] It would have been better if Crabbe
had not needed, as in practice he did, Johnson's help.

'A way of life that has come down to us from the days of Virgil.'[2] But
if it is the continuity of a settled agriculture, it is from very much
earlier than that. The literary reference, for a presumed social fact, is

the really significant structure. It is symptomatic of the confusion which surrounds the whole question of 'pastoral'. . . .

All traditions are selective: the pastoral tradition quite as much as any other. Where poets run scholars follow, and questions about the 'pastoral' poetry or the poetry of 'rural retreat' of our own sixteenth to eighteenth centuries are again and again turned aside by the confident glossing and glozing of the reference back. We must not look, with Crabbe and others, at what the country was really like: that is a utilitarian or materialist, perhaps even a peasant response. Let us remember, instead, that this poem is based on Horace, Epode II or Virgil, Eclogue IV; that among the high far names are Theocritus and Hesiod: the Golden Age in another sense.

It is time that this bluff was called. Academic gloss has made such a habit of tracing influences that it needs the constant correction of a Coleridge, to those

who seem to hold, that every possible thought and image is traditional; who have no notion that there are such things as fountains in the world, small as well as great; and who would therefore charitably derive every rill they behold flowing, from a perforation made in some other man's tank.[3]

And how much more is this necessary when the presumed sources, the other men's tanks, have been so altered and simplified that nobody can easily see what has happened, meanwhile, to the water.

We must therefore use some illusion to render a Pastoral delightful; and this consists in exposing the best side only of a shepherd's life, and in concealing its miseries.[4]

When Pope could say that, the 'tradition' had been altered. 'No longer truth, though shown in verse.' The long critical dispute, in the seventeenth and eighteenth centuries, on the character of pastoral poetry had this much, at least, as common ground. What was at issue was mainly whether such an idyll, the delightful Pastoral, should be referred always to the Golden Age, as Rapin and the neo-classicists argued; or to the more permanent and indeed timeless idea of the tranquillity of life in the country, as Fontenelle and others maintained. In the former case, because it was the Golden Age, there was really peace and innocence. In the latter, there could still be an idea of these, a conventional literary illusion in native and contemporary scenes: 'exposing to the Eye only the Tranquility of a Shepherd's Life, and dissembling or concealing its meanness, as also in showing only its Innocence, and hiding its Miseries.'

It is with this in mind that we can understand Crabbe:

> But when amid such pleasing scenes I trace
> The poor laborious natives of the place,
> And see the mid-day sun, with fervid ray,
> On their bare heads and dewy temples play;
> While some, with feebler heads and fainter hearts,
> Deplore their fortune, yet sustain their parts:
> Then shall I dare these real ills to hide
> In tinsel trappings of poetic pride?

The question 'shall I dare?' carries the felt outrage, at one of those critical moments, a crisis of perspective, when habits, institutions and experiences clash. Who are they, who dare in this way, to whom Crabbe addresses himself?

> Oh trifle not with wants you cannot feel,
> Nor mock the misery of a stinted meal;
> Homely, not wholesome, plain, not plenteous, such
> As you who praise would never deign to touch.
> Ye gentle souls, who dream of rural ease,
> Whom the smooth stream and smoother sonnet please;
> Go! if the peaceful cot your praises share,
> Go look within, and ask if peace be there.

They are a numerous company, these pretenders to simplicity. It is possible to follow a direct line from Virgil, at the end of which, as in the English 'Augustans', the eclogue has become a highly artificial and abstracted form: its simplicities wholly external. But the line runs also from the *Georgics*, and in Politian and Alamanni, for example, in the late fifteenth and early sixteenth centuries, there is inspiration as well as imitation: the verse of Politian's *Rusticus* is in Latin but the working year he describes is that of the Tuscan peasant; Alamanni's *La Coltivazione* is a modern Italian equivalent to the working descriptions of country life of the *Georgics*.

Yet 'pastoral', with its once precise meaning, was undergoing in the same period an extraordinary transformation. Its most serious element was a renewed intensity of attention to natural beauty, but this is now the nature of observation, of the scientist or the tourist, rather than of the working countryman. Thus the descriptive element in original pastoral could be separated out, and a whole tradition of 'nature poetry', strong and moving in these separated ways, could be founded to go on its major course, over several centuries into our own time. The other main element was very different: pastoral became theatrical and romantic, in the strict senses. The pastoral romance, from Boccaccio to Sannazzaro's *Arcadia* (c. 1500), was a new form, in which the eclogue and natural description were absorbed into the essentially different world of an idealised romantic love. That the shepherds in pastoral had sung love-songs was the nominal basis, but the shepherds and nymphs who now begin to appear are lay figures in an aristocratic entertainment. The pastoral drama, beginning with Tasso's *Aminta* (1572), is similarly the creation of a princely court, in which the shepherd is an idealised mask, a courtly disguise: a traditionally innocent figure through whom, paradoxically, intrigue can be elaborated. This filigree game, which continued as a form of aristocratic entertainment as late as Marie Antoinette, and which has left, its physical legacy in its thousands of painted porcelain figures, has more connection, obviously, with the real interests of the court than with country life in any of its possible forms.

Yet this was not always realised. Pope took the game for the fact, in his essay on pastoral, and recommended description 'not . . . as shepherds at this day really are but as they may be conceiv'd to have been; when the best of men follow'd the employment'. If courtiers played shepherd long enough, original shepherds must have been aristocrats.

But the offered simplicity was not only this kind of fancy dress. A second real interest of the time found its way into pastoral: the medieval and post-medieval habit of allegory. Puttenham in 1589 argued that the Eclogue was devised 'not of purpose to counterfeit or represent the rusticall manner of loves or communications: but under the vaile of homely persons, and in rude speeches, to insinuate and glance at great matters'.[5] [See excerpt in Part One, above – Ed.]

He went on to say that this was true of Virgil, and this is the exact process of selective cultural adaptation. Virgil, like Hesiod, could raise the most serious questions of life and its purposes in the direct world in which the working year and the pastoral song are still there in their own right. What happened in the aristocratic transformation was the reduction of these primary activities to forms, whether the 'vaile' of allegory or the fancy dress of court games. It is a significant change, but it has been so prepotent – though its impulses, one would think, had been so long dead – that the ordinary modern meaning of pastoral, in the critical discourse of otherwise twentieth-century writers, has been derived from these forms, rather than from the original substance or from its more significant successors. 'Pastoral' means, we are told, the simple matter in which general truths are embodied or implied: even a modern proletarian industrial novel can be pastoral in this sense! But while as a critical procedure for understanding, say, Spenser, this is fair enough, its extension is absurd, and the absurdity has a point. As in so many other areas of English literary thought, there has been an effective and voluntary congealment at the point of significant historical transition, from a feudal to a bourgeois world. If pastoral is only a disguise or an allegory, Crabbe's question has no point; it is no more than a rude noise. But Crabbe's is a question which has to be answered, if the reality of a major transition is to be acknowledged and understood.

For the pastoral of the courts and of the aristocratic houses was not, as it came through, the really significant development. Isolated in time and in status, its modes and its realities are quite easily understood. What is much more significant is the internal transformation of just this artificial mode in the direction and in the interest of a new kind of society: that of a developing agrarian capitalism. Neo-pastoral as a court entertainment is one thing; neo-pastoral in its new location, the country-house and its estate, is quite another. We must follow the development of the artificial eclogue and idyll, but we shall only arrive at the decisive transition when these have been relocated, in a new ideology, in the country-house . . . .

. . . at the centre of the structure of feeling which is here in question – a relation between the country houses and a responsible civilisation – are the poems to actual places and men: notably Ben Jonson's *Penshurst* and *To Sir Robert Wroth*,[6] and Thomas Carew's *To Saxham*. These are not, in any simple sense, pastoral or neo-pastoral, but they use a particular version of country life as a way of expressing, in the form of a compliment to a house or its owner, certain social and moral values.

> How blest art thou, canst love the countrey, Wroth,
> Whether by choice, or fate, or both;
> And, though so neere the citie, and the court,
> Art tane with neither's vice, nor sport.

The life of a country gentleman is thus celebrated as an explicit contrast to the life of the court and the city. The figures of city lawyer, city capitalist, and courtier, are brought in to point the moral.

In Wroth's rural economy, as the poem proceeds and as 'the rout of rurall folke come thronging in', there is an emphasis on the absence of pride and greed and calculation. And then Jonson can turn, positively, to identify and localise the pastoral convention:

> Such, and no other, was that age of old,
> Which boasts t'have had the head of gold.

But is it really so, past the lattice of compliment? Has a neo-pastoral vision acquired a social base, in a Tudor country house? Some critics have taken it so, but the complexity of *To Penshurst* would in any case make us pause. For what is most remarkable about it, in any open reading, is its procedure of definition by negatives:

> Thou are not, Penshurst, built to envious show
> Of touch, or marble; nor canst boast a row
> Of polish'd pillars, or a roofe of gold:
> Thou hast no lantherne, wherof tales are told;
> Or stayre, or courts; but stand'st an ancient pile,
> And these grudg'd at, art reverenc'd the while;
> . . .
> And though thy walls be of the countrey stone,
> They are rear'd with no man's ruine, no mans grone,
> There's none, that dwell about them, wish them downe.
> . . .
> Now, Penshurst, they that will proportion thee
> With other edifices, when they see
> Those proud ambitious heaps, and nothing else,
> May say, their lords have built, but thy lord dwells.

This declaration by negative and contrast, not now with city and court but with other country houses, is enough in itself to remind us that we can make no simple extension from Penshurst to a whole country civilisation. The forces of pride, greed and calculation are evidently active among landowners as well as among city merchants and courtiers. What is being celebrated is then perhaps an idea of rural society, as against the pressures of a new age; and the embodiment of this idea is the house in which Jonson has been entertained.

This is where the comparison with Carew's *To Saxham* is particularly relevant. For there too, as it happens, there is a definition by negatives, though now in a different house:

> Thou hast no Porter at the door
> T'examine, or keep back the poor;
> Nor locks nor bolts; thy gates have been
> Made only to let strangers in.

Or again, more subtly:

> The cold and frozen air had sterv'd
> Much poore, if not by thee preserv'd,
> Whose prayers have made thy Table blest
> With plenty, far above the rest.

The island of Charity is the house where the poet himself eats; but that it is an island, in an otherwise harsh economy, is the whole point of the successive compliments.

We need not refuse Jonson and Carew the courtesy of their lucky exceptions: their Penshurst and Saxham 'rear'd', unlike others, 'with no man's ruine, no mans grone'; with none, 'that dwell about them', wishing them 'downe'. There were, we need not doubt, such houses and such men, but they were at best the gentle exercise of a power that was elsewhere, on their own evidence, mean and brutal. The morality is not, when we look into it, the fruit of the economy; it is a local stand and standard against it.

It is of course clear that in each of the poems, though more strongly and convincingly in Jonson, the social order is seen as part of a wider order: what is now sometimes called a natural order, with metaphysical sanctions. Certainly nothing is more remarkable than the stress on the providence of Nature, but this, we must see on reflection, is double-edged. What kind of wit is it exactly – for it must be wit; the most ardent traditionalist will hardly claim it for observation – which has the birds and other creatures offering themselves to be eaten? The estate of Penshurst, as Jonson sees it:

> To crowne thy open table, doth provide
> The purpled pheasant with the speckled side:
> The painted partrich lyes in every field
> And, for thy messe, is willing to be kill'd.

Carew extends this same hyperbole:

> The Pheasant, Partridge, and the Lark
> Flew to my house, as to the Ark.
> The willing Oxe, of himselfe came
> Home to the slaughter, with the Lamb,
> And every beast did thither bring
> Himselfe to be an offering.
> The scalie herd, more pleasure took
> Bath'd in the dish than in the brook.

In fact the wit depends, in such passages, on a shared and conscious point of view towards nature. The awareness of hyperbole is there, is indeed what is conventional in just this literary convention, and is controlled and ratified, in any wider view, by a common consciousness. At one level this is a willing and happy ethic of consuming, made evident by the organisation of the poems around the centrality of the dining-table. Yet the possible grossness of this, as in Carew (a willing largeness of hyperbole, as in so many cavalier poems, as the awareness of an alternative point of view makes simple statement impossible) is modified in Jonson by a certain pathos, a conscious realisation of his situation:

> And I not faine to sit (as some, this day,
> At great men's tables) and yet dine away.
> Here no man tells my cups; nor, standing by,
> A waiter, doth my gluttony envy:
> But gives me what I call, and lets me eate.

It is difficult not to feel the relief of that. Indeed there is more than a hint, in the whole tone of his hospitable eating and drinking, of that easy, insatiable exploitation of the land and its creatures – a prolonged delight in an organised and corporative production and consumption – which is the basis of many early phases of intensive agriculture: the land is rich, and will be made to provide. But it is then more difficult to talk, in a simple way, of a 'natural order', as if this was man in concert with nature. On the contrary: this natural order is simply and decisively on its way to table.

Of course, in both Jonson and Carew, though again more convincingly in Jonson, this view of the providence of nature is linked to a human sharing: all are welcome, even the poor, to be fed at this board. And it is this stress, more than any other, which has supported the view of a responsible civilisation, in which men care for each other directly and personally, rather than through the abstractions of a more complicated and more commercial society. This, we are told, is the natural order of responsibility and neighbourliness and charity: words we do not now clearly understand, since Old England fell.

Of course one sees what is meant, and as a first approximation, a simple impulse, it is kindly. But the Christian tradition of charity is at just this point weak. For it is a charity of consumption only, as Rosa Luxemburg first pointed out:

The Roman proletarians did not live by working, but from the alms which the government doled out. So the demands of the Christians for collective property did not relate to the means of production, but the means of consumption.[6]

And then, as Adrian Cunningham has argued, this version of charity – of loving relations between men expressed as a community of consumption, with the Christian board and breaking of bread as its natural images, and the feast as its social consummation – was prolonged into periods and societies in which it became peripheral or even damaging. A charity of production – of loving relations between men actually working and producing what is ultimately, in whatever proportions, to be shared – was neglected, not seen, and at times suppressed, by this habitual reference to a charity of consumption, an eating and drinking communion, which when applied to ordinary working societies was inevitably a mystification. All uncharity at work, it was readily assumed, could be redeemed by the charity of the consequent feast. In the complex of feeling and reference derived from this tradition, it matters very much, moreover, that the name of the god and the name of the master are significantly single – our Lord.

Any mystification, however, requires effort. The world of Pens-

hurst or of Saxham can be seen as a moral economy only by
conscious selection and emphasis. And this is just what we get: not
only in the critical reading I have referred to, but in Jonson's and
Carew's actual poems. There were of course social reasons for that
way of seeing: the identification of the writers, as guests, with the
social position of their hosts, consuming what other men had
produced. But a traditional image, already becoming complicated,
was an indispensable poetic support. It is not only the Golden Age, as
in Jonson to Sir Robert Wroth, though Penshurst, in its first positive
description, is seen through classical literature: the woods of Kent
contain Dryads and Pan and Bacchus, and the providing deities of the
charity are Penates. More deeply, however, in a conventional
association of Christian and classical myth, the provident land is seen
as Eden. This country in which all things come naturally to man, for
his use and enjoyment and without his effort, is that Paradise:

> The early cherry, with the later plum,
> Fig, grape and quince, each in his time doth come:
> The blushing apricot, and woolly peach
> Hang on thy walls, that every child may reach.

Except that it is not seen as Paradise; it is seen as Penshurst, a natural
order arranged by a proprietary lord and lady. The manipulation is
evident when we remember Marvell's somewhat similar lines in *The
Garden*:

> The Nectaren, and curious Peach
> Into my hands themselves do reach;
> Stumbling on Melons, as I pass,
> Insnar'd with flowers, I fall on grass.

Here the enjoyment of what seems a natural bounty, a feeling of
paradise in the garden, is exposed to another kind of wit: the easy
consumption goes before the fall. And we can then remember that the
whole result of the fall from paradise was that instead of picking easily
from an all-providing nature, man had to earn his bread in the sweat
of his brow; that he incurred, as a common fate, the curse of labour.
What is really happening, in Jonson's and Carew's celebrations of a
rural order, is an extraction of just this curse, by the power of art: a
magical recreation of what can be seen as a natural bounty and then a
willing charity: both serving to ratify and bless the country land-
owner, or, by a characteristic reification, his house. Yet this magical
extraction of the curse of labour is in fact achieved by a simple
extraction of the existence of labourers. The actual men and women
who rear the animals and drive them to the house and kill them and
prepare them for meat; who trap the pheasants and partridges and

catch the fish; who plant and manure and prune and harvest the fruit trees: these are not present; their work is all done for them by a natural order. When they do at last appear, it is merely as the 'rout of rurall folke' or, more simply, as 'much poore', and what we are then shown is the charity and lack of condescension with which they are given what, now and somehow, not they but the natural order has given for food, into the lord's hands. It is this condition, this set of relationships, that is finally ratified by the consummation of the feast. It is worth setting briefly alongside this a later description of a country feast, by one of the labourers: Stephen Duck, in the late 1720s:

> A Table plentifully spread we find,
> And jugs of huming Ale to cheer the Mind,
> Which he, too gen'rous, pushes round so fast,
> We think no Toils to come, nor mind the past.
> But the next Morning soon reveals the Cheat,
> When the same Toils we must again repeat;
> To the same Barns must back again return,
> To labour there for Room for next Year's Corn.[7]

It is this connection, between the feast and work, that the earlier images significantly obscure, taking the passing moment in which anyone might forget labour and acquiesce in 'the Cheat', and making it 'natural' and permanent. It is this way of seeing that really counts. Jonson looks out over the fields of Penshurst and sees, not work, but a land yielding of itself. Carew, characteristically, does not even look:

> Though frost, and snow, lock'd from mine eyes
> That beauty which without door lyes;
> . . .
> Yet (Saxham) thou within thy gate
> Art of thy selfe so delicate,
> So full of native sweets, that bless
> Thy roof with inward happiness;
> As neither from, nor to thy store,
> Winter takes ought, or Spring adds more.

So that here not only work, but even the turning produce of the seasons, is suppressed or obscured in the complimentary mystification: an innate bounty: 'native sweets'. To call this a natural order is then an abuse of language. It is what the poems are: not country life but social compliment; the familiar hyperboles of the aristocracy and its attendants.

The social order within which Jonson's and Carew's poems took conventional shape was in fact directly described, in another kind of country poem, of which Herrick's *The Hock-Cart* (1648) is a good example. Here the fact of labour is acknowledged:

> Come Sons of Summer, by whose toile
> We are the Lords of Wine and Oile:
> By whose tough labours, and rough hands,
> We rip up first, then reap our lands.
> Crown'd with the eares of corne, now come,
> And to the Pipe, sing Harvest home.

But this is that special kind of work-song, addressed to the work of others. When the harvest has been brought home, the poem continues:

> Come forth, my Lord, and see the Cart.

This lord is (in the poem's address) the 'Right Honourable Lord Mildmay, Earle of Westmorland', and Herrick places himself between the lord and the labourers to make explicit (what in Jonson and Carew had been implicit and mystified) the governing social relations. The labourers must drink to the Lord's health, and then remember all to go back to work, like the animals:

> . . .   Ye must revoke
> The patient Oxe unto the Yoke
> And all goe back unto the plough
> And Harrow (though they're hang'd up now)
> And, you must know, your Lord's word's true,
> Feed him ye must, whose food fills you.
> And that this pleasure is like raine
> Not sent ye for to drowne your paine
> But for to make it spring againe.

It is crude in feeling, this early and jollying kind of man-management, which uses the metaphors of rain and spring to see even the drink as a way of getting more labour (and more pain). But what is there on the surface –

> Feed him ye must, whose food fills you

– is the aching paradox which is subsumed in the earlier images of natural bounty. It is perhaps not surprising that *The Hock-Cart* is less often quoted, as an example of a natural and moral economy, than *Penshurst* or *To Saxham*. Yet all that is in question is the degree of consciousness of real processes. What Herrick embarrassingly intones is what Jonson and Carew mediate. It is a social order, and a consequent way of seeing, which we are not now likely to forget.

SOURCE: extracts from ch. 3, 'Pastoral and Counter-Pastoral', in *The Country and the City* (London, 1973), pp. 13–14, 18–22, 27–34.

NOTES

[Reorganised and renumbered from the original – Ed.]

1. The evidence for this amendment is Boswell's *Life of Samuel Johnson*, ed. J. W. Croker (London, 1831), v, p. 55.

2. G. Ewart Evans, *The Pattern under the Plough* (London, 1966), p. 17.

3. Preface to *Christabel*, in S. Potter (ed.), *Select Poetry and Prose of S. T. Coleridge* (London, 1950), p. 58.

4. Pope, 'A Discourse on Pastoral Poetry'; said by Pope to have been written in 1704, first published in 1717.

5. G. Puttenham, *The Arte of English Poesie* (1589), ed. G. D. Willcock and A. Walker (Cambridge, 1936), p. 36.

6. R. Luxemburg, 'Socialism and the Churches'; cited by A. Cunningham, *Catholics and the Left* (London, 1966), pp. 83–4.

7. Stephen Duck, 'The Thresher's Labour', in *Poems on Several Occasions* (London, 1736).

Peter Weston   The Noble Primitive as Bourgeois Subject   (1984)

'Men make their own history', wrote Marx, 'but they do not make it just as they please; they do not make it under circumstances chosen by themselves, but under circumstances directly encountered, given and transmitted from the past.' Precisely at times of rapid social change, when something quite new is emerging, he argues, people borrow 'names, battle cries and costumes' from the past. 'Cromwell and the English people had borrowed speech, passions and illusions from the Old Testament for their bourgeois revolution. When the real aim had been achieved, when the bourgeois transformation of English society had been accomplished, Locke supplanted Habakkuk.'[1]

The progressive discovery by Europeans of the indigenous people of the Americas during the sixteenth and seventeenth centuries was a significant part of the profound challenge to the medieval Christian world-view which goes under the metaphorical title of 'renaissance'. What was eventually 'born' was the bourgeoisie: but the 'conception' was mediated by names, costumes and illusions from earlier discourses of European culture and history. The hitherto unknown races of North America at first found their way into English culture, or became conceivable for that culture, only through identification with earlier forms and ideas produced by that culture. However, by the time of Locke, the new bourgeois 'subject' – that autonomous, unitary self which lies at the very heart of bourgeois notions of identity and freedom – had, philosophically, fully emerged, and this made it possible for the 'noble savage', as a paradigm of that very bourgeois subject, to be ratified, as a new conceptual category into which the North American 'Indians' could fit. The story of discovery, then, is one of early uneasy and imperfect accommodation of the American Indian, followed in the late seventeenth century by triumphant misrecognition of the 'noble savage'; followed again, after the brutalities of colonialism during the eighteenth century, by that struggle towards cultural relativism marked en route by the sentimentalism of both terror and nostalgia.

The first official history of the Indies was written (in Latin) by Peter Martyr of Anghiera,[2] an Italian humanist at the Spanish court, and friend of Columbus. The first 'Decade' of his *De Orbe Novo* was published in 1511. The work was translated into English and published in 1555 as *The Decades of the New World or West India*. The fundamental problems which the discovery of a 'new world' posed for philosophy and theology were negotiated by Martyr by a simple, though tentative, equation: the new world is in essence the lost, prelapsarian 'old' world, the classical 'golden age'. Martyr writes:

The inhabitants of these islands have been ever so used to live at liberty, in play and pastime . . . they seem to live in that golden world of which the old writers speak so much, wherein men lived simply and innocently without enforcement of laws, without quarrelling, judges and libels, content only to satisfy nature, without further vexation for knowledge of things to come. . . . For it is certain that among them the land is as common as the sun and water, and that Mine and Thine, (the seeds of all mischief) have no place with them. They are content with so little, that in so large a country they have rather superfluity than scarceness, so that (as we have said before) they seem to live in the golden world without toil, living in open gardens, not entrenched with ditches, divided with hedges, or defended with walls. They deal truly with one another, without laws, without books and without judges.[3]

This description reproduces the essential features of Ovid's Golden Age. George Sandys, who was a colonial administrator in Virginia, published in 1632 his *Ovids Metamorphoses Englished*. The relevant section reads:

> The Golden Age was first; which uncompeld,
> And without rule, in faith and Truth exceld.
> As then, there was nor punishment, nor feare;
> Nor threatning Lawes in brasse prescribed were;
> Nor suppliant crouching pris'ners shooke to see

Their angric Iudge: but all was safe and free.
To visit other Worlds, no wounded Pine
Did yet from Hills to faithlesse Seas decline.
Then, un-ambitious Mortals knew no more,
But their owne Countrie's Nature-bounded shore.
Nor Swords, nor Armes were yet: no trenches round
Besieged Townes, nor strifefull Trumpets sound:
The Souldier, of no use. In firme content
And harmlesse ease, their happy daies were spent.
The yet-free Earth did of her own accord
(Untorne with ploughs) all sorts of fruit afford.
Content with Natures un-enforced food,
They gather Wildings, Strawb'ries of the Wood,
Sowre Cornels, what upon the Bramble growes,
And Acornes, which love's spreading Oke bestowes.
'Twas alwaies Spring; warme Zephyrus sweetly blew
On smiling flowres, which without setting grew.
Forth-with the Earth corne, unmanured, beares;
And every yeere renewes her golden Eares:
With Milke and Nectar were the Rivers fill'd;
And Hony from greene Holly-okes distill'd.[4]

This is a picture of a world not just without law, but without the need for law, because 'all was safe and free', and without war, because 'un-ambitious Mortals' stayed at home. There was also no need for labour, because the 'yet-free Earth' produced food and flowers in variety and abundance. Martyr's appropriation of Ovid for a description of his Indians thus conceptualises them as inhabiting an ahistorical 'natural' world, without toil, ambition or private property. This mythical context (after all, both Martyr and Sandys were agents of aggressive and expanding colonial imperialisms) was readily taken over by the European pastoral verse tradition which structures itself on an opposition between the 'natural' and the 'civilised' (courtly or urban), in favour of the former.

There was, however, another traditional discourse into which it was possible to insert the American Indians in the sixteenth century, and that was that of the 'wild man' of European folklore.[5] As a popular, rather than literary tradition, the 'wild man' myth seems to have been at least as widespread as the Roman Empire, and it seems to have survived into the medieval period through peasant agricultural festivities of which there is no specific record. The attributes of the 'wild man', therefore, vary a great deal, but literary evidence (for example from Arthurian romances of the twelfth century) indicates certain basic features: he was hairy; he was strong, being physically superior to dragons, serpents, bears and bulls; he had mastery over animals; he was aggressive; he lived isolated in woods and ate berries, acorns or raw flesh; he had no language; he had no belief in God; he had no desire for civilisation, and would accept a civilised life only if captured, never spontaneously. His ontological status seems to have been intermediate between beast and human.[6] As a reject from the hierarchical order of feudal society, the wild man nevertheless was held in an ambiguous relationship to that society. In the Arthurian romances, both Yvain and Tristan, for example, repair to the woods and live the life of a wild man in temporary insanity brought on by amorous grief or jealousy, and Orson is brought up by a bear.[7]

Perhaps there was some empirical evidence that the vast stretches of forest between medieval settlements contained outlaws, recluses, the subnormal, or abandoned children, who actually led a bestial life, and thus provided a certain amount of apparent empirical validation for the myth: however, its appropriation by the aristocracy in tapestry, sculpture and heraldic convention from the end of the fourteenth century is a significant shift. Richard Bernheimer proposes that this 'radical archaism' is the result of a crisis in the aristocracy deriving from a decline in the power and relevance of the chivalric code and the ascendance of the citizenry (though we may adduce the financial debilitation caused by the Hundred Years War, as well as agricultural changes, as more material causes of the crisis), and he writes: 'Nothing would have been more radical than the attitude of sympathising or identifying oneself with the wild man, whose way of life was the repudiation of all the accumulated values of civilization.'[8]

Spenser provides examples of both the traditional and aristocratic forms of the wild man in *The Faerie Queene* (1596). In Book IV, the gigantic, hairy, lascivious, carnivorous 'salvage man' (IV vii 5 ff.) captures Amoret, but is eventually killed by Belphebe; but then the 'gentle Squire', as a result of a misunderstanding with Belphebe, himself takes up the life of a wild man becoming almost unrecognisable in his dumbness and 'rude brutishness' (IV vii 45). In Book VI we find a 'salvage man' of 'courtesie' who rescues Sir Calepine from Sir Turpine (VI iv 3 ff.): 'For certes he was borne of noble blood' (VI v 2). Shakespeare's *The Tempest* provides us with the last representation of the wild man on the English stage, in Caliban. Despite the fact that the play is influenced by Florio's translation of Montaigne's *Essays*, published in 1603, in which is to be found (in the essay 'On Cannibals') an influential account of primitive virtue among Brazilian natives, Shakespeare reverts to the popular wild man tradition in his portrayal of Caliban. The name seems to be a metathesis of 'cannibal', which itself is derived from 'Carib' – an etymological indication of the early association of bestiality with transatlantic peoples. Caliban is described in the folio 'Names of the Actors' as a 'salvage and deformed slave', being the offspring of witch and demon. He had no language before Prospero's arrival, and is murderous and lecherous.[9] Dryden was able to write in 1679 that such a figure 'is not wholly beyond the bounds of credibility, at least the vulgar still believe it',[10] though by 1712 the assumption seems to have been that Caliban was a *wholly* original creation. Addison writes: 'It shows a greater Genius in Shakespear to have drawn his Calyban, than his Hotspur or Julius Caesar: The one was to be supplied out of his own Imagination, whereas the other might have been formed upon Tradition, History and Observation.'[11] Thus eighteenth-century rationalism disavows the earlier myth.

The varied forms and attributes of the wild man through the Renaissance is an aspect of the problem faced by the 'civilised' when confronted by the 'natural', its excluded and repressed shadow. For the natural can be both terrifying in its potential savagery, but also exciting and stimulating in its challenge to civilisation that life might be lived in other (better?) ways. Thus, when the voyagers and other writers came to represent the newly discovered people of the Americas in the sixteenth and seventeenth centuries, this same alternative presented itself. They were clearly outside civilisation: but were they depraved beasts beyond redemption, or did they represent an innocent, even unfallen, mankind living in near Golden Age simplicity? Were they deserving of no better fate than enslavement or destruction, or were they a model of perfection, of mankind's lost origins? Scholars disagree as to whether, in the Elizabethan period, favourable reports of the American natives predominate over unfavourable;[12] and, of course, it is doubtless true that other pressures than myth and tradition helped to determine the representation of the American natives in Europe. Since, for example, the Virginia colony was a joint-stock company with shares for sale, there was a strong financial incentive for the presentation of benevolent, passive natives and a fertile land of easy riches.[13] On the other hand, dangerous adventures among hostile, cannibalistic natives made more exciting reading. Thus the *conceptual* problem manifested itself through the mediation of economic constraints and through narrative conventions.

The variety of discourses available for describing the Americas is illustrated if we consider Aphra Behn's *Oroonoko, or the Royal Slave* (1688).[14] The novella tells the story of an African king, Oroonoko, who is tricked into slavery and brought to Surinam in South America, where he leads a slave revolt and dies a heroic death. For her description of Surinam and its natives, Aphra Behn adopts the language of Golden Age description. ' 'Tis there eternal spring', she writes (p. 194), and her excited description of the exotic flora and fauna of the country produces the impression that 'all things by nature there are rare, delightful and wonderful' (p. 196). The natives are naked, 'so like our first parents before the fall' (p. 149), and they 'represented to me an absolute idea of the first state of innocence before man knew how to sin . . . laws wou'd but teach 'em to know offence, of which now they have no notion' (pp. 149–50). This discourse is lightly overlaid with values from European polite society: the natives are very concerned with pretty ornaments and aprons, they behave with 'blushing modesty', and their courtship is in accordance with the strictest codes of romance.

The interesting thing about this is that Aphra Behn, having used George Warren's *Impartial Description of Surinam* (1667)[15] as a source for information about Surinam, rejects his description of the Indians: for Warren they are 'a people cowardly and treacherous', their women are 'generally lascivious', and they inflict 'the most barbaric cruelties' upon their enemies. For Oroonoko himself, however, we find another discourse. As an African king with a European education, he had 'all the civility of a well-bred great man', together with a beauty 'transcending all those of his gloomy race', and a 'softness that was capable of the highest passions of love and gallantry' (pp. 152–3), and so he is produced as a conventional hero of chivalric romance. He is able to represent 'honour' against the morality of profit of the Christian captain of the slaving ship who betrays his trust. But, beneath these literary conventions we find in Oroonoko certain residual elements of the 'wild man'. He is fearless, with striking physical prowess: he kills one tiger, 'a monstrous beast of mighty size and vast limbs who came with open jaws upon him' by 'fixing his awful stern eyes full upon those of the beast', and running a sword through her breast, and he shoots another with an arrow through the eye (pp. 196–8). But the wild man's opposition to civilisation and religion is in Oroonoko changed into a principled repugnance at the calculated betrayal which he suffers, both by the slaving ship's captain in enslaving him and by the deputy-governor of Surinam in crushing the slave revolt which he leads. Oroonoko's stand against the petite-bourgeoisie is from the perspective of his own aristocratic notion of honour, and it is this also which enables Aphra Behn to negotiate the contradiction between Oroonoko's being himself a slave-dealer in Africa, and his anti-slavery rhetoric in Surinam – the fact that, when the slaves desert him, he considers them to be 'by nature slaves . . . dogs, treacherous and cowardly' (p. 212). But the crucial reason why Oroonoko is significant as an early noble primitive is that, despite the restraining conventions of romantic tragedy, and though he speaks an aristocratic rhetoric of honour, he stands as a complete, solitary and alien *individual* against the values of the (colonial) society into which he is inserted.

This moment, around 1688, is, of course, the high moment of the bourgeois transformation of English society, which found its Glorious Revolution in 1689, and its theorist and apologist in 1690, with Locke's publication of his *Two Treatises of Government*, as well as his *Essay Concerning Human Understanding*. Locke's founding myth of bourgeois society is twofold: first, that the state of Nature, 'which all men are naturally in . . . is a state of perfect freedom to order their actions . . . as they think fit', and that the law of Nature, which is 'reason', 'teaches that being all equal and independent, no one ought to harm another in his life, health, liberty, or possessions' (ch. II);[16] second, that having created man, God inclined him towards society, and 'fitted him with understanding and language to continue and enjoy it', whereupon man chooses to assign his 'executive power of the Law of Nature' to the Commonwealth (ch. VII). This is the myth of the free, unitary subject, *prior* to both language and society, who, guided by reason, *chooses* to authorise society to legislate for him. This philosophical position, therefore, not only constructs 'nature' as a state of independence and liberty, but also provides the individual subject an *a priori* ground for criticising, or withdrawing his authorisation from, society. It is here, then, that the 'noble savage' is truly born. (The term is Dryden's, in a play published in 1672).[17] If, into a benevolent nature, such as was depicted in representations of the Golden Age, is inserted a free, unitary subject, with powers of reasoning and a sense of justice, then we have the possibility of a critique of European society in its transition to bourgeois capitalism: a critique which could be located conceptually in an innocent, reasoning state of Nature, but which could be thought to be located geographically as well, often in America.

This literary strategy of confrontation between (American) primitive and (European) civilised was anticipated by Montaigne, in his essay 'On Cannibals' (1580). There he wrote, with reference to some Brazilians who had been brought to France:

What we have seen of these people with our own eyes surpasses not only the pictures with which poets have illustrated the golden age, and all their attempts to draw mankind in the state of happiness, but the ideas and the very aspirations of philosophers as well. They could not imagine an innocence as pure and simple as we have actually seen; nor could they believe that our society might be maintained with so little artificiality and human organisation.

This is a nation, in which there is no kind of commerce, no knowledge of letters, no science of numbers, no title of magistrate or of political superior, no habit of service, riches or poverty, no contracts, no inheritance, no divisions of property, only leisurely occupations, no respect for any kinship but the common ties, no clothes, no agriculture, no metals, no use of corn or wine. The very words denoting lying, treason, deceit, greed, envy, slander, and forgiveness have never been heard.[18]

Then, after a discussion of their reputed cannibalism, he concludes: 'We are justified therefore in calling these people barbarians by reference to the laws of reason, but not in comparison with ourselves, who surpass them in every kind of barbarity.'

Montaigne here reproduces the Ovidian Golden Age out of which he wrests a strikingly radical conclusion. But this is not to say that all representations of Golden Age innocence necessarily have radical implications. The Golden Age is portrayed normally as a series of *negations* of the world produced by history, and in this sense may be considered as a photographic negative, shadowing the real world as an undisposable 'other', the world of desire. It is possible for such a world to be appropriated by a discourse of quiescent, sentimental nostalgia which produces no challenge to the dominant values of European society, and this is a common procedure, in fact, in much verse and prose in celebration of the rural idyll, whether in the New World or closer to home.[19] But the uses of 'utopia' (itself a negative – 'no place'), which is essentially a world without contradictions, can have a radical force. Marx and Engels argued that utopian conceptions of society have a value because 'they attack every principle of existing society' and 'correspond with the first instinctive yearnings . . . for a general reconstruction of society'.[20] And Gramsci maintained the political value of utopia, since, as a result, 'ideas of equality, fraternity and liberty ferment among men, among those strata of mankind who do not see themselves as equals nor as brothers of other men, nor as free in relation to them'.[21] Thus it was when the utopian features of a non-contradictory world outside history became invigorated by the theorisation of the free, non-contradictory bourgeois subject, himself 'prior' to society and therefore outside history, that the literary strategy of confrontation between primitive and civilised could be effectively deployed as a potential radicalism, as it was in certain eighteenth-century texts. One more crucial constraint needs to be noticed. The identification of America as the location of this utopian state of Nature (Locke wrote, 'Thus, in the beginning all the world was America'[22]) was possible, within the realist conventions of eighteenth-century fiction, only if America was relatively unknown and inaccessible. That is why the increasing acquaintance with America which resulted from the colonial wars with France and from the War of Independence helped fatally to undermine the noble savage in this form, though the strategy of potentially radical confrontation was able to shift elsewhere, under the influence of Rousseau.[23]

At about the time when Dryden invented the term 'noble savage' with reference to an American native, the autodidact first appears in English literature, as a complete, realist narrative embodiment of the Lockean myth of the autonomous human subject prior to both language and society. The first of three separate translations of a twelfth-century Arabic romance called *Hai Ebn Yokdan*, meaning 'Alive, Son of Awake', appeared in 1674.[24] It tells the story of a baby, who, washed up on a desert island, is suckled by a roe, and grows up to learn from experience and reason all necessary practical skills, including the use of fire, and to deduce concepts such as the existence of the soul and the existence of God. Eventually he is discovered by a visitor to the island, and taught to speak, after which he is taken to another island where he observes human society for the first time. He is horrified to find that people have been 'overwhelmed by Folly', and so he returns to a life of solitary meditation on his original island. But, just as the conceptualisation in the sixteenth and seventeenth centuries of America as the site of the literal 'realisation' of the Golden Age myth was disappointed during the eighteenth century by increasing knowledge of the real inhabitants as they became incorporated into the colonial struggles of Europe, so too the myth of the autodidact as spontaneous exemplar of the natural laws of reason withered under the influence of the discovery of real children apparently brought up in the wild, such as Wild Peter of Hanover, who was brought to England in 1726.[25]

Nevertheless, there is in English prose fiction of the eighteenth century a potential radicalism based on the strategy of confronting European social values and practices with a primitive, usually native American, figure who represents autonomous natural reason. This potential radicalism is bourgeois to the extent that, as Marx and Engels noted, 'The bourgeoisie, historically, has played a most revolutionary part . . . it has pitilessly torn asunder the motley feudal ties that bound man to his "natural superiors" '.[26] But also, to the extent that an implied utopia is per se an imagination of the end of exploitation, there may be found the seeds within it of a self-critique of bourgeois society, since Nature and Reason, the grounds of primitivist radicalism, are notoriously two-edge weapons. Yet, as a necessary corollary, perhaps, primitivist radicalism in English eighteenth-century fiction remains only 'potential': the conditions of literary production and the conventions of fictional narrative both tend to inhibit direct primitivist social criticism.

The first truly radical noble primitive in English fiction is Adario in the 'Dialogue' in Lahontan's *New Voyages to North America*, published in English in 1703, before its publication later in the year in the original French.[27] From Montaigne, through the Jesuit missionaries (who, in the seventeenth century had sent back from New France – Canada – letters, called 'Relations' which were published at the time, extolling the virtues of the Hurons), through to Rousseau, there was a strong tradition of primitivism in France.[28] Lahontan's book was notorious even a century later.[29] The 'Dialogue' is between the author and Adario, who is a Huron, and deals mainly with a comparison between Huron and European beliefs and practices in religion and law, though matters relating to health and sexuality are also covered. The logical contradictions within Christianity and the injustices and complexity of the legal system are both attacked by Adario, who observes:

He (God) order'd thee to be Born in *France*, with intent that thou shouldest believe what thou neither seest nor conceivest, and me he has caus'd to be Born a *Huron*, to the end that I should give credit to nothing but what I understand, and what my reason teaches me. . . . the Great Spirit has vouchsaf'd us an honest Mould, while wickedness nestles in yours; and . . . he sends you into our Country, in order to have an opportunity of Correcting your Faults, and following our Example.

Having clearly out-reasoned his interlocutor, Adario exclaims:

Ha! long live the *Hurons*, who without Laws, without Prisons, and without Torture, pass their Life in a State of Sweetness and Tranquility, and enjoy a pitch of Felicity to which the *French* are utter Strangers. We live quietly under the Laws of Instinct and innocent Conduct, which wise Nature has imprinted upon our Minds from our Cradles.

Thus that golden age world 'without laws', outside history is the energising force which produces a primitivist radicalism.[30]

The last important war of territorial rivalry in North America between the French and English, which effectively ended French power in North America, took place between 1754 and 1763. The interest in the American Indians which this aroused in England may account for a renewed concern with them in fiction. John Shebbeare's *Lydia: or Filial Piety* (1754),[31] has an important character, an Iroquois chief, Cannassatego, who travels to England to see the king. He is an impressive figure, 'active as the bounding Roe, courageous as the generous Lion, sagacious as the provident Beaver', who will wear only the skins of animals he has killed with his own hands, and who has a strong sense of grievance against the fraudulent treaties of the English and their enslavement of Indian women and children. In England he is disappointed: on meeting coal-miners he asks: 'if the Great Spirit had made two Species of Men, one inferior to another, and the lesser destined to the service of the greater; without this, says he, how is this a Land of Freedom, or how is it reconcilable in Justice, that creatures born in the same Land, of the same Form, and endowed with the same Faculties, should be doomed to this inhuman Labour, whilst others live at ease?'

Thus Cannassatego presents America as a country where 'the primeval laws of Nature still hold their native Sway', where 'high and low, noble and ignoble, find no Distinction from Birth'; and, unlike Adario, who was in favour of commerce, though against crooked dealing, he inveighs against the English as 'slaves of money': 'the Eye sees not, the Ear hears not; all human faculties die before its influence; each liberal Motive of the free-born Soul is quite enraged by that pernicious influence'. In this way the imagination of the Golden Age is directed both against the restrictions resulting from inherited rank and against the destructive effects of the so-called free market. Finally, however, the radicalism of the text is marginalised as Cannassatego slips from the plot, which becomes centrally concerned with the endowment of the eponymous heroine, after many adventures, with a good marriage to (significantly) the Earl of Liberal and a paradise-like country seat in Devon. These contradictions are an example of how the conventions of the eighteenth-century novel run inevitably counter to the radical strategy of a primitivist confrontation with dominant social values.

Lydia is a Fieldingesque novel, but in 1763 an anonymous novel, *Tsonnonthouan*, was published, modelled on *Tristram Shandy*, with its hero a chief of the Roundhead tribe.[32] Like a true Lockean empiricist, his mind is a *'tabula rasa*, or sheet of white paper', but mainly because he forgets things. The first part of the novel is an irreverent attack on religious and medical superstition: 'Christians have a piece of wood, and a string of Wampum (meaning the crucifix and beads) for their manitous, and I think a brandy-bottle or a bear's paw as good as either.' The second part satirises European law, government, monarchy and religion through Roundhead language practice, which follows the principle of Locke that 'so far as words are of use and signification, so far there is a constant connection between the sound and the idea . . . without which application of them, they are nothing but so much insignificant noise'.[33] Thus the Roundheads call physicians 'quacks'; medicines 'poisons'; clergymen 'jugglers'; the law 'that art, or science, whereby it is first proved, and afterwards declared and enacted that black is white and white black'; a lawyer 'a diligent and dexterous pickpocket'; judges 'deputy hangmen'; and government 'a successful conspiracy or combination of a few at their will and pleasure, to lord over, enslave, oppress and destroy the many'. The radicalism of this novel is more effective as a result of its formal rupturing of the conventions of expressive realism: Tsonnon-thouan thus becomes less a 'character' than a 'site' where innocence, honesty, and disillusionment interact in the context of a stylised colonial America.

The year of publication of *Tsonnonthouan*, 1763, was also the year of the appearance in English of Rousseau's *Emile*, in three separate translations.[34] Rousseau's project described in the book was to raise a human subject insulated from ideology:

Emile's knowledge is confined to nature and things. The very name of history is unknown to him, along with metaphysics and morals. . . . He is alone in the midst of human society, he depends on himself alone, for he is all that a boy can be at his age. He has no errors, or at least only such as are inevitable; he has no vices, or only those from which no man can escape. [Bk III, pp. 170–1]

Thus Emile's practical education, without religion or books, is an attempt to retrieve the pre-social, benevolent, wild man in a golden age, from a mythicised America and rediscover him empirically in the child. ' "Reason with children" was Locke's chief maxim; it is in the height of fashion at present, and I hardly think it is justified by the results. . . . With the age of reason the child becomes the slave of the community.' [Bk II, p. 53.] But there is no real conflict with Locke: Rousseau is merely proposing a space in childhood for the free and innocent bourgeois subject to develop *prior* to his entry into 'society'. Thus childhood takes over from Locke's America as the philosophical ground of the myth of the free subject.

This philosophical innovation leads to a shift in the conventions of primitivist radicalism in fiction: a common strategy now is for a European child to be brought up either in comparative Emile-like isolation or among primitives, or in some other way for the 'natural', almost autodidactic, child to be contrasted favourably with the sophisticated life of civilised luxury. *The Adventures of Emmera* (1767), where the heroine's name seems to be an elision of 'Emile' and 'America', tells the story of a girl taken to live in the American wilderness by her father, where the innocent pleasures of the natural paradise are contrasted with the decadent luxury of English upper class life. Emmera, though an heiress, rejects her inheritance during a visit to England, and sails with her husband to America to live among the 'virtuous and amiable' American savages. The following year, 1768, Voltaire's *L'Ingénu; or, the Sincere Huron* had as its hero a Frenchman brought up among Indians, who travels to France in 1689 and confronts religious, political and moral injustice with defiance, for which he is falsely imprisoned. This book had a formative influence on one of the finest radical novels of the 1790s, Robert Bage's *Hermsprong; or, Man as He is Not* (1796), in which the eponymous heir to an English estate advocates the libertarian principles of Paine's *Rights of Man*, though finally he settles down to live on his estate.

We might, therefore, in conclusion see the story of the noble primitive as intimately connected with that critical point of bourgeois ascendancy in the late seventeenth century. The concept of a free, unitary bourgeois subject, source and origin of meaning and morals, legitimator by free choice of 'society', was a radical concept which powerfully subverted social values based on inheritance and tradition. The noble primitive was an appropriation of 'costumes from the past': but its transformation from a phylogenetic myth into the ontogenetic myth of the 'free child', as found in Rousseau's *Emile*, produced a much more powerful, 'new pastoralism', that of the innocent child, outside history, which continued to exert a literary influence through the Romantics, Victorians, to Freud and beyond.

SOURCE: essay written for, and first published, in this Casebook.

NOTES

1. K. Marx, *The Eighteenth Brumaire of Louis Napoleon*; in D. McLellan (ed.), *Karl Marx: Selected Writings* (Oxford, 1977), pp. 300–1.

2. Peter Martyr of Anghiera is not to be confused with Peter Martyr (Pietro Vermigli, 1500–62), the Italian Protestant reformer and Professor of Divinity at Oxford.

3. P. Martyr, *The Decades of the New World or West India*, trans. R. Eden (London, 1555): from First Decade, Bks II and III.

4. In F. Kermode (ed.), *English Pastoral Poetry, from the Beginnings to Marvell* (London, 1952; reprinted New York, 1972), pp. 72–3.

5. See R. Bernheimer, *Wild Men in the Middle Ages* (Cambridge, Mass., 1952); R. Withington, *English Pageantry*, 2 vols (Cambridge, Mass., 1918–20), I, pp. 72–7 ff.; R. H. Goldsmith, 'The Wild Man on the English Stage', *Modern Language Review*, 53 (1958), pp. 481–91; F. Kermode (ed.), 'Introduction' to *The Tempest* (New Arden Shakespeare, London, 1954), pp. *xxxviii–xliii*.

6. Cf. Nebuchadnezzar: *Book of Daniel*, ch. 4, vv. 16, 33.

7. A. Dickson, *Valentine and Orson: A Study in Late Medieval Romance* (New York, 1929), ch. IV (esp. pp. 113–24); Bernheimer, op. cit., p. 18.

8. Bernheimer, op. cit., p. 144.

9. See J. E. Hankins, 'Caliban the Bestial Man', *PMLA*, 62 (1947), pp. 793–801; J. A. S. McPeek, 'The Genesis of Caliban', *Philological Quarterly* (1946), pp. 378–81; see also note 5 above.

10. J. Dryden, 'Preface' to *Troilus and Cressida* (1679); in D. J. Palmer (ed.), *The Tempest* (Casebook series, London, 1968), p. 34.

11. J. Addison, *Spectator* (19 Jan. 1712). Cf. also Joseph Warton: *Adventurer*, no. 97 (1753): 'The monster Calyban [sic] is the creature of [Shakespeare's] own imagination, in the formation of which he could derive no assistance from observation or experience'; in D. J. Palmer, op. cit., p. 42.

12. R. R. Cawley concludes that in the Elizabethan period, 'the favourable reports probably predominate over the unfavourable': *The Voyagers and Elizabethan Drama* (London, 1938), p. 347. But Roy Harvey Pearce argues that Cawley's conclusion 'simply does not hold for the period to 1600': 'Primitivistic Ideas in *The Faerie Queene*', *J. of English & Germanic Philology*, XLIV (1945), p. 151 n.

13. John Donne, as Dean of St Paul's, preached a sermon in November 1622 to counteract the bad publicity of the news of a massacre of Virginia settlers by the Indians that year. See also L. B. Wright (ed.), *The Elizabethans' America: A Collection of Early Reports by Englishmen in the New World* (Cambridge, Mass., 1965).

14. Page references are to the reprinting in P. Henderson (ed.), *Shorter Novels: Seventeenth Century* (London, 1930), pp. 145–224.

15. Warren's Surinam relation (1667) was reproduced in T. Osborne (ed.), *A Collection of Voyages and Travels*, 2 vols (London, 1745), II, pp. 919–31.

16. J. Locke, *Two Treatises of Government* (1690): edn cited (London, 1924), Bk II, pp. 118, 119, 155, 160.

17. Dryden wrote: 'ALMANZOR – I am free as Nature first made man / 'Ere the base laws of Servitude began / When wild in woods the noble Savage ran.': *The Conquest of Granada by the Spaniards* (acted 1670, 1671; published 1672), Part I, Act I, p. 7. But note the conjunction of the two words much earlier. In [Marc Lescarbot], *Nova Francia*, trans. P. Erondelle (London, 1609), there is to be found in the list of contents for Bk II, ch. 21, and also on p. 257, the statement 'the Savages are truely noble'.

18. Michel de Montaigne, *Essays*, trans. J. M. Cohen (Harmondsworth, 1970).

19. See H. N. Fairchild, *The Noble Savage* (New York, 1928); also C. B. Tinker, *Nature's Simple Plan* (Princeton, N.J., 1922), and R. S. Crane's review of Tinker in *Modern Language Notes*, XXXIX (1924), pp. 291–7.

20. K. Marx and F. Engels, *The Communist Manifesto* (Harmondsworth, 1967), p. 116.

21. A. Gramsci, *Selections from 'Prison Notebooks'* (London, 1971), p. 405.

22. J. Locke, *Two Treatises of Government*, op. cit., Bk II, p. 140.

23. R. B. Heilman argues that the War of Independence 'dealt a death-blow to the "noble savage" ': *America in English Fiction, 1760–1800* (Baton Rouge, La., 1937), p. 295.

24. Abu Bakr Ibn Al-Tufail, *An Account of the Oriental Philosophy*, trans. G.

Keith (London, 1674); *The History of Hai Eb'n Yockdan, an Indian Prince*, trans. G. Ashwell (London, 1686); *The Improvement of Human Reason, Exhibited in the Life of Hai Ebn Yokhdan*, trans. S. Ockley (London, 1708). This last version was revised by A. S. Fulton and published under the title *The History of Havy Ibn Yaqzan* (London, 1929).

25. For a documented account of Wild Peter, see J. A. L. Singh and R. M. Zingg, *Wolf Children and Feral Men* (Hamden, Conn., 1966), pp. 182–200. See also the tracts by [Defoe], *Mere Nature Delineated* (London, 1726), and [Swift], *It Cannot Rain but it Pours:, or, London strow'd with Rarities* (London, 1726).

26. Marx and Engels, op. cit., p. 82.

27. Baron de Lahontan, *New Voyages to North America*, ed. R. G. Thwaites, 2 vols (Chicago, 1905). See A. H. Greenly, 'Lahontan: An Essay and Bibliography' *Papers of the Bibliographical Society of America*, 48 (1954), pp. 334–89.

28. See G. Chinard, *L'Amérique et le rêve exotique dans la littérature française au XVIIe et au XVIIIe siècle* (Paris, 1913).

29. Charles Lucas, in *The Infernal Quixtote* (London, 1801), attacks radicalism in many forms, one of which is the sect of 'diabolists' called 'the reasoners'. 'The most common method of the REASONER', he writes, 'is to write a dialogue upon [Christianity] between himself and the savage. He, very kindly, for Christianity; the Savage for himself. Oh! how the Savage cuts him up! See the Travels of the Baron de Hontan, and a few others of the Voltairean school, with his Huron, as a model for them': II, p. 280.

30. Gilbert Chinard has noted the striking similarity between characteristics of Lahontan's Hurons and Swift's Houyhnhnms in his (French) edition of the 'Dialogue' (Baltimore, Md., 1931), p. 61.

31. J. Shebbeare, *Lydia: or, Filial Piety*, 4 vols (London, 1755).

32. Anon., *Memoirs of the Life and Adventures of Tsonnonthouan*, 2 vols (London, 1763).

33. J. Locke, *An Essay Concerning Human Understanding* (London, 1690), Bk III, ch. II.

34. *Emile*: references are to the Everyman edition, trans. B. Foxley (London, 1911).

2. INTERPRETATIONS OF INDIVIDUAL WORKS

Bruno Snell   'Arcadia in Theocritus and in Virgil's *Eclogues*'   (1946)

Arcadia was discovered in the year 42 or 41 BC. Not, of course the Arcadia of which the encyclopedia says: 'The central alpine region of the Peloponnesus, limited off on all sides from the other areas of the peninsula by mountains, some of them very high. In the interior, numerous ridges divide the section into a number of small cantons.' This humdrum Arcadia had always been known; in fact it was regarded as the home of Pelasgus, the earliest man. But the Arcadia which the name suggests to the minds of most of us today is a different one; it is the land of shepherds and shepherdesses, the land of poetry and love, and its discoverer is Virgil. How he found it, we are able to tell in some detail, thanks to the researches of Ernst Kapp.[1] The historian Polybius who came from the humdrum Arcadia cherished a great affection for his country. Although there was not much of interest to be related of this land behind the hills, he could at least report . . . that the Arcadians were, from the days of their infancy onwards, accustomed to practise the art of singing, and that they displayed much eagerness in organising musical contests. Virgil came across this passage when he was composing his shepherd songs, the *Eclogues*, and at once understood it to refer to the Arcadian shepherds; for Arcadia was shepherds' country and the home of Pan, the god of the herdsmen, inventor of the syrinx. And so Virgil located the lives and the poetic contests of his shepherds in Arcadia. 'You Arcadians', he says (x 32), 'who are alone experienced in song.' He mentions two Arcadians 'who are equal in song, and equal to giving response in turn' (VII 5). He remarks on mount Maenalus in Arcadia 'which ever hears the love songs of the shepherds and Pan blowing his pipe' (VIII 23). He calls upon Arcadia to judge a contest between the singers (IV 58). The shepherds whom Virgil introduces in his earliest eclogue are not Arcardian but Sicilian (II 21): this setting comes to him from the idylls of Theocritus, the Hellenistic poet who served as the model for all Roman pastoral poetry. Since the shepherds of Theocritus, too, indulged in responsive singing and competitions, Virgil had no difficulty in linking them with the Arcadians of Polybius.

Theocritus who was born in Syracuse had written about the herdsmen of his own country. Meanwhile, however, Sicily had become a Roman province, and her shepherds had entered the service of the big Roman landlords. In this new capacity they had also made their way into Roman literature; witness Lucilius's satire on his trip to Sicily. But they could no longer be mistaken for the shepherds of song and love. Thus Virgil needed a new home for his herdsmen, a land far distant from the sordid realities of the present. Because, too, pastoral poetry did not mean to him what it had meant to Theocritus, he needed a far-away land overlaid with the golden haze of unreality. Theocritus had given a realistic and slightly ironical description of the herdsmen of his country engaged in their daily chores; Virgil regarded the life of the Theocritean shepherds as a sublime and inspired existence. If we look at the beginning of his earliest bucolic poem: 'The shepherd Corydon loved fair Alexis', it has a different ring from anything comparable that Theocritus might have said. In Greek these names were hardened by daily usage; in Virgil they are borrowed words, cultured and strange, with a literary, an exotic flavour, like the names of the mythical heroes which Virgil had drawn from Greek poetry. The effect of this upon the persons of the shepherds was decisive. Later, when Virgil himself had become an example to be followed, the shepherds of European literature were called Daphnis and Amyntas, but they too were awkwardly out of place in the Cotswolds, or the Cornish heath. In the end, when Johann Heinrich Voss by-passed Virgil and re-established Theocritus as his model, he gave the protagonists of his idylls the good German peasant names Krischen and Lene.

Virgil, then, did not aspire to furnish a realistic portrayal of everyday life, but searched for a land which could harbour herdsmen named Corydon and Alexis, Meliboeus and Tityrus, a land which might be a fitting domicile for everything that seems to be implied in such poetic names. In the tenth eclogue, the latest in date of writing, which more than any other pastoral piece by Virgil stresses the Arcadian milieu, the poet Gallus has been set down in Arcady and there finds himself in the company of the gods and shepherds. The Roman god Silvanus and two Greeks, Apollo god of song and Pan the deity of the Arcadian herdsmen, express their sympathy with his unhappy love. How would this be possible in so near and familiar a setting as Sicily? This scene too has its precedent in Theocritus, but there (1 77 ff.) the gods Hermes, Priapus and Aphrodite are shown paying a visit to the mythical shepherd Daphnis, not just to an ordinary human, much less to an identifiable contemporary of the writer. Theocritus's scene is mythical, and he keeps that mythical atmosphere clear of any intrusions. In Virgil's Arcadia the currents of myth and empirical reality flow one into another; gods and modern men stage meetings in a manner which would have been repugnant to Greek poetry. In actual fact this half-way land is neither mythical nor empirical; to the Roman Virgil and his Roman public, Apollo and Pan convey even less of their divinity, as objects of genuine faith, than they had to Theocritus and his Hellenistic audience. Arcadia is not an area on the map, either; even the person of Gallus appears misty and unreal, which has not, of course, prevented the scholars from trying to penetrate through the mist and identify the historical Gallus.

The air of unreality which hangs over Virgil's poems is thus explained by the fact that he seeks to approximate the world of Theocritus and that of myth, and that therefore he manipulates the traditional mythology with a greater licence than would have been possible for a Greek. The tragedians of the fifth century, to be sure, had begun to elaborate the ancient tales and to interpret them anew, but they had nevertheless maintained the fiction that they were discussing events of the hoary past. Plato's inventions in the mythical genre are often no longer connected with the ancient motifs, but they are always profoundly significant tales, genuinely mythical in tenor and aim. Callimachus says that when he first put his writing-tablet on his knees, Apollo gave him some useful hints for his poetry. But that is obviously a joke; and when he reports that the lock of Queen Berenice was placed among the stars, he bases that on the belief of his time that a great man may after his death be received among the gods. But nobody, prior to Virgil, seriously shows men of the present in close contact, and on an equal footing, with divine beings.

When the early age, during which the Greeks had accepted myth as history, came to a close the tragic writers and the historians of the fifth century divorced the two fields from each other. Myth retired beyond the world of man, and though at first it retained its old function of providing a standard of explanation and interpretation for human experiences, tragedy turned it into a poetic counterpart of reality. With the emancipation of myth came two important changes. On the one hand the ancient heroes and events were interpreted realistically – the psychological approach to the myths is part of this trend – in order to render them more useful to men in their daily lives; and secondly new dramatic situations were invented to the end of adapting the old myths to the stage. Hellenistic poetry carried the psychological interpretation of mythical characters even further, and it made the setting more naturalistic than ever before; but as against this, it also discovered new aesthetic possibilities for the myths. From these up-to-date versions of the ancient tradition, poetry learned to turn its aesthetic energies into the glorification and embellishment of the objects of commonplace reality. In the end, Theocritus domesticated the Sicilian shepherds and made them acceptable to his sensitive art. Virgil, in a certain sense, set about reversing this order of events, and in fact he finally wound up restoring the grand form of the epic. The *Eclogues* contain the first indications of his role which was to exalt the realistic writing which served as his point of departure, viz. the idylls of Theocritus, by suffusing it with elements of myth. Myth and reality are thus once more joined together, albeit in a manner never before witnessed in Greece.

Virgil arranges the meeting between his friend Gallus and Pan and Apollo because Gallus is a poet. As a poet he is on excellent terms with the Arcadian shepherds; Virgil had transferred his shepherds to Arcadia because the inhabitants of that country, as Polybius had informed him, were especially well versed in song. The shepherds of Theocritus, too, delight in song; but the ancestry of the musical herdsman is older yet. To trace it all the way back, we must turn to the age before Homer, for on the shield of Achilles (*Il.* 18 525) we find shepherds rejoicing in the sound of the syrinx. We have already mentioned the fact that it was the Arcadian deity Pan who was responsible for the invention of this instrument. Bucolic poetry, also, is of an ancient vintage. It appears that, about the year 600 BC, Stesichorus introduced it into the repertory of Greek literature, with a choral ode in which he told the story of Daphnis. Daphnis was loved by a nymph; but when, in a bout of drunkenness, he became unfaithful to her, he suffered the punishment reserved for him: he was blinded. This account is obviously based on a simple rustic tale, localised in the vicinity of Himera, the city where Stesichorus lived. In his version, as we might expect in a Greek poetic treatment, the folk-tale is changed into a divine myth, for Daphnis is said to be the son – or, according to others the beloved – of Hermes, and he tends the cattle of Helios. Our information about the poem is, unfortunately, late and imperfect, but we know that an important section of it was a lament for Daphnis. From that time onward the shepherds have been in love, usually without hope of success; either they indulge in their own suffering, or they wring a poetic expression of sympathy from their friends. We cannot say for sure how Stesichorus formulated all this, but it may be supposed that he endowed the pastoral life with some of the subdued lustre which Homer allows to the figure of Eumaeus, the faithful swineherd of Odysseus. The familiar and self-sufficient world of the simple shepherd is rendered in a myth which, though evidently sprung from a folk-tale, is for all that no less real than the myths which tell of heroes and heroic deeds.

More than three hundred years later, Theocritus composes yet another lament for Daphnis. This time it is given out as a song of the Sicilian shepherd Tityrus (7 72); and again as a composition of the herdsman Thyrsis (1 66). Theocritus takes some pains to present a realistic picture of the life led by Sicilian shepherds. But in one respect they are anything rather than country folk: their mood is a literary one. Theocritus engineers a kind of masquerade; he wishes us to recognise poets of his own circle behind the rustic disguise. He adopts the classic motif of the singing and playing shepherd, and develops the scope of the pastoral poem by voicing the literary themes of the day. All this is done in a spirit of good-natured jesting; the dissonance between the bucolic simplicity of the pasture and the literary refinement of the city is never completely resolved, nor was it ever intended to be, for the whole point of Theocritus's humour lies in this dissonance. In the lament for Daphnis we read: 'The trees mourned for him, those which grew along the Himera river, when he melted away like snow on mount Haemus or Athos or Rhodope or on the furthest Caucasus.' This is the speech of the literati, for it is not customary with shepherds to discuss Haemus or Athos, Rhodope or Caucasus; it is the grand style of tragedy.

This high-flown diction must not be compared with the Greek geographical nomenclature with which Horace, who is our best example for this technique, equips his poems. To a Roman ear his place names do not convey the parody of tragedy, but respect for a noble tradition. And that is the spirit in which Virgil purloined his characters from Theocritus. The Roman poets use these strange-sounding names, dignified, as they thought, by the Greek passages in which they had occurred, to add to the statelines of their speech; for the Latin tongue has no poetic diction of its own. The names help to lift the writing to a higher plane of literary art. As far as the Romans were concerned, if we may venture a paradox, all these mountains lie in Arcadia, in the land of Corydon and Alexis, of Pan and Apollo. It would not be fair to suggest that in the Augustan period such places had already degenerated into a kind of scenic backdrop for a poetic stage which may be exchanged at will. But it is certain that they have nothing whatever to do with any real landscape outside the theatre, where you might find ordinary, non-fictional men.

When Theocritus has his shepherds enumerate these mountains, he creates roughly the same impression as when Menander puts his quotations from tragedy in the mouths of uneducated slaves. With deliberate irony he makes his Sicilian shepherds live above their intellectual means. But when Virgil read these passages and others like them, he accepted them in the spirit of the more solemn context from which they had originally come, as expressions of genuine feeling. The tension between the real and the literary world which Theocritus had exploited for its peculiar charms, is brought to nought, and everything shifts back to the even plane of an undifferentiated majesty.

In Theocritus, Daphnis is the shepherd from the myth of Stesichorus. In other works he is just an ordinary herdsman, like Tityrus or Corydon. But he is always either the one or the other. Virgil mentions him already in his earliest eclogue: there he is unquestionably the mythical shepherd (II 26). In two other passages (VII 1 & IX 46) he is a common herdsman. But what is his identity in the fifth eclogue? As in other bucolic poems, two shepherds, Menalcas and Mopsus, want to stage a singing contest. They sing of the death and apotheosis of Daphnis, i.e. apparently the Daphnis of the myth. But this Daphnis had been the friend of Menalcas and Mopsus (line 52); thus he also belongs to the immediate environment of the competing herdsmen. Now at the end of the poem we discover that Virgil is using one of the two men as a mask for his own person. Once Virgil had placed his shepherds in Arcadia, it seems, it was but a short step to blend the bucolic with the mythical. This transition was, of course, facilitated by the fact that Theocritus himself had used the figure of Daphnis in both capacities.

In Theocritus, as in Virgil, the shepherds are less concerned with their flocks than they are interested in poetry and love. In both writers, therefore, they are gifted with passion and intellect, but in different ways. Theocritus's herdsmen, notwithstanding their pastoral status, often prove to be urban intellectuals in disguise. Virgil's shepherds, on the other hand – and it is charming to follow the steady progress from eclogue to eclogue – become increasingly more delicate and sensitive: they become Arcadian shepherds. Theocritus, too, stands at a distance from his shepherds; being a man from the city, he looks down upon them partly with a feeling of superiority, partly with an open mind for the straight simplicity of their primitive life. The simplicity is more ideal than fact, and so his shepherds, in spite of all realism, remain fairly remote from the true life in the fields. But this remoteness is as it should be, for a genuine summons back to nature would silence the whole of pastoral poetry; as it turned out, that is exactly what happened in a later age. Above all, these shepherds are not really taken seriously. Their quarrels have something comical about them; how different from the harsh wrangling between Eumaeus and Melanthius in the *Odyssey*! The violent head-on conflicts which we find in tragedy, even between kings, do not exist in Theocritus, and Virgil goes even further in smoothing the differences. From Theocritus on the shepherds display a courtly behaviour, and this courtliness, or courtesy, remains true of all bucolic poetry. The rustic life is made palatable to good society by its acquisition of manners and taste; if there are any embarrassing features left, the poet neutralises them by making them appear droll, by smiling at them. Virgil is even more intent than Theocritus on toning down the crudeness and coarseness of the shepherds; as a result, he has less occasion to feel superior to them. Furthermore, while endowing the herdsmen with good manners and delicate feelings, he also makes them more serious-minded. But their seriousness differs from that of a Eumaeus; they have no strength to stand up for their genuine interests, nor do they ever clash with one another in open conflict. They are no more conversant with the true elemental passions than the heroes of the *Aeneid* were to be. And it is significant that in those ages when Arcadian poetry was in fashion, and when courtly manners were the order of the day, the *Aeneid* has always been more highly favoured than the *Iliad* or the *Odyssey*.

Virgil's Arcadia is ruled by tender feeling. His herdsmen lack the crudeness of the peasant life as well as the oversophistication of the city. In their rural idyll the peaceful calm of the leisurely evening hours stands out more clearly than the labour for their daily bread, the cool shade is more real than the harshness of the elements, and the soft turf by the brook plays a larger role than the wild mountain crags. The herdsmen spend more time playing the pipe and singing their tunes than in the production of milk and cheese. All this is incipient in Theocritus, but the Alexandrian still shows some interest in realistic detail. Virgil has ceased to see anything but what is important to him: tenderness and warmth and delicacy of feeling. Arcadia knows no reckoning in numbers, no precise reasoning of any kind. There is only feeling, which suffuses everything with its glow; not a fierce or passionate feeling: even love is but a delicate desire, gentle and sad.

Virgil, the discoverer of Arcadia, did not set out to explore new lands. He was no adventurer of the spirit who listens to the call of foreign shores. With utmost modesty he admits that he is proud to have been chosen by the Muse to introduce the Theocritean pastoral among the Romans (vi 1). It was not any wish to be an innovator or reformer which caused him to swerve off the path of Theocritus. We must assume that when in his reading of Theocritus he found the grotesque tale of Polyphemus who tried to find a cure for his love in singing, the figure of the Cyclops changed under his very eyes, while he was yet perusing the tale, and turned into a lonely shepherd who voices his longing (*Ecl.* II). Theocritus says (11 12) that the herds of Polyphemus had to make their way home by themselves in the evenings, because the herdsman forgot all else over his singing. Virgil interprets this as a picture of the golden age when the flocks were able to return to the stables of their own accord, without any herdsman to look after them (IV 21). Or again: Virgil has read that during the noon heat lizards sleep in the thornbush. He had found this in Theocritus, where someone expresses his amazement that another person is up and about during that hour, 'while even the lizards take their siesta' (7 22). Virgil has a shepherd who is unhappily in love sing as follows: 'While the flocks seek the cool shade and the lizards hide in the bushes, I must continually sing of my love' (II 8). Thus the sensible beasts have become the happy beasts. Theocritus concludes a jocular prayer to Pan (7 111) with these words: 'If you do not comply with my prayer, I hope you will pasture your flocks during the winter in icy Thrace on the Hebrus, and during the summer among the Ethiopians in the furthest south.' In Virgil, Gallus mourns (x 65 ff.): 'Nor will my unhappy love subside if I drink from the Hebrus in mid-winter or if I plough through the snowfalls of the Thracian winter, nor if I pasture the sheep of the Ethiopians under the sign of Cancer (i.e. in mid-summer).' The drastic punishment threatened to the shepherd's god is transformed into the sorrows of the unhappy lover who roams through the whole wide world and cannot find a hardship extreme enough to free him from his tortures. These subtle changes are numerous; little by little, without drawing our attention to it, Virgil varies the Theocritean motifs. The transformation is so slight that it took a long time before it was noticed how far Virgil had progressed in his *Eclogues* beyond the pleasantries of the Hellenistic poet. He admired and acknowledged the work of Theocritus, he dwelt lovingly on his scenes; but because he read them with the eyes of the new classicistic age, he slowly came back to the classical Greek poetry, with its earnestness, its deep feeling, its drama. Virgil had not intended to be original; he merely re-moulded Theocritus in the image of what he considered to be characteristically Greek. This was the route by which Virgil discovered Arcadia: without searching for it, without proclaiming his arrival; and so we, for our part, have no easy time in discovering that it was he who discovered the land, and what its discovery means to us . . .

SOURCE: extract from ch. 13, 'The Discovery of a Spiritual Landscape', in *The Discovery of the Mind: The Greek Origins of European Thought* (Cambridge, Mass., 1953), pp. 281–90 – T. G. Rosenmeyer's translation of Snell's *Die Entdeckung des Geistes* (1946).

NOTE

1. See E. Panofsky, 'Et in Arcadia Ego', *Philosophy and History: Essays Presented to Ernst Cassirer* (Oxford, 1935), pp. 295–320.

A. C. Hamilton The Argument of Spenser's *Shepheardes Calender* (1956)

The critical attention given Spenser's *Shepheardes Calender*, apart from praise of the work as a brilliant poetical exercise, has mainly been to identify certain historical allusions. While the poem is deliberately designed, so it would seem, to provoke from the reader E.K.'s delighted response to 'a pretty Epanorthosis in these two verses' or 'a very Poetrical πάθος', its brilliant rhetorical surface deliberately conceals reference, as E. K. hints many times in his glosses, to certain persons and events. [See E. K.'s 'Epistle Dedicatory' in Part One, above – Ed.] Accordingly, the poem provokes the critic to turn from the display of sheer poetic skill in order to uncover some historical allegory. Yet even a probable identification of Rosalind or Dido or Cuddie does not take one very far into the poem which is read then only as a cipher or intellectual puzzle. The poem was not so read in Spenser's own age. In his *Skialetheia* Guilpin praised 'deep Spencer' for 'his profound-prickt layes'; to Whetstone, it was 'a work of deepe learning, iudgment & witte'; while upon the evidence of the *Calender* alone Nashe upheld 'diuine Master *Spencer*, the miracle of wit, to bandie line for line for my life in the honor of *England* gainst *Spaine*, *France*, *Italie*, and all the worlde'.[1] Unless we dismiss this praise as jingoism, we must allow that the poem has depths of meaning which cannot be probed by removing an allegorical veil. This is to say the obvious, perhaps; yet criticism of the *Shepheardes Calender* has not been much more than footnotes to E. K.'s glosses.

What is so perverse about this effort to identify historical allusions is that Spenser has laboured so carefully to conceal them. Why, then, should the critic turn from what the poet says to what he has left unsaid? Certainly parts of the poem 'reflect' – though in no simple one-to-one correspondence – the contemporary historical situation, awareness of which would then provide an added social impact for the contemporary reader; but the poem's substance, its meaning, is not there. Again to say the obvious, Rosalind or Dido or Cuddie is clearly in the poem, while whoever in the age may be doubtfully identified with one of these poetic facts is not, unless we confuse art and life. Spenser conceals private meaning in his poem, it is true; but he does so in order to turn the reader from the particular to the universal. A general moral meaning is dominant throughout the poem: E. K. writes that 'the keeping of sheepe . . . is the argument of *all* Aeglogues', and Spenser affirms that his purpose is 'to teach the ruder shepheard how to feede his sheepe'. Moreover, Spenser insists in the Epilogue that his *Calender* be not confined to any particular historical setting:

> Loe I haue made a Calender for *euery* yeare,
> That steele in strength, and time in durance shall outweare:
> And if I marked well the starres reuolution,
> It shall continewe till the worlds dissolution.

As E. K. paraphrases these lines: 'all thinges perish and come to theyr last end, but workes of learned wits and monuments of Poetry abide for euer'.[2] Spenser is not writing a history of his time, but prophecy; or rather, as the poet he considers in Sidney's terms not 'what is, hath been, or shall be', but ranges 'into the diuine consideration of what may be, and should be'.[3] That Milton read the *Shepheardes Calender* in this way is evident from his comment upon 'that false shepherd Palinode in the eclogue of May, under whom the poet lively personates our prelates, whose whole life is a recantation of their pastoral vow, and whose profession to forsake the world, as they use the matter, bogs them deeper into the world. Those our admired Spenser inveighs against, not without some presage of these reforming times'.[4] Spenser's intent in choosing 'rather to unfold great matter of argument couertly, then professing it', is not to set up an historical maze, but to seek the universal level of significance. By his time, the pastoral form had become the vehicle for such higher meaning. Drayton believed that 'the most High, and most Noble Matters of the World may bee shaddowed in them', and he held Spenser to be 'the prime Pastoralist of England'.[5] [See Drayton's preface in Part One, above – Ed.]

My purpose in this paper is to explore the larger meaning of the *Shepheardes Calender*. To state my own position briefly: I believe that the whole poem is integrated through the form of the Calendar; and I shall attempt here to describe the nature of its meaning as a whole, what may be called the poem's argument. It is generally agreed that the poem lacks unity both in form and content; my purpose is to prove otherwise. Only one critic, to my knowledge, treats the poem as a whole. Hallett Smith writes that Elizabethan pastoral poetry illustrates a 'pastoral idea' which is 'an ideal of the good life, of the state of content and mental self-sufficiency', and that 'the pastoral idea, in its various ramifications, *is* the *Calender*'.[6] His understanding of Spenser's poem is directly opposed to mine. When he analyses the poem he does so through the different kinds of eclogues which he sees illustrating the 'pastoral idea' and not in terms of the poem's internal structure or developing pattern through which it may possess its own organic unity. My approach, too, differs: being not through what the poem has in common with Elizabethan pastoral poetry, but through what is unique in Spenser's recreation of the pastoral form. The beginning, then, of my discussion of the poem's argument is Spenser's use of the Calendar.

Spenser's contribution to the pastoral form was the Calendar. Its use may have been suggested through Virgil's Fourth Eclogue which celebrates the return of the Golden Age, and the subsequent linking of the pastoral with the Nativity. 'In the Angels Song to Shepheards at our Saviours Nativitie', Drayton writes, 'Pastorall Poesie seemes consecrated';[7] and in his 'General Argument' E. K. justifies the poem's beginning with the month of January because of its association with the Incarnation of Christ 'who as then renewing the state of the decayed world, and returning the compasse of expired yeres to theyr former date and first commencement, left to vs his heires a memoriall of his birth'. The year with its cycle of seasons determines the form of the poem. The opening lines announce the poet's Exodus as he 'led forth his flock, that had bene long ypent', and in the wilderness of the winter setting he complains of his suffering through the revolution of the seasons. The contest of the seasons suggests the sequence of winter-summer-winter that dominates the January-June-December eclogues, and through them the shape of the whole poem. The form of the Calendar allows Spenser to return to the ritual origins of the pastoral seen in Bion's *Lament for Adonis*; only now the lament for the dying God becomes the lament for himself. The poet is Adonis, the love-wounded God for whom all Nature laments:

> Thou barrein ground, whome winters wrath hath wasted,
> Art made a myrrhour, to behold my plight:
> Whilome thy fresh spring flowrd, and after hasted
> Thy sommer prowde with Daffadillies dight.
> And now is come thy wynters stormy state,
> Thy mantle mard, wherein thou maskedst late.

> Such rage as winters, reigneth in my heart,
> My life bloud friesing with vnkindly cold:
> Such stormy stoures do breede my balefull smart,
> As if my yeare were wast, and woxen old.   [*Jan.* 19–28]

The ritual quest for the God becomes the quest for himself, and the poem's major theme is the effort to 'find' himself. The association of the Calendar with the Nativity adds the life-death-life sequence, and the mutability of life that brings death within nature is opposed at the end of the poem by the November eclogue where for the first time the pagan mood of despair is supplanted by the full Christian assurance of man's resurrection out of Nature. This assurance, together with the aspiration in October to cast off his shepherd's weeds, brings him to the resolution of the final eclogue when he lays down the oaten pipe and emerges as England's heroic poet. The *Calender* becomes the poet's manifestation, his epiphany to the world. Since the poem is set within the framework of the Nativity, its moment of time is when the pagan world violently confronts the Christian, and the old gods are rejected for the new. The traditional lament, 'Pan is dead' is rendered in Spenser's cry: 'Perdie god was he none'; and in the final eclogue, the pagan pastoral world gives way to the Christian with the poet's prayer to the greater Pan. Since Christ is the second Adam whose birth returns 'the compasse of expired yeres to theyr former date and first commencement', the poem is set also in the framework of the Fall which is constantly echoed and retold throughout.

Within the form of the Calendar, the various eclogues are divided by E. K. into 'three formes or ranckes': the Recreative, the Moral, and the Plaintive. The relationship of these three distinct kinds of eclogues provides the poem's argument; but first it is necessary to see how they are distinct. The pastoral world which provides the poem's setting is traditionally identified with Arcadia, the state of innocence before the Fall. This 'unreal' world, seen in the poem's deliberate artifice with its conventions of the shepherd life, provides the subject of the Recreative eclogues: March with its story of Cupid, April's hymn of praise, and the contest of the shepherds in August. These eclogues exist in the poem as fragments of an earlier pastoral tradition, the idyll, that serve to 'test' the poet's skill. In each he seeks to 'overgo' the traditional form. When this timeless pastoral world is placed in the order of time given by the Calendar form, it is seen from the perspective of the Fall caught in perpetual mutability. The pastoral world of innocence circumscribed by the 'real' world of fallen nature becomes the subject of the moral eclogues with their allegory of the political and religious conditions of England. The simple pastoral life of enjoyable ease must then be rejected for the dedicated life where man does not live according to Nature but seeks escape out of Nature. For this reason the pastoral life is identified with the antagonists in the moral eclogues: Cuddie's 'flowring youth' (*Feb*., 31), Palinode's yearning for 'lustihede and wanton meryment' (*May*, 42), the wanton poets

singing 'rymes of rybaudrye' (*Oct.*, 76), and Morrell upon the hill
identified with the Garden of Eden where 'vsed shepheards all to
feede theyr flocks at will, / Till by his foly one did fall, that all the rest
did spill' (*July*, 65–8). The good shepherds of the moral eclogues, such
as Thomalin, know that since the Fall 'shepheardes bene foresayd
from places of delight' (*July*, 69–70). In the moral eclogues the
pastoral conventions become radically allegorical; simple lyricism is
replaced by satire, irony and open denunciation. The poet's relation
to the simple pastoral world of innocence becomes the subject of the
Plaintive eclogues. Within the pastoral world he is the melancholy
shepherd dominated by the elusive and faithless Rosalind. While
Hobbinoll, the shepherd of the pastoral world, may find Paradise, the
poet Colin Clout must journey through a wilderness:

> O happy *Hobbinoll*, I blesse thy state,
> That Paradise hast found, whych *Adam* lost.
> Here wander may thy flock early or late,
> Withouten dreade of Wolues to bene ytost:
> Thy louely layes here mayst thou freely boste.
> But I vnhappy man, whom cruell fate,
> And angry Gods pursue from coste to coste,
> Can nowhere fynd, to shroude my lucklesse pate. [*June*, 9–16]

(Significantly, the last lines echo Virgil's opening description of
Aeneas.) Paradise, tempting man to return to the life of pleasurable
ease, is evil; for life lived merely according to Nature, as portrayed
through the device of the Calendar, yields eternal death. For this
reason the poet withdraws from the pastoral world, signified in the
opening eclogue by the act of breaking the shepherd's pipe, and
remains disguised until he may find his rightful place in the real world
reflected in the moral eclogues. The mode of the plaintive eclogues is
the pastoral elegy with its central theme of death and rebirth: hence at
the beginning, middle, and end of the poem the poet laments his
present 'death' until the climax in December: 'winter is come, that
blowes the balefull breath, / And after Winter commeth timely death'
(149–50). At this moment when the year begins to descend through
another cycle of seasons, the poet casts off his pastoral disguise, turns
from Pan to address the greater Pan, and frees himself from bondage
to the pastoral life:

> Adieu delightes, that lulled me asleepe,
> Adieu my deare, whose loue I bought so deare:
> Adieu my little Lambes and loued sheepe,
> Adieu ye Woodes that oft my witnesse were:
> > Adieu good *Hobbinol*, that was so true,
> > Tell *Rosalind*, her *Colin* bids her adieu.

This sudden and climactic resolution coming with full force only in the final line suggests that the poet's release is achieved through the act of writing the poem.

The kinds of eclogues are carefully juxtaposed: in the first half of the poem there is the movement from the opening plaintive eclogue to the moral eclogue and to the recreative eclogue which is repeated, then returning to the moral and to the plaintive eclogue of June; in the second half, there is the same descent from the plaintive to the moral and to the recreative, then returning as before to the moral eclogue which is repeated and to the final plaintive eclogues which resolve the argument of the whole poem.[8] Within this structure Spenser explores the roles of the poet and pastor in society. The subject of the eclogues alternates from the poet to the pastor regularly (the pair of recreative eclogues March and April being taken as one), until October where the poet aspires to fulfil the pastor's role in society. Thus the eclogues form pairs: what is first treated in terms of the poet is then expanded in religious terms. The patterning of the eclogues, as I seek to establish now, provides the developing argument of the poem.

The two opening eclogues serve as prelude to the poem, even as January and February precede the natural year. In January, the poet as Colin is identified with Nature, being at one with Nature, reflected by and reflecting Nature, as he invokes the Nature God Pan. Brought to despair through his vain love for Rosalind, he may only withdraw and break his pipe: 'both pype and Muse, shall sore the while abye. / So broke his oaten pype, and downe dyd lye' (71–2). His complaint, 'such rage as winters, reigneth in my heart' is expressed in the following eclogue through Cuddie's lament against 'rancke Winters rage'; and in reproof Thenot moralises upon the mutability of the world which must go 'from good to badd, and from badde to worse, / From worse vnto that is worst of all, / And then returne to his former fall' (12–14). He illustrates the world's mutability through the fable of the Oak that 'had bene an auncient tree, / Sacred with many a mysteree' but later is cut down through the complaints of the ambitious Briar. Whatever particular meaning the fable may hold, the 'morall and generall' meaning is dominant, as E. K. declares: it stands as an allegory of the dangers of Reformation, the Oak being the Catholic Church which suffers reform by the Established Church under Elizabeth (the Briar with 'colours meete to clothe a mayden Queene'). Cutting the tree corresponds to breaking the shepherd's pipe: the January eclogue stands, then, as an allegory of the aspirations of the Renaissance poet. It expresses the desire of England's 'new Poete', the successor of the old Poet Chaucer, to escape the pastoral form.[9] The poem becomes his 'retracciouns' of 'many a song and many a leccherous lay' – his Dreams, Legends, Courts of Cupid, and his Dying Pelican – and the record of his dedication to the higher argument of the heroic form.

'The yeare beginneth in March' and 'proportioned' to that season is a recreative eclogue describing the pastoral world of Flora who 'bids make ready *Maias* bowre', and leads the shepherds to 'sporten in delight' / And learne with Lettice to wexe light' (17, 19–20). The fable of the discovery of Cupid whose wound, the shepherd complains, 'ranckleth more and more, / And inwardly it festreth sore' (100–1) presents allegorically the state of human nature within the natural world. The eclogue defines the world out of which the poet seeks escape. E. K. writes in the 'Epistle' that the poet's purpose in his poem is to warn others against his folly, for 'his vnstayed yougth had long wandred in the common Labyrinth of Loue'. In the following eclogue the poet as Colin is described as one who 'doth forbeare / His wonted songs' for 'Loue hath wounded [him] with a deadly darte' (22). This account is juxtaposed to the intensely lyrical hymn of praise to the Queen who appears as Flora attended with her nymphs, being crowned with flowers and surrounded by 'this beuie of Ladies bright' (118). She inspires him to song, and he dedicates to her his poetic labours:

> To her will I offer a milkwhite Lamb:
> She is my goddesse plaine,
> And I her shepherds swayne,
> Albee forswonck and forswatt I am.   [96–9]

The counterpart of April is the May eclogue: here Palinode the dedicated shepherd-pastor delivers his hymn of praise to Lady Flora who is a parody of the Virgin Queen, being the companion of 'a lusty Tabrere' (22). (The two eclogues are companion pieces on the themes of sacred and profane love.) As the shepherds in March are led by Flora to 'sporten in delight', so Palinode lusts after the 'great sport' of Lady Flora and her Nymphs. The protagonist, Piers, reproves Palinode's recantation of the dedicated life for 'shepheard must walke another way, / Sike worldly souenance he must foresay' (81–2), and denounces any temporizing between them. Piers's declaration completes the first part of the poem's argument: by withdrawing from the pastoral life the poet need not be, as Palinode, a 'worldes childe' but may lead a dedicated life within but not of the world. Milton understood that the eclogue shows how one must 'learn first to renounce the world and so give himself to God, and not therefore give himself to God, that he may close the better with the world'.[10] Hence with June the poet returns to the pastoral setting being now prepared to forsake the pastoral Paradise for a dedicated life. His poetical ambitions are expressed through Hobbinoll's advice to leave the pastoral world for the court. But he dare not as yet aspire to a higher muse, though he hopes to be baptised by Chaucer, and rejects the ambition that would lead him to 'presume to *Parnasse* hyll' (70). Thus the first part of the poem treats of the individual self and points forward to the truly dedicated life. There remains the problem treated in the second part, how one may lead the dedicated life within the fallen world. In July, the companion eclogue to June, the same theme of aspiration is given for the shepherd-pastor. Morrell, the proud and ambitious pastor inhabits the hill which is identified with seven different hills (signifying the seven hills of Rome and therefore the fallen world) including Eden and Parnassus. As the poet in June would not climb Parnassus, so the good pastor Thomalin scorns the hill and loves the low degree.

The August eclogue is a recreative interlude displaying the poet's skill through the traditional singing-contest in which the shepherds' praise of love is significantly opposed by his lament upon love. Renwick calls the eclogue an 'allegory of the new poetry: the simple swains sing merrily enough, but a grave, elaborate, Italianate song of *Colin's* hushes them in admiration, their simple impromptu is overshadowed'.[11] The September and October eclogues conclude the debate upon the role of the poet-pastor in society. In September, the allegorical veil is removed and Diggon denounces openly the corruption of pastors in England. His denunciation summarises the attacks made previously against the shepherds who 'bene ydle and still, / And ledde of theyr sheepe, what way they wyll' (as Palinode), those who 'bene false, and full of couetise, / And casten to compasse many wrong emprise' (such as Morrell), and those represented by the Briar who 'ne in good nor goodnes taken delight: / But kindle coales of conteck and yre' (80–7). Corrupt pastors ('badde is the best') corrupt the sheep who do not listen to their voice but 'wander at wil, and stray at pleasure, / And to theyr foldes yead at their owne leasure' (144–5). October presents a similar complaint against the corrupt age; and at this moment of crisis the poet aspires to become the heroic poet who may fulfil the role of the pastor and through his work move the infected will:

> O what an honor is it, to restraine
> The lust of lawlesse youth with good aduice:
> Or pricke them forth with pleasaunce of thy vaine,
> Whereto thou list their trayned willes entice.   [21–4]

In the May eclogue Piers upheld the dedicated life within the world;

now he advocates the life of service dedicated to the Queen. He urges the poet to 'lyft vp thy selfe out of the lowly dust', and Colin is inspired by that love which 'lyftes him vp out of the loathsome myre' and may 'rayse [his] mynd aboue the starry skie' (92, 4). That man may be lifted out of the lowly dust and raised above the starry sky becomes the theme of the November eclogue which treats the death and resurrection of Dido. E. K.'s claim that this eclogue surpasses all others in the book is a measure of its significance. Here, for the first time, is shown the ultimate defeat of Nature with man's release from the state of mutability. The assurance of resurrection out of the state of Nature resolves, as it does for Milton in *Lycidas*, the problems which led to writing the poem. Then with the return to the pastoral setting in the concluding eclogue, the poet prays to the great Pan who is Christ: to Him he addresses his complaint against life confined to the state of Nature, and at the end abandons the pastoral world.

The argument of the *Shepheardes Calender* is, then, the rejection of the pastoral life for the truly dedicated life in the world. For Spenser, this life is that of the heroic poet whose high religious calling is to serve the Queen by inspiring her people to all virtuous action. Upon the level of merely private allusion, the poem may refer covertly to Spenser's circle of friends, to local gossip and other topical matters; but such allusion is carefully submerged, being occasional, digressive and extrinsic to the poem's organic unity. Upon another level, the personal, the poem records Spenser's progress from his apprenticeship to pastoral poetry towards the heroic poem. Like the Red Cross Knight, he is a 'clownishe younge man' described in the 'Letter to Ralegh' who 'rested him on the floore, vnfitte through his rusticity for a better place' until the Faery Queen appoints him his task. (A year after the *Calender* appeared, Spenser started to write *The Faerie Queene*.) This level of meaning is transmuted through the pastoral conventions and the Calendar form into an allegory of human life within the order of Nature. Through the device of the Calendar, human life is seen in the perspective of the Fall and the Nativity: the one bringing the state of death out of which man must escape through rejecting the pastoral Paradise, the other promising rebirth which he may gain through seeking the truly dedicated life in the world.

SOURCE: article in *English Literary History*, 23, no. 3 (Sept. 1956), pp. 171–82.

NOTES

[Reorganised and renumbered from the original – Ed.]

1. *Skialetheia or, A Shadowe of Truth* (1598) E1ʳ; *Sir Phillip Sidney, his honorable*

198 R. L. COLIE (1974) – 'AS YOU LIKE IT'

life . . . by G. W. (1586) B2ᵛ Margin; Nashe, Preface to Greene's *Menaphon*, in G. Gregory Smith (ed.), *Elizabethan Critical Essays* (Oxford, 1904), I, p. 318.

2. Gloss on December Emblem. All quotations of the poems are from E. de Selincourt (ed.), *Spenser's Minor Poems* (Oxford, 1910).

3. *An Apologie for Poetrie*, ed. J. Churton Collins (Oxford, 1907), p. 11.

4. *Animadversions* in F. Patterson (ed.), *The Student's Milton* (New York, 1933), p. 500.

5. Drayton, 'To the Reader of his Pastorals' in J. Hebel (ed.), *Works* (Oxford, 1932), II, pp. 517–8.

6. Hallett Smith, *Elizabethan Poetry* (Cambridge, Mass., 1952), pp. 2, 46.

7. Drayton, op. cit., II, p. 517.

8. The juxtaposition of the eclogues may be given diagrammatically:

```
PLAINTIVE      1          6              11——12
MORAL            2      5    7      9 — 10
RECREATIVE         3 — 4            8
```

9. The antithesis between the old poet and the new is carefully made in E. K.'s 'Epistle': 'the new Poete . . . the olde famous Poete Chaucer . . . that good old Poete . . . this our new Poete.'

10. *Animadversions*, op. cit., p. 500.

11. W. L. Renwick, *The Shepherd's Calendar* (London, 1930), p. 206.

Rosalie L. Colie   On *As You Like It*   (1974)

. . . *As You Like It* miraculously collects the major themes of pastoral, manipulating and juxtaposing them so as to bring that rich mix under critical scrutiny. Not only is the classic pastoral dramatic pattern its basic fiction – exile from court: country restoration; triumphant return to court – but so also are the themes of nature and nurture, of art and nature, of art and artifice, of court and country debated in eclogue-like exchanges uttered by representatives of pastoral and non-pastoral (sometimes even anti-pastoral) positions. The 'parallel and parody' of the play, so well analysed by Jay Halio and others,[1] works beautifully to undermine doctrinaire attitudes, social, moral or literary. The play's perspectivism is sufficient exposure of the implications of the *vie sentimentale* for which pastoral had come so masterfully to stand.

Even satire and folly, embodied in Jaques and Touchstone, in turn set into *agon*, come to challenge and to reinforce the values of this pastoral. The love at the center of the play is not a particularly pastoral love, save in that the playwright works toward eliminating the artificial and non-natural aspects and elements of love; but the pastoral tradition, with its exquisite concentrations upon the emotional nuances and values of love, offered a superb literary opportunity for examining the love-subject.

Nor is love the only topic so scrutinised: Corin speaks of his content in the life he leads, in open contrast to Touchstone's obvious dependency upon his ladies, yet we know from his own mouth that Corin is shepherd to another man and not, in Fletcher's sense, one of the true literary shepherds who are 'owners of flockes and not hyerlings'.[2] Corin qualifies his own position: so does Touchstone who, praising the court above the shepherd's life, by his witty chop-logic lays open the shabbiness of the court's customs. Shepherd and jester are brothers, after all, under the skin: Touchstone, remembering Jane Smile, recalls that early love in the generic language of the peasant Corin. The 'country copulatives' comment on each other, and on the courtiers: Orlando, courtly mock-shepherd genuinely disinherited, dotes on Rosalind; Silvius, a real shepherd who has learned his love-role as thoroughly as Orlando has his, dotes upon Phebe; Phebe, a real shepherdess struck by the *coup de foudre* prescribed by Marlowe (to whom they refer as 'the dead shepherd', in pure literary idiom), dotes upon Ganymede; and Ganymede dotes, as he insists, upon no woman.

All of them, even the trim Ganymede, smugly apart from their encirclement, show some aspects of pastoral loving; all of them, in turn, have been called (like all fools) into a circle. Ganymede assumes with his disguise (Shakespeare's one-upmanship is manifest in this boy-actor-disguised-as-a-girl-disguised-as-a-boy-acting-the-part-of-a-girl) one proper pastoral love-attitude, that conventionally assigned the shepherdess, of coolness to the lover. Orlando may not have been given a gentleman's education by his hard-hearted brother, but he knows all the same that proper pastoral lovers hang poems on trees. Silvius loves his lady totally, as if she were perfectly beautiful, in spite of Rosalind's rebuke to Phebe; and Phebe illustrates, before our very eyes, how totally love can wipe out all other considerations, particularly those of common sense.

Yet all shall be changed: though in the beginning each loves the wrong person, we see Phebe settle for Silvius; we see Touchstone, clad in his courtly aura as well as in motley, win the goat-girl Audrey from the well-to-do rural William – win her, then, by his courtly 'rank'. We

see Aliena paired with the repentant Oliver, both of them struck as
finally as Phebe by Marlovian love at first sight. And we see, by a
magic attributable to her forest-character, Ganymede-Rosalind
claim her lover Orlando. Only Silvius and Phebe, of the whole crowd,
are what they seem and no more: the others, one way or another, have
been disguised from others and from themselves. And all of them,
save Silvius and Phebe, must cope with the undisguising: Audrey
must be either taken to the court by her fool or brutally abandoned:
Aliena-become-Celia at once threatens her lover's recent vow of
shepherdhood, that sign of his reconciliation with kind nature;
Orlando must learn what his beloved is to inherit.[3]

Desengaño does not rob the pastoral of its sweetness in *As You Like It*.
These considerations do not intrude upon the play itself, in which,
however much pastoral love is mocked, its sweet fidelities are
rewarded, too. By making fun of Orlando's language, Rosalind jokes
him into ever-increasing avowals of his love for her. She may seem to
mock all lovers, but at the news of Orlando's hurt by the lion faints
like a green girl. Touchstone does not want to be in Arden and
contrasts Corin's life unfavorably with what he had known at the
court, but he makes the best of his forest opportunities, and his logic
actually recoils on him, to endorse the simplicities Corin embodies.
The melancholy-satiric Jaques comes to scoff at pastoral sentimentalism, but he is scoffed at in his turn – and for pastoral sentimentalism
at that. The data of various literary modes are mocked and yet,
through all the mockery, reaffirmed: questioned, teased, tested, found
wanting – and found valuable in spite of manifest weaknesses.

In this way, perspectivism is built into this play; it is the play's
method, but it relies on traditional implications within the mode, by
developing an inherent dialectical tendency in pastoral eclogues to an
astonishing degree. Many contests question the traditions which
ultimately they endorse: the lovers' fourfold catch suggests the
merry-go-round illusion of the experience of loving; Corin and Silvius
speak not just about love, but about the kinds of love appropriate to
the different ages of man, and Jaques deals with love as developmen-
tal folly in his far more total indictment of man's ages and the illusions
of each age. Touchstone and Corin debate the life of court and
country to demonstrate the limitations of both. Jaques marches
through the play, in his melancholy isolation a challenge to
everyone's social assumptions and conclusions: like Philisides, Sidney's name for his symbolic self in the *Arcadia*, Jaques has retired to
the forest in disappointment with the world's offerings. Though
established in Arden, Jaques is characterised as a traveller, a
continentalised Englishman who (as the character-books assure us)

can never find aught at home good again. He is also – a bit
unexpectedly – the superpastoralist of the play, speaking out for the
pathetic identification of creatural suffering with human unhappiness. He it is who criticises the Robin Hood band of gentlemen around
Duke Senior for their unbrotherly attacks upon the deer-
commonwealth, whose 'fat burghers' are slaughtered for men's
whims and pleasure; but all this while he is also unpastorally
melancholy, unpastorally anti-social. As we look at him more
narrowly, of course, we see the social role his melancholy fulfills, and
how consistently Jaques acts the part the Duke's men expect of him. It
is he who recognises a freedom even greater than that of the forest in
his cry, 'Motley's the only wear!' He knows how to call all fools into a
circle; he, in short, reminds us by most unpastoral means that Arden
is a pleasaunce, that for all its rough weather, the forest is also
Cockayne, where all is upside down to be set aright. He knows what
his fellow-fool recognises at sight: 'Ay, now I am in Arden; the more
fool I; when I was at home I was in a better place; but travellers must
be content.' And yet Arden is his home, as he chooses to remain in the
forest now solitary enough for his nature.

What the forest is, is never made entirely clear, although it *is*
obvious that, even with the season's difference, the forest is a better
place than the usurper's court. In the forest there is no need for 'new
news o' the new court'; fashionable gossip is irrelevant to the
fundamental constants of courtesy, civility and humanity. And yet,
for all the talk of the golden world, Arden is never 'really' that –
Corin's master was of churlish disposition and inhospitable, ready to
sell his sheepfarm for gold. Unprofessional cleric that he is, Sir Oliver
Martext is nonetheless at home in Arden; Duke Senior's fellow exiles
do not hesitate to comment on the bitter wind, painful to them if less
'unkind' than man's ingratitude. The moral arrangements of the
golden world are, come wind come weather, scrupulously observed,
together with the pastoral delusions. The melancholy Jaques is
courteously received, his idiosyncrasies are respected, enjoyed, and
even admired; when Orlando, assuming the role of salvage man,
bursts in upon the *fête champêtre*, he is welcomed, not repulsed, in spite
of his words and his sword; the country lovers ultimately accept each
other with grace. The Duke lives, 'the Robin Hood of England' to
whom young gentlemen flock 'every day, and fleet the time care-
lessly', so that such rank as he has is, like Robin Hood's, only first
among equals. To the forest come Rosalind and Celia. Touchstone
faithfully in attendance; to the forest comes Jaques; to the forest
comes the outlawed Orlando, with old Adam on his back. In the forest
Oliver de Boys and Duke Frederick make their moral recoveries and

find their various rewards. In the forest, the fairy-tale world rules: a serpent and a lion, hitherto inconceivable, threaten the only new-comer distinguished for his savagery: in token of his recognition of the beast within, Oliver had become a hairy man.[4] In Arden, an untaught innocent younger-brother-hero can save that newcomer from these creatures by the 'kindness' of his 'nature', which marks him as trueborn in spite of his deprivation of nurture. In the forest, whatever nature's natural drawbacks, nature makes written calendars irrele-vant: there are no clocks in the forest, and there is time enough for everyone's inner and social needs: the forest, as C. L. Barber reassuringly claims, induces and confirms holiday humor.[5]

Time does not pass, theoretically at least, in the golden world – but this rule does not hold for our play, where we are endlessly made aware, both in earnest and in jest, of the passage of time: in the confrontation of generations (Silvius and Corin, dukes and daugh-ters, Sir Rowland's sons and his aged servant Adam); Orlando comes late to his appointments with Ganymede, who rates him for that – because she is a young girl in love: as she tells us in her psychological typology of time, time trots hard with her. A living emblem of the last age of man, the nearly dying Adam is brought in to emphasise Jaques's classic oration. In other words, this forest is at once ideal and real; the inhabitants of Arden insist that their life is unvaried, as in the Golden Age; but the play works in the rhythms of experience's human actuality. On one side, Arden *is* holiday, and thus timeless; it offers a chance for recovery and redemption, a parodic, exalted imitation of the real world, now corrected and purged. In Arden, fools are visibly in circles, men feast graciously on venison and wine – but time passes as they do so, as we are continually reminded, and men ripen and rot in spite of the lack of clocks.

What the forest offers is its liberties: love finds what it seeks: Jaques is allowed to criticise as he likes; Touchstone may mock, Corin may be threatened with impoverishment. But nothing untoward happens; the forest offers restitution to the dispossessed as well as the far more important imaginative freedom in which the natural spirits of men and women may expand. Duke Senior, Rosalind and Orlando know that this forest is their goal; there they find a world where even real brothers can be brothers. For with the psychological flowering favored in Arden, we are reminded that all life is not so free: Cain and Abel patterns recur in the play, in each generation. Even in *that* pattern, indeed, one can find a pastoral analogue: the pastoral Abel is the contemplative man, Cain the cultivator, the active man, the man of violence prepared to defend the value of his way of life and its produce. In his underpopulated world, Cain felt he had to savage his brother, as Duke Frederick and Oliver seek to savage their brothers. When these romance-brothers enter the forest, however, reformation strikes at once; the virtuous maintain and corroborate their gentility and their gentleness, and the evil recover or discover the gentleness in themselves they had denied. Orlando's lapse into savagery, so clearly motivated by his concern for old Adam, is immediately reversed by the gentleness with which his threat of violence is received. As is usual in these discussions of pastoral nature, we find throughout the play the terms which form its structure: nature, natural; kind, kindness; civil, civility; gentle, gentleness. For nature is kind, and kindness is a recognition of one's kind, a response designed to protect and to strengthen whatever is mutually human.

Against this background, Orlando's complaint against his unnatural nurture makes full sense. His brother owed him, as kin, to raise him as the gentleman he is, but chose instead to rob him of his rights and to cast him, if he could, as a type of Prodigal Son. Finally, Oliver even tried to kill the boy, in an unmotivated gesture of the supreme unkindness. Oliver is presented, as Iago was to be, as simply evil – 'simply' evil. The question of nature and nurture running through so much of the play is nowhere debated outright, but from the start the debaters are given real parts in the play. In contrast to his brother, Orlando is, as his behavior consistently confirms, preternaturally 'gentle', even though he is also preternaturally strong. Actually, as he and we come to recognise, he has no need of that mysterious education he laments, and grows into a symbolic portion far grander than his inheritance would have been. Orlando assumes responsibility for Adam, grown old in his father's service, to the extent that he violates his own nature by attempting to steal for his sake. He cannot pass by on the other side and let the lion attack his sleeping brother, for all that his brother has done against him. His natural qualities caused him to fall in love with Rosalind, and her to fall in love with him. He speaks of his own gentility ('Yet am I inland bred') and recognises the same 'inland' quality in Ganymede's speech, anomalously cultured for the child of the forest he claims to be. Folk hero that he is, Orlando, the youngest of three sons, is eminently suited to take his place at the head of his family and to marry the Duke's daughter at the end of the play, to return with daughter and Duke to the court, confident of exhibiting the courtliness he has always naturally displayed.

The debate between nature and nurture overlaps the problem of nature and art: nurture is education, altering, improving, grafting, conventionally taken as 'good'. In Orlando's case, it turns out that the art of which he laments the lack is in fact superfluous. He is what he is 'by nature' – and when he assumes various stylised, courtly poses, such as in his role of pastoral lover, Rosalind makes fun of his efforts. As often happens in Shakespeare's versions of pastoral, the nature-nurture debate is skewed and ultimately denied, as received dialectical opposites are shown to be fused in the person (Orlando, Perdita, Arviragus, Guiderius) whose gentle birth marches with his courteous nature. Nurture is not necessary for such as these: all the education in the world had failed to improve Oliver, until he experienced his brother's miraculous assertion of kindness. In Jaques, we see that education has even weakened his feelings for his kind. Rosalind is not the nutbrown boy she pretends she is; her cultivated ancestry of magicians is a fiction to account for the cultivation of her nature and her breeding. In her case, indeed, the diguise which makes it possible for her to take her place in Arden is a fiction in itself. Though she is spokeswoman for what is natural, real, and psychologically sincere, and persuades Orlando to natural and unstylised love, she is of course always neither simple nor boy.

The forest, then, shelters a counter-society, idyllic and playful, offering a model of possibility to the real world, a counter-society made up on the one hand by the fictions of a literary convention and on the other by the types of that convention, determined to express the goodness of their natures. The pastoral second chance offered by the Forest of Arden is not just a second chance for the people in the play; it is equally a second chance for the larger society of which the *dramatis personae* are representatives. As the procession troops courtward, men with antlers on their heads, girls dressed as country brother and sister, nut-brown from sun or dye, dukes and reconciled brothers, we believe in the escapade and in their unlikely return, believe in their capacity to maintain reform, because of the upright good sense they have demonstrated or learned in the forest, because of their natural courtesy, kindness and radiant moral strength. But we believe in them also because the pastoral refuge has acknowledged the flawed realities of the workingday world; the holiday has recognised real experience. Touchstone is not the only character on whom the truth of experience can be proved: all of them try, assay, essay the pastoral myth, each from his own perspective, and all of them find at its heart the recreative values of nature, kind and kindness promised by the tradition. The play's perspectivism insists also upon the convergence of all views at its central and controlling point, the symbolic, simple truth of this most artificial of literary constructs. . . .

SOURCE: extract from *Shakespeare's Living Art* (Princeton, N.J., 1974), pp. 253–61.

NOTES

[Reorganised and renumbered from the original – Ed.]

1. Jay L. Halio, 'Introduction' to *As You Like It': Twentieth-Century Views* (Englewood Cliffs, N.J., 1968).
2. See T. G. Rosenmeyer, *The Green Cabinet: Theocritus and the European Pastoral Lyric* (Berkeley, Cal., 1969), pp. 99–103.
3. For the convention of disguise as written into pastoral drama and interlude, see Walter R. Davis, 'Masking in Arden', *Studies in English Literature*, v (1965), pp. 151–63.
4. See Richard Bernheimer, *Wild Men in the Middle Ages* (Cambridge, Mass., 1952).
5. C. L. Barber, *Shakespeare's Festive Comedy* (New York, and London, 1959).

Northrop Frye   Literature as Context: Milton's *Lycidas*   (1958)

... *Lycidas* ... is an elegy in the pastoral convention, written to commemorate a young man named Edward King who was drowned at sea. The origins of the pastoral are partly classical, the tradition that runs through Theocritus and Virgil, and partly Biblical, the imagery of the twenty-third Psalm, of Christ as the Good Shepherd, of the metaphors of 'pastor' and 'flock' in the Church. The chief connecting link between the traditions in Milton's day was the Fourth or Messianic Eclogue of Virgil. Hence it is common enough to have pastoral images echoing both traditions at once, and not surprising to find that *Lycidas* is a Christian poem as well as a humanistic one.

In the classical pastoral elegy the subject of the elegy is not treated as an individual but as a representative of a dying spirit of nature. The pastoral elegy seems to have some relation to the ritual of the Adonis lament, and the dead poet Bion, in Moschus's poem, is celebrated with much the same kind of imagery as Bion himself uses in his lament for Adonis. The phrase 'dying god', for such a figure in later pastoral, is not an anachronism: Virgil says of Daphnis, for example, in the Fifth Eclogue: *'deus, deus ille, Menalca'* ['a god, he is a god, Menalca']. Besides, Milton and his learned contemporaries, Selden, for example, or Henry Reynolds, knew at least as much about the symbolism of the 'dying god' as any modern student could get out of *The Golden Bough*, which depends mainly on the same classical sources that were available to them. The notion that twentieth-century poets differ from their predecessors in their understanding or use of myth will not bear much scrutiny. So King is given the pastoral name of Lycidas, which is equivalent to Adonis, and is associated with the cyclical rhythms of nature. Of these three are of particular importance: the daily cycle of the sun across the sky, the yearly cycle of the seasons, and the cycle of water, flowing from wells and fountains through rivers to the sea. Sunset, winter, and the sea are emblems of Lycidas's death; sunrise and spring, of his resurrection. The poem begins in the morning, 'Under the opening eyelids of the morn', and ends with the sun, like Lycidas himself, dropping into the western ocean, yet due to rise again as Lycidas is to do. The imagery of the opening lines, 'Shatter your leaves before the mellowing year', suggests the frosts of autumn killing the flowers, and in the great roll-call of flowers towards the end, most of them early blooming flowers like the 'rathe primrose', the spring returns. Again, the opening invocation is to the 'Sisters of the sacred well', and the water imagery carries through a great variety of Greek, Italian and English rivers to the sea in which the dead body of Lycidas lies.

Lycidas, then, is the 'archetype' of Edward King. By an archetype I mean a literary symbol, or cluster of symbols, which are used recurrently throughout literature, and thereby become conventional. A poetic use of a flower, by itself, is not necessarily an archetype. But in a poem about the death of a young man it is conventional to associate him with a red or purple flower, usually a spring flower like the hyacinth. The historical origin of the convention may be lost in ritual, but it is a constantly latent one, not only in literature but in life, as the symbolism of the scarlet poppies in World War I shows. Hence in *Lycidas* the 'sanguine flower inscrib'd with woe' is an archetype, a symbol that recurs regularly in many poems of its kind. Similarly Lycidas himself is not only the literary form of Edward King, but a conventional or recurring form, of the same family as Shelley's Adonais, the Daphnis of Theocritus and Virgil, and Milton's own Damon. King was also a clergyman and, for Milton's purposes, a poet, so, having selected the conventional archetype of King as drowned young man, Milton has then to select the conventional archetypes of King as poet and of King as priest. These are, respectively, Orpheus and Peter.

Both Orpheus and Peter have attributes that link them in imagery with Lycidas. Orpheus was also an 'enchanting son' or spirit of nature; he died young, in much the same role as Adonis, and was flung into the water. Peter would have drowned too without the help of Christ; hence Peter is not named directly, but only as 'The Pilot of the Galilean Lake', just as Christ is not named directly, but only as 'Him that walked the waves'. When Orpheus was torn to pieces by the Maenads, his head went floating 'Down the swift Hebrus to the Lesbian shore'. The theme of salvation out of water is connected with the image of the dolphin, a conventional type of Christ, and dolphins are called upon to 'waft the hapless youth' just before the peroration begins.

The body of the poem is arranged in the form ABACA, a main theme repeated twice with two intervening episodes, as in the musical rondo. The main theme is the drowning of Lycidas in the prime of his life; the two episodes, presided over by the figures of Orpheus and Peter, deal with the theme of premature death as it relates to poetry and to the priesthood respectively. In both the same type of image appears: the mechanical instrument of execution that brings about a sudden death, represented by the 'abhorred shears' in the meditation on fame and the 'grim two-handed engine' in the meditation on the corruption of the Church. The most difficult part of the construction is the managing of the transitions from these episodes back to the main theme. The poet does this by alluding to his great forerunners in the pastoral convention, Theocritus of Sicily, Virgil of Mantua, and the legendary Arcadians who preceded both:

> O fountain Arethuse, and thou honour'd flood,
> Smooth-sliding Mincius, crown'd with vocal reeds,
> . . .

and later:

> Return, Alpheus, the dread voice is past
> That shrunk thy streams: return, Sicilian Muse,
> . . .

The allusion has the effect of reminding the reader that this is, after all, a pastoral. But Milton also alludes to the myth of Arethusa and Alpheus, the Arcadian water-spirits who plunged underground and reappeared in Sicily, and this myth not only outlines the history of the pastoral convention, but unites the water imagery with the theme of disappearance and revival.

In pastoral elegy the poet who laments the death is often so closely associated with the dead man as to make him a kind of double or shadow of himself. Similarly Milton represents himself as intimately involved with the death of Lycidas. The theme of premature death is skilfully associated in the opening lines with the conventional apology for a 'harsh and crude' poem; the poet hopes for a similar elegy when he dies, and at the end he accepts the responsibilities of survival and turns 'Tomorrow to fresh woods, and pastures new', bringing the elegy to a full rich *tierce de Picardie* or major chord. By appearing himself at the beginning and end of the poem, Milton presents the poem as, in a sense, contained within the mind of the poet.

Apart from the historical convention of the pastoral, however, there is also the conventional framework of ideas or assumptions which forms the background of the poem. I call it a framework of ideas, and it may also be that, but in poetry it is rather a framework of images. It consists of four levels of existence. First is the order revealed by Christianity, the order of grace and salvation and of eternal life. Second is the order of human nature, the order represented by the Garden of Eden in the Bible and the Golden Age in classical myth, and which man in his fallen state can, up to a point, regain through education, obedience to law and the habit of virtue. Third is the order of physical nature, the world of animals and plants which is morally neutral but theologically 'fallen'. Fourth is the disorder of the unnatural, the sin and death and corruption that entered the world with the Fall.

Lycidas has his connections with all of these orders. In the first place, all the images of death and resurrection are included in and identified with the body of Christ. Christ is the sun of righteousness, the tree of life, the water of life, the dying god who rose again, the saviour from the sea. On this level Lycidas enters the Christian heaven and is greeted by the 'Saints above', 'In solemn troops, and sweet societies', where the language echoes the Book of Revelation. But simultaneously Lycidas achieves another apotheosis as the Genius of the shore, corresponding to the Attendant Spirit in *Comus*, whose habitation is said to be a world above our own, identified, not with the Christian heaven, but with Spenser's Gardens of Adonis. The third level of physical nature is the world of ordinary experience, where death is simply a loss, and those who mourn the death have to turn to pick up their tasks again. On this level Lycidas is merely absent, 'to our moist vows denied', represented only by the empty bier with its flowers. It is on this level too that the poem is contained within the mind of the surviving poet, as on the Christian level it is contained within the body of Christ. Finally, the world of death and corruption holds the drowned corpse of Lycidas, which will soon come to the surface and 'welter to the parching wind'. This last is an unpleasant and distressing image, and Milton touches it very lightly, picking it up again in an appropriate context:

> But swoln with wind and the rank mist they draw,
> Rot inwardly,   . . .

In the writing of *Lycidas* there are four creative principles of particular importance. To say that there are four does not mean, of course, that they are separable. One is convention, the reshaping of the poetic material which is appropriate to this subject. Another is genre, the choosing of the appropriate form. A third is archetype, the use of appropriate, and therefore recurrently employed, images and symbols. The fourth, for which there is no name, is the fact that the forms of literature are autonomous: that is, they do not exist outside literature. Milton is not writing an obituary: he does not start with Edward King and his life and times, but with the conventions and archetypes that poetry requires for such a theme.

Of the critical principles illustrated by this analysis, one will be no surprise . . . . *Lycidas* owes quite as much to Hebrew, Greek, Latin and Italian traditions as it does to English. Even the diction, of which I have no space to speak, shows strong Italian influence. Milton was of course a learned poet, but there is no poet whose literary influences are entirely confined to his own language. Thus every problem in literary criticism is a problem in comparative literature, or simply of literature itself.

The next principle is that the provisional hypothesis which we must adopt for the study of every poem is that that poem is a unity. If, after careful and repeated testing, we are forced to conclude that it is not a unity, then we must abandon the hypothesis and look for the reasons why it is not. A good deal of bad criticism of *Lycidas* has resulted from not making enough initial effort to understand the unity of the poem. To talk of 'digressions' in *Lycidas* is a typical consequence of a mistaken critical method, of backing into the poem the wrong way round. If, instead of starting with the poem, we start with a handful of peripheral facts about the poem, Milton's casual knowledge of King, his ambitions as a poet, his bitterness against the episcopacy, then of course the poem will break down into pieces corresponding precisely to those fragments of knowledge. *Lycidas* illustrates, on a small scale, what has happened on a much bigger scale in, for example, the criticism of Homer. Critics knowing something about the fragmentary nature of heroic lays and ballads approached the *Iliad* and the *Odyssey* with this knowledge in mind, and the poems obediently split up into the pieces that they wished to isolate. Other critics came along and treated the poems as imaginative unities, and today everyone knows that the second group were more convincing.

The same thing happens when our approach to 'sources' becomes fragmented or piecemeal. *Lycidas* is a dense mass of echoes from previous literature, chiefly pastoral literature. Reading through Virgil's Eclogues with *Lycidas* in mind, we can see that Milton had not simply read or studied these poems: he possessed them; they were part of the material he was shaping. The passage about the hungry sheep reminds us of at least three other passages: one in Dante's *Paradiso*, one in the Book of Ezekiel, and one near the beginning of Hesiod's *Theogony*. There are also echoes of Mantuan and Spenser, of the Gospel of John, and it is quite possible that there are even more striking parallels with poems that Milton had not read. In such cases there is not *a* source at all, no one place that the passage 'comes from', or, as we say with such stupefying presumption, that the poet 'had in mind'. There are only archetypes, or recurring themes of literary expression, which *Lycidas* has recreated, and therefore re-echoed, yet once more.

The next principle is that the important problems of literary criticism lie within the study of literature. We notice that a law of diminishing returns sets in as soon as we move away from the poem itself. If we ask, who is Lycidas? the answer is that he is a member of the same family as Theocritus's Daphnis, Bion's Adonis, the Old Testament Abel, and so on. The answer goes on building up a wider comprehension of literature and a deeper knowledge of its structural principles and recurring themes. But if we ask, who was Edward King? What was his relation to Milton? How good a poet was he? we find ourselves moving dimly in the intense inane. The same is true of minor points. If we ask, why is the image of the two-handed engine in *Lycidas*? we can give an answer, along the lines suggested above, that illustrates how carefully the poem has been constructed. If we ask, what is the two-handed engine? there are forty-odd answers, none of them completely satisfactory; yet the fact that they are not wholly satisfactory hardly seems to be important.

Another form of the same kind of fallacy is the confusion between personal sincerity and literary sincerity. If we start with the facts that *Lycidas* is highly conventional and that Milton knew King only slightly, we may see in *Lycidas* an 'artificial' poem without 'real feeling' in it. This red herring, though more common among third-rate romantics, was dragged across the study of *Lycidas* by Samuel Johnson. [See the 1780 excerpt from Johnson in Part One, above – Ed.] Johnson knew better, but he happened to feel perverse about this particular poem, and so deliberately raised false issues. It would not have occurred to him, for example, to question the conventional use of Horace in the satires of Pope, or of Juvenal in his own. Personal sincerity has no place in literature, because personal sincerity as such is inarticulate. One may burst into tears at the news of a friend's death, but one can never spontaneously burst into song, however doleful a lay. *Lycidas* is a passionately sincere poem, because

Milton was deeply interested in the structure and symbolism of funeral elegies, and had been practising since adolescence on every fresh corpse in sight, from the university beadle to the fair infant dying of a cough.

If we ask what inspires a poet, there are always two answers. An occasion, an experience, an event, may inspire the impulse to write. But the impulse to write can only come from previous contact with literature, and the formal inspiration, the poetic structure that crystallises around the new event, can only be derived from other poems. Hence while every new poem is a new and unique creation, it is also a reshaping of familiar conventions of literature, otherwise it would not be recognisable as literature at all. Literature often gives us the illusion of turning from books to life, from second-hand to direct experience, and thereby discovering new literary principles in the world outside. But this is never quite what happens. No matter how tightly Wordsworth may close the barren leaves of art and let nature be his teacher, his literary forms will be as conventional as ever, although they may echo an unaccustomed set of conventions, such as the ballad or the broadside. The pretence of personal sincerity is itself a literary convention, and Wordsworth makes many of the flat simple statements which represent, in literature, the inarticulateness of personal sincerity:

> No motion has she now, no force:
> She neither hears nor sees;
>   . . .

But as soon as a death becomes a poetic image, that image is assimilated to other poetic images of death in nature, and hence Lucy inevitably becomes a Proserpine figure, just as King becomes an Adonis:

> Rolled round in earth's diurnal course
> With rocks, and stones, and trees.

In Whitman we have an even more extreme example than Wordsworth of a cult of personal statement and an avoidance of learned conventions. It is therefore instructive to see what happens in *When Lilacs Last in Dooryard Bloomed*. The dead man is not called by a pastoral name, but neither is he called by his historical name. He is in a coffin which is carried the length and breadth of the land; he is identified with a 'powerful western fallen star'; he is the beloved comrade of the poet, who throws the purple flower of the lilac on his coffin; a singing bird laments the death, just as the woods and caves do in *Lycidas*. Convention, genre, archetype and the autonomy of forms are all illustrated as clearly in Whitman as they are in Milton.

Lycidas is an occasional poem, called forth by a specific event. It seems, therefore, to be a poem with a strong external reference. Critics who cannot approach a poem except as a personal statement of the poet's thus feel that if it says little about King, it must say a good deal about Milton. So, they reason, *Lycidas* is really autobiographical, concerned with Milton's own preoccupations, including his fear of death. There can be no objection to this unless Milton's conventional involving himself with the poem is misinterpreted as a personal intrusion into it.

For Milton was even by seventeenth-century standards an unusually professional and impersonal poet. Of all Milton's poems, the one obvious failure is the poem called *The Passion*, and if we look at the imagery of that poem we can see why. It is the only poem of Milton's in which he is preoccupied with himself in the process of writing it. 'My muse', 'my song', 'my harp', 'my roving verse', 'my Phoebus', and so on for eight stanzas until Milton abandons the poem in disgust. It is not a coincidence that Milton's one self-conscious poem should be the one that never gets off the ground. There is nothing like this in *Lycidas*: the 'I' of that poem is a professional poet in his conventional shepherd disguise, and to think of him as a personal 'I' is to bring *Lycidas* down to the level of *The Passion*, to make it a poem that has to be studied primarily as a biographical document rather than for its own sake. Such an approach to *Lycidas* is apt to look most plausible to those who dislike Milton, and want to see him cut down to size.

One more critical principle, and the one that I have written this paper to enunciate, seems to me to follow inevitably from the previous ones. Every poem must be examined as a unity, but no poem is an isolatable unity. Every poem is inherently connected with other poems of its kind, whether explicitly, as *Lycidas* is with Theocritus and Virgil, or implicitly, as Whitman is with the same tradition, or by anticipation, as *Lycidas* is with later pastoral elegies. And, of course, the kinds or genres of literature are not separable either, like the orders of pre-Darwinian biology. Everyone who has seriously studied literature knows that he is not simply moving from poem to poem, or from one aesthetic experience to another: he is also entering into a coherent and progressive discipline. For literature is not simply an aggregate of books and poems and plays: it is an order of words. And our total literary experience, at any given time, is not a discrete series of memories or impressions of what we have read, but an imaginatively coherent body of experience.

It is literature as an order of words, therefore, which forms the primary context of any given work of literary art. All other contexts – the place of *Lycidas* in Milton's development; its place in the history of English poetry; its place in seventeenth-century thought or history – are secondary and derivative contexts. Within the total literary order certain structural and generic principles, certain configurations of narrative and imagery, certain conventions and devices and *topoi*, occur over and over again. In every new work of literature some of these principles are reshaped.

Lycidas, we found, is informed by such a recurring structural principle. The short, simple, and accurate name for this principle is myth. The Adonis myth is what makes *Lycidas* both distinctive and traditional. Of course if we think of the Adonis myth as some kind of Platonic idea existing by itself, we shall not get far with it as a critical conception. But it is only incompetence that tries to reduce or assimilate a poem to a myth. The Adonis myth in *Lycidas* is the structure of *Lycidas*. It is in *Lycidas* in much the same way that the sonata form is in the first movement of a Mozart symphony. It is the connecting link between what makes *Lycidas* the poem it is and what unites it to other forms of poetic experience. If we attend only to the uniqueness of *Lycidas*, and analyse the ambiguities and subtleties of its diction, our method, however useful in itself, soon reaches a point of no return to the poem. If we attend only to the conventional element, our method will turn it into a scissors-and-paste collection of allusive tags. One method reduces the poem to a jangle of echoes of itself, the other to a jangle of echoes from other poets. If we have a unifying principle that holds these two tendencies together from the start, neither will get out of hand.

Myths, it is true, turn up in other disciplines, in anthropology, in psychology, in comparative religion. But the primary business of the critic is with myth as the shaping principle of a work of literature. Thus for him myth becomes much the same thing as Aristotle's *mythos*, narrative or plot, the moving formal cause which is what Aristotle called the 'soul' of the work and assimilates all details in the realising of its unity.

In its simplest English meaning a myth is a story about a god, and Lycidas is, poetically speaking, a god or spirit of nature, who eventually becomes a saint in heaven, which is as near as one can get to godhead in ordinary Christianity. The reason for treating Lycidas mythically, in this sense, is conventional, but the convention is not arbitrary or accidental. It arises from the metaphorical nature of poetic speech. We are not told simply that Lycidas has left the woods and caves, but that the woods and caves and all their echoes mourn his loss. This is the language of that curious identification of subject

and object, of personality and thing, which the poet has in common
with the lunatic and the lover. It is the language of metaphor,
recognised by Aristotle as the distinctive language of poetry. And, as
we can see in such phrases as sun-god and tree-god, the language of
metaphor is interdependent with the language of myth.

I have said that all problems of criticism are problems of
comparative literature. But where there is comparison there must be
some standard by which we can distinguish what is actually
comparable from what is merely analogous. The scientists discovered
long ago that to make valid comparisons you have to know what your
real categories are. If you're studying natural history, for instance, no
matter how fascinated you may be by anything that has eight legs,
you can't just lump together an octopus and a spider and a string
quartet. In science the difference between a scientific and a pseudo-
scientific procedure can usually be spotted fairly soon. I wonder if
literary criticism has any standards of this kind. It seems to me that a
critic practically has to maintain that the Earl of Oxford wrote the
plays of Shakespeare before he can be clearly recognised as making
pseudo-critical statements. I have read some critics on Milton who
appeared to be confusing Milton with their phallic fathers, if that is
the right phrase. I could call them pseudo-critics; others call them
neo-classicists. How is one to know? There is such a variety of even
legitimate critics. There are critics who can find things in the Public
Records Office, and there are critics who, like myself, could not find
the Public Records Office. Not all critical statements or procedures
can be equally valid.

The first step, I think, is to recognise the dependence of value
judgements on scholarship. Scholarship, or the knowledge of literature, constantly expands and increases; value judgements are produced by a skill based on the knowledge we already have. Thus
scholarship has both priority to value judgements and the power of
veto over them. The second step is to recognise the dependence of
scholarship on a co-ordinated view of literature. A good deal of
critical taxonomy lies ahead of us. We need to know much more than
we do about the structural principles of literature, about myth and
metaphor, conventions and genres, before we can distinguish with
any authority a real from an imaginary line of influence, an
illuminating from a misleading analogy, a poet's original source from
his last resource. The basis of this central critical activity that gives
direction to scholarship is the simple fact that every poem is a member
of the class of things called poems. Some poems, including *Lycidas*,
proclaim that they are conventional, in other words that their
primary context is in literature. Other poems leave this inference to

the critic, with an appealing if often misplaced confidence.

SOURCE: A paper delivered to the Second Congress of the International Literature Association, University of North Carolina (1958); reproduced in David Lodge (ed.), *20th Century Literary Criticism* (London, 1972), pp. 433–41.

James Turner 'Katherine Philips's Country Life' (1979)

The subject of this book [from which our excerpt is taken – Ed.] is *topographia*, the literary depiction of rural places and the life they support. I attempt to explain its form, its application to political thinking, and its unspoken assumptions and contradictions.

Rural poetry flourished in the crisis of 1630–1660. There is a great increase in the number and quality of retirement and garden poems, of rural celebrations like 'The Hock Cart', of poems on actual places or modelled on landscape painting. The theatre introduces landscape scenery and creates a topographical genre. Amateur theatricals dramatise the setting of country houses. Long descriptions of imaginary landscape are introduced into fiction, either as similes or as settings for amorous retreat. Rural and topographical imagery is central to the poetry of this period. Yet it was a time of disaster in the countryside. Beyond the magic circles of Windsor, Belvoir and Penshurst was a land racked by bad harvests, unprecedented poverty and oppression, peasant rebellion and the devastations of civil war. The country was also a place of social and cultural bleakness,

> Perpetual *Winter*, endless *Solitude*,
> Or the society of men so rude
> That it is ten times worse.

This picture of desolation is derived partly from historical sources but partly from those very poets who idealise country life elsewhere. Stuart culture was courtly and metropolitan, though its wealth was based on country estates. To resolve this contradiction, the rural element of the gentleman's life must be identified as exceptional, a *villeggiatura* or rustic episode in which the real business of life is left behind. Literature, with its separate reality and its watertight genres and *topoi*, plays an important role in this ideology of dissociation. Country literature cannot be reduced to 'depiction' of the actual state of the countryside – that is its whole point. It works on historical reality, and produces something different. It works, moreover, in a variety of ways – insisting on the irrelevance of the world, or suppressing its painful contradictions, or interrogating, transforming or inverting it. This book tries to reconstruct the meaning of rural poetry in its complex collision with the economic processes of rural life and the theories evoked to explain them in their own time.

The poem has a double status. It is an exercise in rhetoric, elaborating purely literary and aesthetic effects, and it is a version of the world, which is to say an interpretation, an ideological statement. This may be seen in any piece of rural verse – for example, 'A Country-Life', by Katherine Philips:[1]

> How Sacred and how Innocent
>   A Country-life appears,
> How free from Tumult, Discontent,
>   From Flattery or Fears!
> This was the first and happiest Life,
>   When man enjoy'd himself;
> Till Pride exchanged Peace for Strife,
>   And Happiness for Pelf.
> 'Twas here the Poets were inspir'd,
>   Here taught the multitude;
> The brave they here with Honour fir'd
>   And civiliz'd the rude.
> That Golden Age did entertain
>   No Passion but of Love;
> The thoughts of Ruling and of Gain
>   Did ne'er their Fancies move.

This happy state is vanished from the world, but still lives on in the country life:

> What Blessings doth this World afford
>   To tempt or bribe desire?
> Her Courtship is all Fire and Sword,
>   Who would then retire?

She praises the innocence she has achieved in retirement and satirises the wretched entertainments of Hyde Park, Spring-Garden and the Exchange. She is 'resolved from within, Confirmed from without'; only Friendship and Honesty are valuable in this life, and these can only be found in a country hermitage. Philips's poem is certainly amiable, and parts of it are honest – though not perhaps in the way she intended:

> Opinion is the rate of things,
>   From hence our Peace doth flow;
> I have a better fate than Kings,
>   Because I think it so.

This is true; the poem embodies an *opinion* of country life, though in the guise of an experience. If we take seriously its implicit claim to be a personal utterance, great cracks of irony open up:

> When all the Stormy World doth roar
>   How unconcern'd am I!
> I cannot fear to tumble lower
>   Who never could be high,
> Secure in these unenvi'd walls
>   I think not on the State
> . . .

She is indeed 'unconcern'd' with politics, and she does write 'secure' within a country dwelling; but of what kind? Katharine Philips was a London merchant's daughter, 'who never could be high' in a caste sense. She married James Philips, a parliamentary colonel who distinguished himself both during and after the civil war by ferocious suppressions of local royalist rebellions. The poet is therefore acutely qualified to attest the cruel world's 'Fire and Sword', and the freedom of the countryside from tumult and strife. Did not the colonel himself guarantee this happy state, and bravely 'civilise the rude'? The lack of Pelf and Thoughts of Gain in the local populace can also be attributed to James Philips. He personally sequestered at least eleven estates in South Wales. He became wealthy enough, through plunder and judicious marriage, to maintain a London home and a splendid country-house in Wales; this explains the poet's expertise in condemning the fashionable places of London, and throws some light on her recommendations:

> It is not brave to be possest
>   Of Earth, but to despise.
> . . .
> Them that do covet only rest
>   A Cottage will suffice.

This particular Cottage was roofed not with thatch but with lead; in fact colonel Philips stripped off the entire roof of St David's cathedral and transferred it to his own house – the 'Hermitage' where his wife felt able to praise the sacredness as well as the innocence of country life.

Katharine Philips was, of course, herself a victim of the colonel's sequestrations. We should not chide her too fiercely for having to gain financial security by marriage; no one would want to undergo the sexual and social abuse levelled at women who earned their living – especially if it was by the pen. Her poetry is designed to express her freedom of spirit, her ability to transcend the material base of her existence; the exact lineaments of that existence are nonetheless preserved in what she writes. Horace put the praise of country life into the mouth of a city money-lender in his Epode 'Beatus ille qui procul negotiis', but this irony was too near the knuckle for most of his seventeenth-century followers. They could not tolerate explicit contradictions in the text, itself produced from contradiction: the graceful articulation of the *beatus ille* theme, the quintessence of rural poetry, was a mark of the writer's urbanity; Katherine Philips's life was the diametric opposite of what she purports to celebrate. The meaning of 'A Country-Life' cannot be adequately grasped without relating it to this matrix of contradiction and suppression. . . .

SOURCE: extract from the Introduction, 'The Poetry of Place', in *The Politics of Landscape* (Oxford, 1979), pp. 1–4.

NOTE

1. [Ed.] Katherine Philips (1631–64), daughter of John Fowler. To frequenters of her literary salon, 'The Society of Friendship', she was the 'Matchless Orinda'. Her earliest verses were prefixed to Henry Vaughan's *Poems* (1651), and her collected poetry was published in 1667. Cowley wrote an elegy on her death.

Hoyt Trowbridge   Pope, Gay and The Shepherd's Week   (1944)

The Shepherd's Week, John Gay's cycle of pastoral eclogues, was published on 15 April 1714. Writing to his friend John Caryll about two months later, Pope represented Gay's poem as an attack on Ambrose Philips, presumably a burlesque of his *Pastorals*. Philips, Pope wrote, had intentionally withheld payment of the subscription money he had collected for Pope's Homer, and it is to this behavior, he said, that 'the world owes Mr Gay's Pastorals'.[1]

This letter is so explicit and so well known that none of Gay's critics has failed at least to allude to it, but even in the eighteenth century, when most readers knew of Pope's quarrel with Philips, critics tended to minimise its importance in the interpretation of Gay's poem. There has been a general conviction, still operating in the most recent studies of Gay, that Pope's testimony is untrustworthy and may be dismissed, that Gay had no sufficient motive for attacking Philips, and finally that the poem itself does not bear out Pope's statement of its satiric purpose. On these grounds it has been inferred that Pope was either lying or exaggerating, or at best was mistaken; and *The Shepherd's Week* has therefore usually been described in terms quite different from his – as a realistic picture of country life, as a burlesque of pastoral poetry in general, or as a Virgilian parody.

In reply to these objections, it may readily be admitted that Pope was an interested party, and that in writing to Caryll he may have had some reason – whether spite, or vanity, or merely the instinctive mendacity of 'one of the most consummate liars that ever lived'[2] – for misrepresenting Gay's purposes. Beyond this we may even admit that his statement cannot be taken too literally, for we know from a letter he wrote to Swift in December 1713, that Gay's pastorals were begun several months before Philips held up delivery of Pope's subscription money.[3] On the other hand, the statement to Caryll may well have been not a lie but rather a simplification, ascribing to one very recent act of Philips an attitude towards him (on Gay's part and Pope's own) which was actually grounded on many earlier events. In that case Pope's interpretation of the poem might be sound although we rejected his explanation of its specific motive.

The second objection, Gay's lack of adequate motive, could be removed by showing that he had in fact several reasons both for disliking Philips and for despising his verse; this part of the case will be examined in the paragraphs immediately following. The third objection, that *The Shepherd's Week*, apart from some few incidental gibes, does not carry sufficient internal evidence of a desire to burlesque Philips, can only be refuted by examining the poem itself. This will be done in the third section of this paper.

Without such supporting evidence we should not be justified in accepting Pope's definition of Gay's aims, but if his statement is borne out by the biographical evidence and by an analysis of the poem itself there seems no good reason to continue to reject it. Gay himself left no record of his intentions, and Pope, as one of his most intimate friends, was certainly in a position to know them; it is not reasonable, out of a general suspicion of Pope's veracity, to reject the only direct testimony we have on the purposes for which Gay wrote his poem. At all events, this paper is intended to support Pope's interpretation: in other words, to argue that burlesque of Philips was the basic motive of *The Shepherd's Week* and that the poem is most fully understood in the light of that controlling purpose.

Ambrose Philips was one of the minor Whig writers of Pope's time, a member of Addison's 'little senate' at Button's coffee-house and author of plays and periodical essays as well as poems. Later known, because of his children's verses, as 'Namby Pamby', in the period with which we are concerned he seems to have been generally known as 'Pastoral' Philips. His eclogues were published, as Pope's were, in the sixth part of Tonson's *Poetical Miscellanies* (1709).

Pope, whose *Pastorals* had certainly not been underpraised, had no reason to be jealous of Philips's performance, and he shows no evidence of having been so.[4] By 1713 he was deeply engaged in new and quite different projects, and without some special impulse from outside it is unlikely that he would have paid any particular attention to his rival pastoralist. They were by this time acquainted, met frequently at Button's, and were both generally counted as members of the Addisonian group.

From the beginning, however, Philips's Whig friends had been persistent and exaggerated in their praise of his poems. He was complimented in the *Tatler* and half a dozen times in the *Spectator*;[5] elsewhere Welsted and Tickell, both Whig writers, had singled him out for special praise.[6] This advertising campaign reached its climax in the spring of 1713 in a series of five essays on pastoral poetry, probably written by Tickell, in the *Guardian*.[7] Tickell stated that his rules were drawn from the practice of 'our countrymen Spenser and Philips' and concluded the series by asserting that Theocritus 'left his dominions to Virgil; Virgil left his to his son Spenser; and Spenser was succeeded by his eldest-born Philips'. Though Pope was quoted in one of the earlier numbers, he was not mentioned in the concluding essay. [See the 1713 essays by Tickell and by Pope in Part One, above – Ed.]

Pope replied to this lopsided estimate by submitting to the *Guardian*, to which both he and Gay were occasional contributors, an anonymous essay (published 27 April 1713), which ironically applied Tickell's critical principles to a direct comparison, ostensibly in Philips's favor, between his *Pastorals* and Pope's own. Tickell, presenting the conventional golden-age theory of pastoral (to which Pope also subscribed), had emphasised simplicity and innocence as the leading characteristics of the form. He argued, however, that these qualities should be adapted to the writer's own country and time. 'What is proper in Arcadia, or even in Italy, might be very absurd in a colder country', and the English pastoralist should represent English scenes, dress, superstitions, customs and sports. Tickell praised Philips for his realistic English settings and commended his Theocritan or 'Doric' style.

Pope, ironically accepting these principles and judgements, implied by various devices that Philips's simplicity was tasteless and inane, that he imitated the ancients with excessive 'order and method', that his country proverbs were puerile, and that his descriptive passages violated decorum. Pope burlesqued Philips's 'elegant dialect' in a pastoral dialogue, purporting to be the work of an 'old west-country bard'. . . . Pope's eclogues, the essay concluded, must on the whole be excluded from the pastoral class. Lacking Philips's 'beautiful rusticity', they are evidently not pastorals at all, 'but something better'.[8]

The immediate consequences of Pope's essay are somewhat obscure. Pope believed that Philips, incapable of a direct reply, secretly tried to get revenge by alienating Addison from Pope,[9] but there was apparently no open break. When the proposals for Pope's translation of Homer were published (October 1713), the group at Button's gave it at least nominal support, and Philips himself was responsible for collecting the guineas of the Hanover Club members. It is certain, however, that by the beginning of 1714 the 'little senate' had openly declared war on Pope. In February he was gazetted as an enemy of the 'Grand Societé' at Button's; and although this action 'was laughed at by the chief of my whig friends and my tory friends',[10] it was a clear indication of the attitude among the lesser Whig writers, the friends and supporters of Philips. It was at this time, too, that Philips held up the subscription money, and in April Pope was attacked, along with Gay and Rowe, in Gildon's *New Rehearsal*. *The Shepherd's Week* was published in the same month, and Parnell's squib, *The Bookworm*, in which Philips was laughed at along with Dennis (Pope's other enemy), appeared at about the same time.[11] In view of the time-sequence, it is difficult to believe that these pieces, Parnell's and Gay's, do not represent counter-attacks by the friends of Pope.

Some critics have treated the warfare between Pope and the 'little senate' as a private affair in which Gay could not have been intimately concerned. Dobson, for instance, says that Pope 'decoyed' Gay into 'his own war' with Philips.[12] Professor Irving states that, in the letter to Caryll, Pope 'sought to suggest' that *The Shepherd's Week* was an attack on Philips and remarks that Gay "indeed may have encouraged Pope to think so'.[13]

To my mind, this view has no real plausibility. Even if Philips had been a purely personal enemy of Pope's, Gay had sufficient motive for attacking him. From the beginning of their acquaintance, as Johnson said, Pope had received Gay into his inmost confidence, and their friendship 'lasted to their separation by death, without any known abatement on either part'.[14] Gay had already come to Pope's support, in another quarrel, by ironically dedicating his play, *The Mohocks* (April 1712), to John Dennis; he was to support him again in January 1715, by collaborating on *The What D'Ye Call It*, in which Pope and Gay mock Philips's play, *The Distressed Mother*, and even poke mild fun at Addison. Friendship for Pope was in itself sufficient reason for aiding him in his battles.

But Philips was not merely a personal enemy of Pope's. His friends had identified Gay with Pope and had attacked them both; he was Gay's own enemy as well as Pope's. Furthermore, Philips was both a Whig and a dunce, and in either capacity he was Gay's natural foe; Gay was much more a Tory than Pope, and just as much an enemy of fools. Philips was in fact a favorite butt for the whole Scriblerus Club group; Parnell, Pope and Swift at one time or another all attacked him, and Gay had the same motives, both literary and political, for doing so. There is no reason, then, to suppose that Pope had to 'incite' or 'decoy' him into such a project. On the contrary, Philips was a natural target for Gay's wit, and it is entirely credible that Gay, even without encouragement from Pope or Swift, might have conceived and carried out a plan for burlesquing Philips's insipid *Pastorals*. Though Pope oversimplified Gay's motives for such an attack, the biographical evidence makes a strong *prima facie* case for Pope's description of *The Shepherd's Week* as a satire on Philips. It is plausible, and indeed very likely, that the poem had this purpose. With this probability in mind, we may turn to the poem itself.

The Shepherd's Week consists of six pastoral eclogues accompanied by a rather elaborate critical apparatus: a proeme [See Part One, above – Ed.], a prologue, a number of notes, and a word-index. A large part of the poem's charm comes from its vivid rural details – accounts of hobgoblins and gypsies, descriptions of cheese- and butter-making, of sheep-tending and hog-feeding, of country wrestling matches, dances, and games. Gay's purpose, however, was not descriptive and realistic but comic, and the rural characters and scenes are distorted and exaggerated for comic effect. Like Shakespeare's artisans, shepherds and squires, Gay's rustics have a certain naïve charm, but from the sophisticated urban point of view which Gay (like Shakespeare) expected in his readers, these dairymaids and swineherds are ludicrous – delightful but absurd.

Gay's comic pastorals are relevant to Philips in two ways: first through direct verbal parody, and secondly through Gay's adoption of a pastoral formula, a style and manner of treatment, which is meant to be understood as imitating that of Philips. Critics have recognised the element of direct parody in *The Shepherd's Week* but have considered it to be incidental and comparatively unimportant, a superficial factor in a poem with quite different basic purposes. The other aspect of Gay's satire on Philips seems to have escaped attention.

Gay's direct imitations of Philips add little to Pope's ironic analysis in the *Guardian*. In the following tabulation I have tried to indicate both the extent of Gay's parody and the closeness with which it paralleled Pope's attack. To save space I have omitted most of the illustrative passages which might be quoted, but even with a minimum of detail the range and quantity of parody are, I think, impressive.

1. *Obsolete or 'Doric' language.* Pope ironically praised Philips for using antiquated terms like *welladay*, *whilom*, *make mock*, and *witless younglings*. Spenserian diction is the most obvious aspect of Gay's parody of Philips. Besides the terms mentioned by Pope, Gay has scores of Spenserianisms such as *adown*, *erst*, *dearlings*, *ween*, *plain*, etc., all of which appear in Philips, along with others from the general Spenserian stock. Many of these have comic glosses, evidently burlesquing those contributed by E. K. to the *Shepherd's Calendar*.

2. *Rustic names.* Pope commended Philips's choice of names 'peculiar to the country, and more agreeable to a reader of delicacy; such as Hobbinol, Lobbin, Cuddy, and Colin Clout'. Gay uses the same Spenserian names, describing them in the proeme as 'right simple and meet for the country', and also invents several comic names analogous to these. The most obvious instance is Blouzelind for the Rosalind of Spenser and Philips, but Grubbinol, Cloddipole, Hobnelia and Bumkinet have the same comic relevance to Philips. Lightfoot, a dog mentioned by Philips, also appears in *The Shepherd's Week*.[15]

3. *Violations of decorum.* Pope said that 'Mr. Philips hath with great judgement described wolves in England' and praised him for showing flowers of all seasons in bloom at once. Gay says in the proeme that his shepherd does not defend his flock from wolves, because in England there are none. Among several passages imitating Philips's flower descriptions, the following is representative:

> My *Blouzelinda* is the blithest lass,
> Than primrose sweeter, or the clover-grass.
> Fair is the king-cup that in meadow blows,
> Fair is the daisie that beside her grows,

> Fair is the gillyflow'r, of gardens sweet,
> Fair is the mary-gold, for pottage meet.
> But *Blouzelind's* than gillyflow'r more fair,
> Than daisie, mary-gold, or king-cup rare.
>
> ['Monday', 41–8]

4. *Platitudinous proverbs*. Philips excels in country proverbs, according to Pope, who quoted some very flat examples. Gay has six or seven similarly banal maxims, all italicised for emphasis.[16]

5. *Pseudo-simplicity*. Pope: 'In the first of these authors [i.e., Philips], two shepherds thus innocently describe the behavior of their mistresses.'

> *Hobb*. As Marian bath'd, by chance I passed by;
> She blush'd, and at me cast a side-long eye:
> Then swift beneath the crystal wave she try'd
> Her beauteous form, but all in vain, to hide.
>
> *Lanq*. As I to cool me bath'd one sultry day,
> Fond Lydia lurking in the sedges lay;
> The wanton laugh'd and seem'd in hast to fly;
> Yet often stopp'd, and often turn'd her eye.
>
> [Philips, *Pastorals*, vi 69–76]

Gay burlesques this rather coy passage as follows:

> *Lobbin*. On two near elms, the slacken'd cord I hung,
> Now high, now low my *Blouzelinda* swung.
> With the rude wind her rumpled garment rose,
> And show'd her taper leg, and scarlet hose.
>
> *Cuddy*. Across the fallen oak the plank I laid,
> And my self pois'd against the tott'ring maid,
> High leapt the plank; adown *Buxoma* fell;
> I spy'd – but faithful sweethearts never tell.
>
> ['Monday', 103–10]

6. *Inanity*. Pope quoted from Philips's second eclogue:

> Ah me the while! ah me, the luckless day!
> Ah luckless lad, the rather might I say;
> Ah silly I! more silly than my sheep,
> Which on the flow'ry plains I once did keep. [ii 57–8, 61–2]

Gay has:

> Ah woful day! ah woful noon and morn!
> When first by thee my younglings white were shorn,
> Then first, I ween, I cast a lover's eye,
> My sheep were silly, but more silly I.   ['Tuesday', 25–8]

Pope, again quoting Philips:

> O woful day! O day of woe, quoth he,
> And woful I, who live the day to see.   [IV 47–8]

Gay's parody of this passage:

> I rue the day, a rueful day, I trow,
> The woful day, a day indeed of woe!   ['Thursday', 5–6]

In the light of the tabulation given above, it is difficult to accept the traditional view that parody of Philips is superficial or infrequent in *The Shepherd's Week*. The verses quoted are scattered throughout the poem; none of its six eclogues is without some passage of direct burlesque. It seems unlikely that such extensive parody could have been added, as Professor Irving thinks, 'in the later stages of composition'.[17]

This brings us to the second aspect of Gay's burlesque, his adoption of a style and manner modelled on those of Philips. The clue to Gay's intentions is to be found in the proeme, where he explains, for those who can read between the lines, both his purpose and his comic method. The proeme has been underemphasised by most critics; it has also been misunderstood through a failure to realise that it is consistently ironic. Gay does not express his own views but assumes throughout the proeme the character and attitudes of a rustic bard, signing himself 'Thy loving countryman, JOHN GAY'. Not only the proeme and the prologue but the notes and the eclogues themselves are assumed to have been written by the 'painful hand' of this naïve and earnest swain. His opinions, it need hardly be said, are very different from Gay's own.

In the proeme Gay rejects with indignant scorn the sort of pastoral Pope wrote. He dismisses the theory of the golden age as a 'rout and rabblement of critical gallimawfry' and describes the diction of contemporary pastoral as 'the fine finical new-fangled fooleries of this gay Gothic garniture'. His own eclogues, by contrast, combine Theocritan realism and Spenserian dialect. In his matter, following 'the true ancient guise of Theocritus', the poet claims to represent the scenes and manners of actual country life, as they exist in his own country and in his own time. Instead of idly piping on oaten reeds, his shepherdesses milk the kine and drive the straying hogs to the sties. In his diction, however, 'thy loving countryman' confesses that he has departed from Theocritus, who copied genuine vulgar usage, the rural dialect actually spoken in his time. The poet concedes that the language of his own eclogues is spoken neither in the country nor at court, that it never has been spoken, and, 'if I judge aright, will never be uttered in times future'. Such language must soon turn to rubbish and ruins, and the bard can find no rational motive for adopting it. He has been led into it, he says, by 'deep learned ensamples'. The bard has a good deal of hearty common sense, but he is simple and modest and wants to do everything in the proper way.

Gay's 'ensample', of course, was Philips. Philips had professed to be a disciple of Virgil, Theocritus and Spenser.[18] His materials were mainly Virgilian (as Gay's therefore also were), but he had imitated Spenser's dialect and had attempted, by the description of English settings and rural customs, to achieve a Theocritan local realism. Tickell, while accepting the assumptions of prevailing pastoral theory, had contended that English eclogists should give their poems a specifically English flavor. Commending Philips as a true-born son of Theocritus and Spenser, Tickell had praised his 'Doric' language, his simplicity, and his 'beautiful rusticity'. Pope ironically accepted this definition of Philips's work and carried it to a ludicrous extreme in the vulgar and barely intelligible ballad of the 'old west-country bard'.

The Shepherd's Week has the same relation to Philips that Pope's *Guardian* essay had. With an irony paralleling Pope's, Gay indicates that he takes Philips as his model. His purpose is to reveal the artistic fatuity of Tickell's pastoral theory and of Philips's practice; his method is to illustrate their principles and definitions in a series of comic eclogues. Gay imitates Virgil, Theocritus, and Spenser because Philips had done so. His shepherds are low-comedy bumpkins because he wished to imply that Philips's style, if consistently followed out, could lead to no other effect; if, as Tickell claimed, the rules of pastoral were to be drawn from the practice of Philips, this was the sort of poem which must result. This idea, implicit in Gay's proeme and consistently applied in the eclogues themselves, is the organising principle of *The Shepherd's Week*. It is this idea which gives the poem a coherent artistic plan.

Johnson remarked, in reviewing Gay's poem, that it had been read with pleasure by 'those who had no interest in the rivalry of the poets, nor knowledge of the critical dispute'. This is undoubtedly true. The comic formula adopted in *The Shepherd's Week* is sufficiently general to be amusing apart from any specific satiric object; as in *The Beggar's Opera*, the topical allusions may be disregarded. I believe, however, that *The Shepherd's Week* was designed as a burlesque of Philips's *Pastorals* and that its particular combination of qualities, its content, form, manner and diction, were determined by this purpose. On any other hypothesis, important features of the poem must be disregarded or left unexplained. It can be fully understood – and fully enjoyed too – only against the background of controversy in which it originated. . . .

SOURCE: article in *Modern Language Quarterly*, v (March 1944), pp. 79–88; reproduced in an adapted form in the author's *From Dryden to Jane Austen* (Albuquerque, N.M., 1977).

NOTES

[Reorganised and renumbered from the original – Ed.]

1. Pope to Caryll (8 June 1714): *Works*, ed. Elwin & Courthope, (London, 1871–79), VI, p. 210. Warburton's account, ibid., I, pp. 233–4.

2. Sir Leslie Stephen, *Hours in a Library* (London, 1892), I, p. 141. This conception of Pope's character, taken for granted a generation ago, has been considerably undermined by the new evidence and the more sympathetic interpretation presented in George Sherburn's *Early Career of Pope* (Oxford, 1934).

3. Pope to Swift (8 Dec. 1713): *Works*, VII, p. 6.

4. In a letter to Henry Cromwell on October 28, 1710, Pope gives qualified but sufficiently generous praise to Philips's eclogues; see *Works*, VI, p. 106.

5. *Tatler*, no. 10; *Spectator*, nos 223, 229, 336, 400, 578.

6. Leonard Welsted, *Remarks on the English Poets* (1712), and _homas Tickell, *The Prospect of Peace* (1712).

7. *Guardian*, nos 22, 23, 28, 30, 32.

8. Ibid., no. 40.

9. Pope to Jervas (27 Aug. 1714): *Works*, VIII, pp. 8–9.

10. Pope to Caryll (25 Feb. 1714): *Works*, VI, pp. 202–3.

11. Thomas Parnell, *Poems on Several Occasions* (London, 1770), pp. 102–7.

12. Austin Dobson, *Dictionary of National Biography*, ed. Leslie Stephen, VII, 962–9.

13. W. H. Irving, *John Gay, Favorite of the Wits* (Durham, N.C., 1940), p. 83.

14. Johnson, *Lives of the English Poets*, ed. G. B. Hill (1905), II, p. 268.

15. Philips, *Pastorals*, II, 29: in *Poems*, ed. Mary G. Segar (Oxford, 1937), p. 11. Gay, 'Prologue'. 43.

16. 'Monday', 8, 98; 'Tuesday', 18, 102; 'Wednesday', 31; 'Friday', 151–2: cf. Philips, II, 55–6, 79–80; IV, 121–2; VI, 16.

17. Irving, op. cit., p. 83.

18. See his preface to the *Pastorals*: Segar, op. cit., p. 3.

Michael Squires　　　'Wordsworth's Pastoral
Realism and the Pastoral Novel'　(1975)

. . . It is usually agreed that *Lyrical Ballads* (1798) marks a change in
the nature and direction of English literature. But *Lyrical Ballads* also
inaugurates a change in attitude toward peasants and rural life.
Wordsworth proves highly significant to our study not only because of
this change but because his ideas and attitudes strongly influenced
George Eliot, who in turn provided fictional direction for Thomas
Hardy and the early D. H. Lawrence. The critical document that
illustrates this change is Wordsworth's 'Preface' to the 1800 edition of
Lyrical Ballads in which he proposes to treat incidents and situations
from humble, rustic life and to relate them 'in a selection of language
really used by men'. Here Wordsworth, aided by Samuel Johnson
half a century earlier, deals the blow that destroys traditional pastoral
as a vital source of inspiration to men of letters. [For other aspects of
Wordsworth's argument, and for Johnson's 1750 essay, see Part One,
above – Ed.] The result: conventional pastoral completes its
metamorphosis into a form of pastoral heavily mixed with real rural
life. If simplicity and a love of nature were already part of traditional
pastoral, mimetic representation was not. Wordsworth in the 'Preface' invites us to reconsider rural life sincerely and directly, to
rediscover its permanent value. M. H. Abrams has written that the
poet's criticism reflects the discovery of literary subject matter in the
habits and speech of those living close to the soil, comparatively
insulated from urban contact. 'Wordsworth, by doctrine and example, brought into the literary province the store of materials which
has been richly exploited by writers from Thomas Hardy to William
Faulkner.' The essential character of the pastoral novel develops from
the subtle and artistic blending of the newly realistic Wordsworthian
materials with some techniques and patterns of traditional pastoral.

Yet how is Wordsworth a pastoral poet when many of his
characteristic figures – Michael, the old leech-gatherer, the old
Cumberland beggar – appear to be realistic? After traditional
pastoral undergoes a metamorphosis, it gradually emerges as modern
or realistic pastoral, a variation of the conventional genre. Pastoral, as
it represents rural life, is brought from a remote and artificial world
into a real world. Although Wordsworth adopts in his poetry several
characteristics of traditional pastoral – rustic life as poetic setting,
sharp contrast between rural and urban, idealisation, simplification,

harmony of man and nature – his typical figures are more realistic than typical figures of traditional pastoral. He maintains loyalties to both camps, as does the pastoral novel later. His figures and landscape are partly idealised, yet partly realistic. David Ferry has said that Wordsworth's poetry, though inimical to prettification or falsification, is 'in a serious . . . sense a version of pastoral'.[2]

Several of Wordsworth's finest poems show elements of pastoral and so help to define his relationship to the pastoral tradition. 'Michael' (1800), subtitled 'A Pastoral Poem', shows most clearly the change in attitude toward traditional pastoral. By his subtitle he intends to suggest a poem not about refined shepherds remote from actuality but about real contemporary shepherds. Following the lead of eighteenth-century rationalist and pre-Romantic critics, Wordsworth in this poem puts into literary practice the change in attitude toward traditional pastoral and dramatises the suffering of a humble rustic family when their only son Luke is corrupted by the 'dissolute city'. By interlacing work and sorrow with pastoral occupations, harmony, and simplicity, Wordsworth in 'Michael' makes pastoral realistic. Michael and his wife Isabel are 'a proverb in the vale / For endless industry' (94–5).[3] The insistence that 'The Shepherd went about his daily work / With confident and cheerful thoughts' offers an obvious literary antecedent for the preoccupation with work in George Eliot's early novels, especially *Adam Bede*, and in the pastoral novels of Hardy and Lawrence as well. *Adam Bede* and *Silas Marner* are, in fact, adaptations of 'Michael'.

. . . Michael and his family not only toil diligently but, like their neighbors, lack material wealth. Yet though they toil and are poor, Wordsworth praises the life they live. He says of Michael:

> Those fields, those hills – what could they less? had laid
> Strong hold on his affections, were to him
> A pleasurable feeling of blind love,
> The pleasure which there is in life itself.   [74–7]

The shepherd's calling, stripped of ease and luxury, is nonetheless glorified, as in traditional pastoral. Nature, a benign and cheerful influence, accompanies Michael in his daily work. Toward the close of the poem, Wordsworth expresses the rural-urban dialectic essential to pastoral. When Michael recognises at last the necessity of Luke's departure for the city to redeem their patrimonial fields, he intuitively fears that evil men will 'Be thy companions'. Once in the city, Luke succumbs to urban temptations and, forgetting duty,

> He in the dissolute city gave himself
> To evil courses: ignominy and shame

> Fell on him, so that he was driven at last
> To seek a hiding-place beyond the seas.   [444–7]

The poem explicitly criticises urban life. In contrast, rural life functions as a version of the Golden-Age criterion by which poet and reader judge the corrupting atmosphere of the city. Like Hetty Sorrel in *Adam Bede* or Godfrey Cass in *Silas Marner*, Luke fails in his duty when exposed to materialism and the lures of the city. But the invasion of urban values on Luke also affects the rural world and its simple round of duty; when news of his son reaches Michael, he stops work on the sheepfold: 'many a day he thither went, / And never lifted up a single stone' (465–6). The rural world is disrupted by outside forces. After the death of the old couple, the immemorial family farm, like the farms in Vergil's first and ninth eclogues or like the Saxtons' farm in *The White Peacock*, 'went into a stranger's hand'.

Although a number of Wordsworth's poems manifest elements of pastoral[4] (and still others, such as 'Simon Lee', tend to be anti-pastoral), the poem that most clearly reveals Wordsworth's attitudes toward pastoral is *The Prelude* – particularly Book VIII, the pastoral book. Here he reconsiders his first twenty-one years in order to detect the transfer of his early love of nature to shepherds and other humble people, like Michael or the leech-gatherer or the Highland reaper, who perform their solitary duty as though they were mobilised objects in the landscape. Wordsworth, in showing his early appreciation of the dignity and sacred value of man, comments significantly and in detail on traditional pastoral, distinguishing his own version of pastoral from that of convention in much the same way that George Eliot contrasts Vergil's shepherds to those she describes in *Adam Bede* ... or the way Lawrence treats the pastoral picnic in *The White Peacock*. ...

The opening portion of Book VIII hails the joyful marriage of man and nature in Wordsworth's native countryside. The landscape and the shepherds who live among the mountains, in creating his most vivid impressions of the Lake District, shaped in his boyhood mind a version of the Golden Age. Throughout his early manhood, this version offered recurrent inspiration, and his first human love inclined toward shepherds in particular. With its majestic sights, his native region appeared more exquisite 'Than is that Paradise of ten thousand Trees, / Or Gehol's famous Gardens . . .' (VIII 122–3).[5] Lovelier by far was his native countryside than the paradises typically featured in romances: his native region was tangible, inhabited by real shepherds. Though shepherding and agriculture rank as ancient occupations, the shepherds and other humble people of Wordsworth's native region differ from shepherds of traditional pastoral:

> Smooth life had Flock and Shepherd in old time,
> Long Springs and tepid Winters
> . . .
> . . .   where the Pipe was heard
> Of Pan, the invisible God, thrilling the rocks
> With tutelary music, from all harm
> The Fold protecting. . . .   [312–13, 321–4]

But Wordsworth's shepherds inhabit, he says, another world. They are

> Not such as in Arcadian Fastnesses
> Sequester'd, handed down among themselves,
> So ancient Poets sing, the golden Age;
> Nor such, a second Race, allied to these,
> As Shakespeare in the Wood of Arden plac'd
> Where Phoebe sigh'd for the false Ganymede,
> . . .
> Nor such as Spenser fabled. . . .   [183–8, 191]

The Arcadian shepherds of Sidney, Shakespeare or Spenser, inhabiting literary pastoral, had only love and pleasure to occupy their days.

Wordsworth distinguishes his shepherds equally from rustics who inhabited the alleged golden age of rural England. Although Spenser and others may have observed such quaint rural customs as the Maypole Dance, these festivities represent for Wordsworth only imaginative fragments of yet another ideal world which can have no validity because it has no reality. However beautiful as a memory, this idealised folk world alas

> Was but a dream; the times had scatter'd all
> These lighter graces, and the rural custom
> And manners which it was my chance to see
> In childhood were severe and unadorn'd,
> . . .
> Yet beautiful, and beauty that was felt.   [204–7, 210]

This passage is critical because it illustrates the double nature of Wordsworth's version of pastoral. The rural life which he had observed all his life is simple yet substantial, unadorned yet attractive, and above all severe yet beautiful. Wordsworth's version of pastoral inclines toward both realism and idealism, directly anticipating the pastoral novel.

In distinguishing his pastoral region from all ideal worlds, Wordsworth also considers a contemporary form of the Golden Age of classical pastoral – Goslar, Germany – a region offering a 'Smooth life' of 'Long Springs and tepid Winters', and a pastoral 'Pleasure-ground' where the shepherd strays, having 'no task / More toilsome than to carve a beechen bowl / For Spring or Fountain' (VIII 343–5). But Wordsworth's pastoral region is harsher, a more realistic form of pastoral where a sweet life is challenged by suffering and real obstacles, where ' 'tis the Shepherd's task the winter long / To wait upon the storms' (VIII 359–60).

The shepherd of Wordsworth's pastoral earns praise because, being free, he 'feels himself' in those vast regions where he works. He lives a 'life of hope *and* hazard' and of 'hard labour *interchanged* / With that majestic indolence so dear to native Man' (VIII 389–90; my italics). Both sides of the coin matter, yet as a child Wordsworth saw only the idealised form of the shepherd, glorified and ennobled. The reader suspects that it is this form of pastoral man that dominated his imagination throughout 1797–1806, the period of his finest poetry. Of his representative shepherd Wordsworth recalls feeling his presence 'As of a Lord or Master; or a Power / Or genius, under Nature, under God'. Then come the critical lines:

> His Form hath flash'd upon me, glorified
> By the deep radiance of the setting sun:
> . . .
> . . .   Thus was Man
> Ennobled outwardly before mine eyes.   [404–5, 410–11]

The idealised figure of the solitary shepherd yet 'Was not a Corin of the groves', but a man who 'suffer'd with the rest / From vice and folly, wretchedness and fear'. Yet throughout *The Prelude* the form glorified and ennobled is the form we grasp imaginatively, seldom the form that suffers with the rest of mankind. Thus two conceptions intermingle: the idealised shepherd of Wordsworth's boyhood; and the partly real, partly ideal shepherd of his early adulthood, which derives from his childhood impression. David Ferry argues that Wordsworth confuses 'his vision of man as ideal and his insistence that this ideal *in fact* exists in such persons as the shepherds of his country'.[6] Interestingly, the revisions for the 1850 text of *The Prelude* show that, with the passing of time, his conception of the Lake District shepherd gradually became more realistic, thus anticipating the fictional development of George Eliot and Thomas Hardy.

Book VIII of *The Prelude*, then, stands as one of many versions of traditional pastoral. Idealised shepherds, with enviable occupations and lives, inhabit a real Golden Age in the near past. Wordsworth intensifies this pastoral feeling when he says that he discovered the 'great City' to be almost like 'A heart-depressing wilderness indeed', almost like 'a wearisome abode':

> . . .   therefore did I turn
> To you, ye Pathways, and ye lonely Roads
> Sought you enrich'd with everything I prized,
> With human kindness and with Nature's joy.   [XIII 123–6]

As in the pastoral of tradition, the creation of a beautiful and harmonious Golden Age invites a criticism of the complex urban life opposed to it. Wordsworth values highly his retreat into the rural world because he found there

> Hope to my hope, and to my pleasure peace
> And steadiness, and healing and repose
> To every angry passion. There I heard,
> From mouths of men obscure and lowly, truths
> Replete with honour; sounds in unison
> With loftiest promises of good and fair.
> [XIII 180–5; 1850 text]

Wordsworth is not writing as a traditional pastoralist. Nor is he literal, like Crabbe, in interpreting humble and rustic life. Put simply, he alternates between realism and idealisation in his treatment of rural life. His affinities with traditional pastoral are several. He mistrusts the city, and prefers Nature to Art. Harmony and beauty provide central themes; shepherd and setting conjoin. As Herbert Lindenberger comments, 'Wordsworth idealises not only his individual shepherds, but the whole society of dalesmen who, in their ordered, traditional way of living, are contrasted with the brute masses of the city'.[7] He renounces worldly ambition for peace and rural solitude. And though it is different in character from traditional pastoral in its preference for realistic details, he creates of his native countryside a Golden Age, a metaphor for the creative potential of the imagination, a landscape of the mind as much as of observed reality. Wordsworth, insisting that his shepherds are not of the golden age, is yet nostalgic for that age and eagerly celebrates it. The anti-pastoral passages in his poetry show, along with his 'Preface', how sharply he intended to break from the artificiality of conventional pastoral. But, as his critics have pointed out, Wordsworth simply replaced one kind of pastoralism with another. By creating a realistic pastoral, Wordsworth succeeded however in modifying traditional pastoral. Acknowledging the real, Wordsworth still considers rural life of the Lake District to be the best life attainable, thereby shifting the Golden Age from the long ago of older forms of pastoral to the recent past of his childhood memories.

Two things bring about this change in the conception of pastoral: Wordsworth's frequent mention of toil and hardship, and his desire to take his settings literally. Instead of functioning to disguise the poet's cultured stance, Wordsworth's shepherd comes out of his setting literally.[8] The fundamental pastoral impulse, hardened into the convention of traditional pastoral, needed to be revitalised and brought once again near its roots in country life. After Wordsworth, pastoralism becomes increasingly oriented toward realism and becomes, as it travels through the nineteenth century, increasingly broadened in scope. Renato Poggioli argues that 'while creating quasi-pastoral utopias, the modern world destroyed the conventional and traditional pastoral through four cultural trends that arose together and partly coincided. There were the humanitarian outlook, the idea of material progress, the scientific spirit, and artistic realism.'[9] In its many modern transformations, the pastoral artist's eye rests more closely on his subject matter than before; he respects fact. Science and empiricism have deeply impressed the literary imagination. Moreover, although the modern pastoralist is nostalgic for the past, he is less inclined to treat the past as allegory or as a landscape of the mind. The modern pastoralist, although he is committed to a portrayal of the positive relationship between man and nature, is less interested in the *otium* of the pleasance than in representing faithfully the spirit of the rural life he either sees or recalls.

Whereas conventional pastoral had demanded that the pastoral world be free from toil and that leisure to sing and pipe be unbroken, the most significant change in the nineteenth-century transformation of the pastoral impulse is the recognition, even glorification, of work. One writer has said that 'the bucolic, unlike the georgic, exalts the innocent leisure of the shepherd over the peasant's hard task'.[10] After Wordsworth the pastoral form verges toward the georgic, the literary work which glorifies the toil of the agricultural sphere and which finds supreme expression in Vergil's *Georgics*. A second significant change in pastoral is the shift – anticipated by Wordsworth in the prose-poetry of 'Michael' and much of *The Prelude* – to the use of prose rather than poetry in works inspired by the pastoral impulse. A final change occurs in the virtual abandonment of allegorical uses of landscape and character – an interest less in a perfect and pure world of the imagination, and more in a world of imagined reality that depends upon verifiable local details. . . .

SOURCE: extract from 'The Development of the Pastoral Novel' in *The*

Pastoral Novel: Studies in George Eliot, Thomas Hardy and D. H. Lawrence (Charlotteville, Va., 1975), pp. 43–9.

NOTES

[Reorganised and renumbered from the original – Ed.]

1. M. H. Abrams, *The Mirror and the Lamp* (New York, 1953), pp. 112–13.
2. David Ferry, *The Limits of Mortality* (Middletown, Conn., 1959), p. 91.
3. All quotations are from E. de Selincourt (ed.), *The Poetical Works of William Wordsworth* (1940), rev. edn by Helen Darbishire (Oxford, 1952–8).
4. 'Resolution and Independence' (1802) is, William Empson has said, 'a genuine pastoral if ever there was one': *Some Versions of Pastoral* (London, 1935; rev. edn, 1979), p. 263.
5. Quotations are from the 1805 text.
6. Ferry, op. cit., p. 95.
7. H. Lindenberger, *On Wordsworth's 'Prelude'* (Princeton, N.J., 1963), p. 249.
8. See John Stevenson, 'Arcadia Re-settled: Pastoral Poetry and Romantic Theory', *Studies in English Literature*, 7 (1979), p. 636.
9. Renato Poggioli, *The Oaten Flute* (Cambridge, Mass., 1975), p. 175.
10. Ibid., p. 161.

John Bayley   'Tolstoy and the Pastoral Perspective: *War and Peace*'   (1966)

. . . By 'Pastoral' – not the ideal term but I cannot think of another which suggests the same range of literary effect – I understand the process of making everything in a work of literature *characteristic*. There may be many motives for doing this, straightforward and deliberate or undeclared and almost unconscious. In his book, *Some Versions of Pastoral*, William Empson used the term to cover a wide range of effect in which the unifying factor is 'putting the complex into the simple', so that a readily accepted convention exerts social, political or emotional influence on the reader in ways to which he is partly conditioned, but to which the skilled or inspired pastoralist will give an unexpected turn. [See excerpt in Part One, above – Ed.]

Almost all literature is pastoral to the extent in which it accepts conventions, characters and situations without attempting to see them – at some stage of the creative process – in the uncharacteristic, unframed and unproffered way in which they appear to the seeing eye of quotidian experience. Documentaries, biographies, detective stories, historical novels, all make use of pastoral for seeing their subjects in a given frame from which they cannot be allowed to escape except at the pastoralist's pondered behest. A detective story may have a mad detective, a blind detective, a religious detective, or an elderly female one – it will always have a detective. The individual must be determined by his setting and be a part of it, however eccentric or unexpected a part. A coalminer, or a retired colonel in Camberley, are seen by pastoral in their functions and their characters – the fact that they may not feel like or be aware of themselves as a coalminer and a colonel cannot be considered.

Conrad's *Nostromo* is a *tour de force* and a remarkable novel, but it is a pastoral novel. The politico-romantic framework of the imaginary South American state of Costaguana holds and determines the characters in a way in which the ship-board setting of *The Shadow Line* or *The Nigger of the Narcissus* does not; for the sea for Conrad is not a pastoral setting but the natural and instinctive setting of felt and experienced life.

Many of Tolstoy's most enthusiastic critics and supporters have seen *War and Peace* as the most sublime and complete of all pastorals. It says (they imply): 'this is what human life should be like and shall be like'. They confuse the involuntary ideality of the work with a conscious pastoral ideal. Considered pastorally, the characters of *War and Peace* at once become lifeless and almost repellent. We must return to this, but let us first notice an important difference between the two main uses of pastoral ideology today. In the east it is used as an image of what human life shall be like in the good or Socialist State: in the west it is the image of what human life eases itself of the perpetual burden of humanity by seeing itself *as*. Soviet man (or woman) is an ideal: 'Mrs (or Mr) 1970' is an opiate. Only superficially does the Western pastoral image call: come and be like me! Deeper down, its function as art is sedative; it calls us, as sleep does, towards passivity and non-existence. Our need for this kind of pastoral expresses our deep hunger for something apparently the same as ourselves but in fact quite different – our desire for a mirror world in which every activity, every gesture, every garment, exists beatifically in and for itself.

At the level of art what we may call the Eastern and the Western pastoral join hands: the Communist ideological image and the capitalist advertising image function through much the same techniques. The Western critic and consumer is less likely than his Eastern counterpart to see art (and even the greatest) as serving, in some sort, the social functions of pastoral. Our conception of those functions is defeated, knowing, stopped off. Our pleasure in everyday pastoral images assumes that they are incapable of high artistic achievement. But the deeply learned and perceptive Marxist critic, Lukács, is predisposed by his faith to see not only Tolstoy but the whole tradition of European realism in the novel as disposed towards pastoral and capable – by reason of their very excellence – of serving its ideological ends.

The tradition of realism in the novel can be so understood by Lukács precisely because its realism can be interpreted according to the highest pastoral standards. It is as far as possible from being escape art, in the sense that popular novels are escape art. *The Quiet Don*, Sholokhov's post-Tolstoyan novel, is totally a pastoral, but it is also a fine novel in the highest traditions of realism. It is conceived out of a complete love and understanding. But this process of affection is also a process of enclosure, of caging. Its mode of *possession* reminds us not of Tolstoy but of Balzac.

The Comédie Humaine is the most gigantic pastoral enterprise ever undertaken by a novelist. Balzac intended it to do for moden society what Scott in the *Waverley Novels* had done for the past. Both Scott and Balzac love to contemplate human beings in their habits as they lived, or are living. But Scott was a poet in a sense that Balzac was not; and his greatest creations, though seen and loved because they are *characteristic*, are also coloured by the subjective dream of his historical imagination. Balzac's enthusiasm for the characteristic is more earthy, more lovingly factual. Pastoral realism does not put the complex into the simple. Its purpose is to enfold a total complexity in terms of itself, so that it does not merge with the uncharacteristic and transparent being of our own lives.

Pastoral experiences continually occur to us in life of course. We have one when we acquire a new name or a new suit,[1] move into a newly done-up flat or are promoted to a new status. For a while the whole of our experience is seen by ourselves in terms of this new circumstance, which determines what we do and how we feel – we do not behave in our normal transparent and open way in terms of our own consciousness, but see ourselves behaving in a novel and limiting character. Very soon the new circumstance becomes submerged in the general flow of life and ceases to dictate a consciousness suited to itself. But in pastoral art the authority of the circumstance remains constant, fixed: we continue, as it were, to see ourselves within the definition of circumstance: there is no play between the fixity of character and the freedom of consciousness.

The morale of a revolutionary state depends upon conditioning its members to see themselves in a pastoral character – indeed the desire to bring about a pastoral state in which everyone can be seen to be playing an appropriate part is an aspect of revolutionary mythology. In practice this state of affairs can hardly endure for long, but the function of revolutionary literature is to assume that it does, and to continue to present a total pastoral image. Hence the gap between the image of living in Soviet literature and the reality of doing it day by day. Hence, too, our tendency to see Russians and Chinese in a pastoral light, as we see people set in a historical novel, set in the past or the future. Socialist realism is pure pastoral, for the reality exists as a means towards a given end, and the whole tradition of realism can be absorbed and seen as stages in the process. Even epic can be seen in this way. Lukács comments on the fact (first noticed by Lessing in the *Laokoon*) that it is the manufacture rather than the appearance of Achilles's armour which Homer describes, the dynamic process rather than the static detail. This is the clue to Lukács's distinction between *realism*, in which the 'totality of objects' is integrated in the processes of living, and *naturalism*, in which objects and people are seen in great detail but as dead matter.[2] Not only Balzac and Tolstoy, but Homer and Shakespeare, are for Lukács examples of the first: Flaubert and Zola of the second.

This is a just distinction, but unfortunately it ignores the issue of pastoral. There is an immense difference between the world of *War and Peace* and the world of epic pastoral, whether in Homer or in Balzac. Tolstoy's characters are never contemplated; they are never seen doing what characters of their sort do. Balzac and Homer would know, cherishingly, what Andromache or Eugénie Grandet were doing at any moment of the day, and it would always be the right thing. But we can no more say what Natasha or Pierre or even Kutuzov would be doing than we can say what we ourselves would be doing – they seem a part of Tolstoy's and our own indistinguishable activity. Eugénie Grandet, by contrast, seems a kind of relief from Balzac's human activity; she joins the vast capital of his repose, despite the fact that we see the making of money in this and in Balzac's other novels as we see the making of arms in Homer. Eugénie and her father are magnificent examples of pastoral creation, and the theme of money is perfectly suited to creation of this type. Balzac's leisurely, loving, long-distance account of how old Grandet continued to make money during successive regimes – revolution, empire and restoration – persuades us without apparent intention that nothing but money is real. It is as completely in control of society as the Grandets are controlled by Balzac's pastoral.

Tolstoy can use pastoral, but he never allows it to dominate his creative imagination because he neither accepts the heroic world as

Homer does, nor sets out as Balzac does to accomplish what Lukács sees as the task of the great realist – 'to depict man as a whole in the whole of society'. General Bagration, for example, is seen almost entirely in terms of heroic pastoral, as natural and inevitable a fighter as Achilles.

His face wore the look of concentrated and happy determination seen on the face of a man who on a hot day takes a final run before plunging into the water. . . . The round hard eagle eyes looked ecstatically and rather disdainfully before him, obviously not resting on anything, though there was still the same deliberation in his measured movements.

But Tolstoyan reality interposes at the moment when he enters the English club for the dinner given in his honour, 'wearing a sort of naïvely festive air, which, in conjunction with his determined and manly features, gave an expression positively rather comic to his face'. Even Bagration is not always permitted, as he would be in total pastoral, to do *the right thing*.

The most remarkable use of pastoral by Tolstoy for his own purposes takes place at the end of *War and Peace*, and the change it makes in our conception of the characters shows how different they were before. Natasha, in particular, becomes fixed in Tolstoy's contemplation of marriage – she becomes a figure of repose. All the details about her, the nappies, the preoccupations, the disregard for her own appearance, become the *right* details, not for the individual she has been but for Tolstoy's conception of the ideal married woman: she is now fixed in her fated social and historical background. The partial alienation we feel from her at the end is extraordinarily right in terms of the whole natural scope of the work, but it is not, I think, intended by Tolstoy. It is the consequence of his use of her as a conclusion in terms of pastoral, in which his own vision of what is right and characteristic dominates over all earlier individualities and episodes. We must return to this when we consider the ending of *War and Peace*. . . .

SOURCE: extract from *Tolstoy and the Novel* (London, 1966), pp. 147–52.

NOTES

[Reorganised and abbreviated from the original – Ed.]

1. When Natasha decided to put on her dress 'which had the property of producing cheerfulness in the morning', she was courting a pastoral experience, and we are seeing the act and the wish from the inside. The heroine of a pastoral novel would be wearing an appropriate garment as part

of her *character*, and we would be invited to contemplate the tableau from the outside.

2. See Georg Lukács, *Studies in European Realism* (London, 1972).

J. R. Ebbatson   A Darwinian Version of Pastoral: Hardy's *Tess*   (1980)

Hardy accompanied his poem 'Nature's Questioning' with the sketch of a broken key in a lock. This emblematically sums up his insistence, both intellectual and emotional, on the unknowability of the universe and man's bafflement at his role within it. 'Nature', Hardy observed in 1887, 'is played out as a Beauty but not as a Mystery.' In *Tess of the d'Urbervilles* Hardy dramatised the contrary views of nature espoused by science and art, synthesising them in the varied career of his heroine. The novel turns, that is to say, on an ambiguity in the face of nature – a factor which helps to account for the rich, confusing power of the book. As a metaphysician, D. H. Lawrence once remarked, Hardy 'makes a poor show'. However this may be, it is true that the articulation of the nature-theme in the novel stands creatively poised between images of romantic pastoral and scientific battleground. The protagonists act within a landscape of which, as in romantic versions of pastoral, they are an integral part; at the same time they are unwitting agents of evolutionary change.

Discussion of *Tess of the d'Urbervilles* might fruitfully begin with Mrs Durbeyfield's exclamation after the seduction: ' 'Tis nater, after all, and what do please God' (p. 117).[1] The novel reads as an extended gloss on this claim, consisting as it does in essence of definition and redefinition of the term 'nature'. In 1890, while working on the text, Hardy complained that contemporary fiction was devoid of 'treatment which seeks to show Nature's unconsciousness not of essential laws, but of those laws framed merely as social and expedient by humanity'. Never before had Hardy portrayed characters so connected, in the romantic tradition, with nature – landscape, birds, animals – and yet subject to the unremitting agency of sexual selection and struggle for survival, that 'stubborn and resistless tendency', as he characterises it, through which 'the great passionate pulse of existence, unwarped, uncontorted, untrammelled' is made manifest with a force which is 'not to be controlled by vague lucubrations over the social rubric'. The pervasive motif of 'flux and reflux', typical of the circularity insisted on by seasonal traditions of pastoral, collides with the linearity of modern evolutionary thought. Indeed this seminal collision of two worlds of value is cunningly imaged in the intervention of the advanced man, Angel Clare, at the May Day dance at Marlott. It was the 'becoming' of the world, Hardy once wrote, which created sadness: 'If the world stood still', then 'there would be no sadness in it'. This is an illuminating remark, implying as it does a backward glance to versions of pastoral no longer available to a writer in the agriculturally depressed Wessex of late Victorian times. The Durbeyfields, of aristocratic lineage and history, go down to extinction to be replaced by the *nouveaux riches* Stoke d'Urbervilles.

One vital strand of the novel typifies life close to nature as a good, not only at the pastoral climax of the book at Talbothays, but also in the comparison between the primitive life of Cranborne Chase and the 'Slopes', the bogus house of the Stoke d'Urbervilles, and between Sandbourne, a 'glittering novelty' of a pleasure-city, and that 'tawny piece of antiquity', Egdon Heath. Even the sluttish field-women experience a species of romantic pantheism in their drunken revels, 'themselves and surrounding nature forming an organism of which all the parts harmoniously and joyously interpenetrated each other' (p. 98) – the oblique sexual reference wholly appropriate, since Car Darch was 'till lately a favourite of d'Urberville's', and repeated at Talbothays, where the 'ready bosoms existing there were impregnated by their surroundings' (p. 189). But it is Tess who is crucially 'Pantheistic as to essence' (p. 213); she is created by Hardy in terms of a proliferation of bird and animal imagery. Her baby is a 'bastard gift of shameless Nature who respects not the social law' (p. 131), and after his death it becomes clear that the 'recuperative power which pervaded organic nature was surely not denied to maidenhood alone' (p. 135). What the narrator terms her 'essentially naturalistic' beliefs (p. 205) enable her, in administering the *coup de grâce* to the injured pheasants, to embrace 'Nature's teeming family' (p. 324).

Against the free life of nature, at Talbothays and elsewhere, Hardy counters the claustrophobic life-denying moral law of human society which traps Tess 'like a bird in a springe' (p. 238). The subtly coercive power of opinion is epitomised in the paradoxically harmless figures of Mercy Chant and the Clare brothers, or by the anonymous landlord who expels the Durbeyfields. Hardy almost obsessively expands this sense of social conformity as inimical to human potential by introducing repeated blows of fate or chance. Tess is raised in a sequestered spot where 'fatalism is a strong sentiment' (p. 186), and her sufferings lead her to a partial acceptance of the fatalistic convictions 'common to field folk' (p. 244) and exemplified in her mother's reliance on the *Compleat Fortune Teller* or Dairyman Crick's faith in the son of Conjuror Trendle. The d'Urberville traditions heighten the sense of fatality right up to the seemingly inevitable murder of Alec. After the seduction Tess feels 'she could have hidden herself in a tomb' (p. 119), and this image of simultaneous surrender to and flight from society reverberates into the sleep-walking scene, Alec's concealment in the d'Urberville tombs, and Tess's sleep on the sacrificial stone. Tess is dogged by a long 'family of waiters on Providence' (p. 66) and by the sense that she is 'one of a long row only' (p. 165). The movement of the novel thus vacillates creatively between freedom and naturalness and repression and subjection; the image of herons which fly out of the Froom Valley is finally traduced into the 'Herons' boarding house, presided over by Mrs Brooks, with her 'enforced bondage to that arithmetical demon Profit-and-Loss' (p. 431).

This doubleness of vision centres on Tess. The feeling about her is both that she represents the decline of the pastoral mode of life and that her human potential is thrown away through ill choice and satires of circumstance. It is thus vital that we read the central act as one which had energised pastoral: seduction of the rural by the urban. Indeed, both of Tess's lovers are urbanised, cut off from the natural world which she embodies. On first meeting Alec, she is startled; she had dreamt of 'an aged and dignified face, the sublimation of all the d'Urberville lineaments' (p. 69), but instead she discovers the young man lurking behind a 'blue narcotic haze' (p. 71) as he will lurk again in the weird allotment scene. Like the murderer discussed at Talbothays who has 'brimstone flames around him' (p. 147), Alec likes to dramatise himself as a 'lost soul' who was 'born bad' (p. 112). His role is foreshadowed in the flowers and fruit, the wild ride, and the rose-prick which will echo in Tess's blow with the glove at Flintcomb-Ash. The roses and strawberries at the Slopes are forced, products of the world Alec represents – money, as against the certainties of the pastoral order. Angel, though more sympathetically conceived, is also denatured. At the outset he is little more than a mouthpiece for secularist formulae. When he comes to work for Dairyman Crick he attains a new baptism in a deeper pastoral reality, just as Mill was redeemed from barren rationalism by *Lyrical Ballads*. Yet both Angel and Tess are blind at Talbothays. Although Angel adapts to become something of a votary of nature and a practical farmer, his courtship with Tess is flawed by his idealism. Hardy's analysis of the type is careful, precise and sympathetic. Angel is compulsively led to etherealise Tess into 'a visionary essence of woman' (p. 170) whose life seems to him 'actualised poetry' (p. 205). Tess is also blinded by passion: she sees Angel as 'godlike', with the 'soul of a saint' and the intellect of a seer (pp. 222, 234). In exposing Angel's vulnerability to convention Hardy shows great art. Thinking he has lit upon a 'new-sprung child of nature', Angel later condemns her as 'the belated seedling of an effete aristocracy' (p. 275) – terms of approbation and abuse which derive clearly from the pastoral mode. Clare had, Hardy notes, 'persistently elevated Hellenic Paganism at the expense of Christianity; yet in that civilisation an illegal surrender was not certain disesteem' (p. 389). With 'more animalism' he might have been 'the nobler man' (p. 287), but he is sent off to Brazil under 'the shade of his own limitations' (p. 309). His education through suffering finally allows Clare to share the second, doomed honeymoon with Tess.

Thus both men fail Tess, and each perverts pastoral life in his own way, agents of a dehumanisation which is going on progressively in humanity, through industrialisation, education and all the weapons of the modern state. Yet things are not as simple as this: as he contemplates the mess of the Durbeyfield household Hardy berates Wordsworth and demands to know where the poet gets his authority 'for speaking of "Nature's holy plan" ' (p. 51). This outburst lays bare the polar opposition of the novel, the tensions between two views of nature. On the one side stands the beneficent pastoral of romanticism and on the other the Darwinian perspective of struggle in nature intensified by random chance. Thus Tess, viewed as a child of nature in a recognisably Wordsworthian sense, is instructed by her brother that she is an inhabitant of a blighted star, and later falls victim to 'the vulpine slyness of Dame Nature' (p. 287) at Talbothays. Lesser characters like the milkmaids, those traditional denizens of pastoral tradition, here writhe 'feverishly under the oppressiveness of an emotion thrust on them by cruel Nature's law' (p. 187). The cornered animals in the hayfield, the rats in the corn-rick, the dying pheasants – all enforce this interpretation, a patterning which runs counter to the poetic concept of nature elsewhere.

The crux in Hardy's imaginative recreation is neatly defined in the contrast between Talbothays and Flintcomb-Ash, the one romantic pastoral, the other naked Darwinian struggle. The abundant creativity, fertility and potency of natural forces are beautifully embodied in the almost paradisal radiance of the Talbothays scenes. Nonetheless, buried beneath the pastoral golden age and ultimately subverting it lies the modern myth unveiled by Darwin. The scene in which sexual selection declares itself is the one closest in tone to a classical pastoral encounter – the allurement of Tess by Angel's harp:

> The outskirt of the garden in which Tess found herself had been left uncultivated for some years, and was now damp and rank with juicy grass which sent up mists of pollen at a touch; and with tall blooming weeds emitting offensive smells – weeds whose red and yellow and purple hues formed a polychrome as dazzling as that of cultivated flowers. She went stealthily as a cat through this profusion of growth, gathering cuckoo-spittle on her skirts, cracking snails that were underfoot, staining her hands with thistle-milk and slug-slime, and rubbing off upon her naked arms sticky blights which, though snow-white on the apple-tree trunks, made madder stains on her skin; thus she drew quite near to Clare, still unobserved of him.
>
> Tess was conscious of neither time nor space. The exaltation which she had described as being producible at will by gazing at a star, came now without any determination of hers; she undulated upon the thin notes of the second-hand harp, and their harmonies passed like breezes through her, bringing tears into her eyes. The floating pollen seemed to be his notes made visible, and the dampness of the garden the weeping of the garden's sensibility. Though near nightfall, the rank-smelling weed-flowers glowed as if they would not close for intentness, and the waves of colour mixed with the waves of sound. (pp. 161–2)

Like the sword-play between Troy and Bathsheba, this is a scene double-dyed in Darwinism, presenting Tess as a victim lured 'like a fascinated bird' (p. 161). The syntactic complexity loops together strings of dependent clauses which enact Tess's trance-like movement through the garden and creates a typically Hardyesque tableau in its enactment of the attraction / repulsion of the plants. The supplanting of garden flowers by somewhat exotic weeds hints both at the deracinating effect of Clare's intellection on an agricultural community and at Tess's 'idolatry' of him, designated as 'too rank, too wild, too deadly' (p. 256). T. H. Huxley had written of how, under Darwinian law, 'the very plants are at war': 'The ground is full of seeds that cannot rise into seedlings; the seedlings rob one another of air and light and water, the strongest robber winning the day, and extinguishing his competitors.'[2] Just so does Tess unwittingly extinguish Izz Huett and other 'competitors' for Angel at Talbothays, and just so does Angel virtually extinguish her own will to live: within the paradisal setting the law of survival and sexual selection works ineluctably, the ambiguous tones of the second-hand harp replacing, imitating and mocking the oaten flute of pastoral convention. In a passage redolent with literary echoes, the gleanings from Milton, *Hamlet* and the Bible serve to conceal the most seminal of Hardy's subtexts, *The Origin of Species*. In Talbothays garden, perhaps for the first time, the reader may sense that something has gone awry with the pastoral as an imaginative recreation of reality.

That supposition is confirmed at Flintcomb-Ash. Here the beneficent potential of life is withdrawn in a bleak upland setting. The girls are reduced to wage-slaves by undeviating harshness in work and environment, surviving through sheer will-power. Their only visitants are the 'strange birds from behind the North Pole' who have witnessed 'scenes of cataclysmal horror' in polar regions, arrivals from a region of white obliteration. In this sequence, with the death of nature and hope, one senses Hardy turning towards the mode of classical pastoral elegy of which he was so personally fond. The elegy arose out of rituals based in the cycle of natural fertility; Tess and her career thus come to symbolise the decline of a whole way of living, just as the pastoral elegy recorded both personal and seasonal death. The sufferings of winter continue into spring, with the arrival of the steam-threshing machine, 'the engine which was to act as the *primum mobile* of this little world' (p. 372). The machine inexorably reduces the farm-labourers to exhausted automata serving the cause of blind process. The irruption of Alec, whose money was made from usury, and Tess's blow on the mouth, serve to body out the implications of the arrival of the 'machine in the garden', implications which are redoubled by the hinted recollection of the more leisurely and graceful pastoral of the reaping at Marlott in which Tess had participated as a nursing mother. A dehumanising mechanism which reorders pastoral rhythms contrives to coexist here with a highly characteristic Victorian sense of power and mystery:

> . . . ever-rising, on its mystic stair
> In the dim light, from secret chambers borne,
> The straw of harvest, sever'd from the corn,
> Climb'd, and fell over, in the murky air.[3]

Through a dramatic synthesis of meaning the tyranny of the machine may be taken as metaphor for the iron law of the universe disclosed by evolution theory: the pastoral values of the natural organism (the universe as tree) are in continuous dialectic with mechanism (universe as machine) which crushes out natural life. The sufferings of Tess and her fellows on the rick, the cruelty to the cornered rats, Tess's arrest and execution all act out the confusions of moral purpose to which evolutionary theory had given rise. Huxley himself, in his 1893 Romanes lecture, would speak of the muddle caused by mixing up 'fittest' and 'best', and argue that no ethical principle could be founded upon processes of random survival. Yet the raising of the black flag over Wintoncester Gaol is not the novelist's final word: the drawing together of Angel Clare and Liza-Lu in the closing paragraph hints at the creative power, the renewal and rebirth which define pastoral forms, inherent in a universe whose purposes remain unknown and unknowable to the human community.

The modern pastoral idiom of the romantic movement, it has been suggested, is a fundamentally private myth which replaced the universal classical myth of Arcadia. In *Tess of the d'Urbervilles* Hardy comes to grips with difficult areas of modern experience – social mobility, agricultural distress, female sexuality, the decay of religious belief, the claims of the individual, the impact of the machine – against a background of unified pastoral simplicity. In this Empsonian imaginative act of 'putting the complex into the simple' Hardy seizes on the heroic individual rather than, as in classical pastoral, on the type: Tess, Henchard, Jude achieve massively significant proportions under his hand, developing into archetypes of that 'ache of modernism' which split the consciousness of their creator. Hardy, haunted by family ghosts and pervaded by an abiding sense of loss, turned emotionally to this romantic form of pastoral, with its evocation of a returning past. But paradoxically, as a man infected by the thought of his time, he embraced intellectually the evolutionary theory which must destroy that promise in its insistence upon unceasing linear progression. If Talbothays is an ambivalently pastoral bower of bliss, Flintcomb-Ash stands uncompromisingly for the Darwinian landscape of the future in which Jude will wander towards his death. It was perhaps partly the recognition of the demise of the pastoral ideal at the hands of Darwin which led the novelist to lay down his pen and retreat into the private communings of an increasingly past-haunted poetic art.

SOURCE: adapted for this Casebook by the author from ch. 4 of *Lawrence and the Nature Tradition* (Brighton, 1980).

NOTES

1. Reference is to the paperback version of the New Wessex edition (London, 1974).

2. T. H. Huxley, *Man's Place in Nature and Other Essays*, Everyman edition (London, n.d.), pp. 348–9.

3. C. Tennyson Turner, 'The Steam Threshing-Machine' (1868).

John F. Lynen   'Frost's New England and Arcadia'   (1960)

. . . In studying Frost's pastoralism we must recognise that it is an art which did not, and could not have, developed within the old framework. As a matter of fact one of Frost's earliest poems shows very clearly how remote the conventions of pastoral were from his own interest. In 'Pan with Us' he uses the imagery of Arcadia to symbolise all the genteel poetic styles which were dying out during the period of his literary apprenticeship. In despair, Pan throws away his oaten pipes:

> They were pipes of pagan mirth,
> And the world had found new terms of worth.
> He laid him down on the sun-burned earth
>   And raveled a flower and looked away –
> Play? Play? – What should he play?

The question posed in these lines is directly relevant to his own verse. If the pastoral tradition had long since lost its validity, how was he to write a poetry essentially pastoral? The answer to this question becomes apparent when one recalls the distinction between pastoralism as a kind of poetic structure and pastoralism in the narrower sense of a particular tradition. It was the tradition that had withered; the fundamental form remained as a potential. Occasionally this potential was realised, notably in the works of Burns, and in Wordsworth's 'Michael' and a few of his short lyrics. Frost's achievement as a pastoral poet, like Burns's and Wordsworth's, is a distinctly individual triumph. It has resulted from his discovery of a new and realistic basis for examining the rural scene within the structure of pastoral.

To say this is to say that Frost discovered a new myth of rural life. When he wrote the lines quoted above he had not yet arrived at this; and I do not mean to suggest that the discovery was a conscious, reasoned one. As a poet Frost matured late; his early verse reveals a constant searching for an idiom and a subject. From the beginning his instincts drew him towards rural subjects, but in the long period of experiment we find him writing of these in an elegant manner reminiscent of late Victorian nature poetry. Only when he learned to adopt the perspective of pastoral and wrote from the point of view of an actual New England farmer did he come into his own as an artist.

The change was a sudden one; it occurred when his imagination grasped the poetic possibilities of the region he knew so well, when, by leaving home for a brief sojourn in old England, he came to see in the life of rural New England a remote, ideal world which could serve the same function as Arcadia. The important role of regionalism in Frost's poetry is a large subject, and we will therefore have to explore his myth of New England more fully later on. For the moment, let us accept it as a myth. Our present purpose is to consider somewhat further the kind of poetry it makes possible.

Frost, like the writers of old pastoral, draws upon our feeling that the rural world is representative of human life in general. By working from this nodal idea he is able to develop in his poems a very broad range of reference without ever seeming to depart from particular matters of fact. He says nothing of other places and other times – he gives us only the minute particulars of his own immediate experience; yet . . . in 'Stopping by Woods', the things described seem everywhere to point beyond the rural world. The effect is to create a remarkable depth of reference. One senses a powerful symbolism at work in the poem, but when one attempts to specify just what the images refer to their meaning proves too delicate, too elusive to capture. One can define the poem's meaning in general terms, as I have done, but this is not entirely satisfactory. Such a definition can give only a flat, abstract statement of theme, whereas the beauty of such poetry consists in the presence of manifold particular references lurking behind the symbols.

A symbolism of this kind is neither defined by traditional references nor shaped through such devices as metaphor, but emerges, like the three dimensional effects of painting, from the very perspective of the poet's vision. Pastoralism, as we have noted, is characterised by a basic duality: it portrays rural life, but it always does this with reference to the great world beyond. Its essential technique is that of creating a sharp contrast between the two. The pastoral poet tends to emphasise the great distance which separates the shepherd from the aristocrat and the rustic setting from the city and court. His method is paradoxical in that his intent is to portray universal experience by revealing the basic realitites common to both worlds, yet he achieves this by insisting upon their dissimilarity. If the country is to become the microcosm of the great world it must be pictured as a little world in itself, one which is separate from the realm of ordinary experience even though, in another sense, it displays the familiar reality. It is, then, by making his Arcadia remote that the pastoral poet transforms it into a symbolic world. And since the rustic scene in its entirety is taken as representative of all other levels of being, the things that belong to it – the shepherds and farmers, their tasks, amusements and concerns, the simple objects familiar to them and the scenic aspects of their surroundings – are all infused with symbolic suggestions.

It is just such a perspective and such a method of pastoral contrast that gives the simple scenes and episodes Frost describes their extraordinary breadth of reference. When one considers his Yankee poems, one begins to notice a number of fundamental similarities between them and the old pastorals. His New England, like Arcadia, is a distinct plane of existence portrayed in such a way that a comparison with the outer world is always strongly implied. It is isolated from ordinary experience, a society with its own folkways, customs, and ideals, a locality with its own distinctive landscape. Like the old pastoralists, he emphasises the uniqueness of his rural world. It is an agrarian society isolated within an urbanised world, and its country folk are separated from the modern reading public by a gulf of social, cultural and economic differences nearly as broad as that dividing the swain of the old pastoral from the courtly reader. If the awareness of class differences, which is so prominent in traditional eclogues, is necessarily much less important in Frost's pastorals, regionalism provides another means for creating the effect of remoteness. He sets his rural world apart by stressing its distinctly local traits and portraying Yankee life as quite different from that in the cosmopolitan urban society. And as in the old pastoral, awareness of differences leads to a recognition of parallels. The more unusual and remote from everyday life his rural New England appears, the more effectively he can use it as a medium for the symbolic representation of realities in other areas of experience.[1]

Frost's method as pastoral poet is nicely illustrated by one of his most familiar lyrics, 'The Pasture'. This poem is of particular interest in that the poet has for many years used it as the epigraph for editions of his collected verse, a fact which suggests that he regards it as a symbol of the kind of poetry he writes. 'The Pasture' may at first appear very simple indeed, since the materials of which it is composed are so slight. It seems merely to describe a few casual details of farm life which the poet sees in going about his tasks. But as in 'Stopping by Woods', the bits of description somehow cohere to form a pattern which expresses a much broader meaning than is overtly stated. It is important to note that the poem is an invitation: the poet invites someone, perhaps a person he loves, perhaps just a friend, to come with him and see the glimpses of delicate beauty to be found in the pasture. The implication is that the person invited knows little of such things. More important, he will have to be initiated into the special way of looking at them which makes them precious and meaningful.

The leaves floating in the pasture spring, the little calf, so young it totters when its mother licks it, have the simplicity and innocence of pristine reality, and the poem implies that the average person, like the person invited, could not see the beauty in such natural, everyday things without the poet as guide. To appreciate these, he will have to abandon knowledge as the great world understands it and learn to adopt the poet's special way of seeing.

The poet's invitation is really to a kind of vision, and this vision is to be understood through its implicit difference from the common view of reality. But the invitation is also to a place, the pasture itself, for only within the humble, out-of-the-way rural world is this special mode of perception possible. The pasture, then, is both the subject of the vision and its perspective; the mode of perception is embodied in the images themselves. For all its sweetness the poem is not tainted by sentimentality, because while it describes the charming aspects of the pasture, it is concerned less with beauty for its own sake than with the organic wholeness which makes this beauty meaningful. Frost's theme here is the coherence of the rural scene, the unity between the things observed and the way of seeing, between objects and thought, between man's work – the speaker of the poem must clean the spring and fetch the young calf – and his aesthetic experience. This unity raises the world of the pasture above other realms of human life by showing it as an ordered world where the significance of things is simple and apparent. This is manifest in the symbols themselves: the spring and the calf represent the source, the simple, pure, innocent beginnings of things.

Yet the special value of this world is paradoxical in that the pasture embodies a humble and naïve level of being. The reader is to admire the pasture as a world better than his own because it is more natural, more neatly organised, and more meaningful, but he is also aware that it is a plane of existence inferior in many respects to that on which he lives. The contrast between the country and the town which we have noted in pastoral is clearly the essential element in the design of this poem. By making the rural scene remote from ordinary life and by implying that to understand it we must learn to adopt its special perspective, Frost establishes a comparison between the pasture and the outside world. It is from this implied comparison that the poem's elusive symbolism grows. The calf and the pasture spring emerge as symbols because they exist within a world which is viewed in its relation to other places and other modes of experience. . . .

SOURCE: extract from 'The Pastoral Mode' in *The Pastoral Art of Robert Frost* (New Haven, Conn., 1960), pp. 17–23.

[Renumbered from the original – Ed.]

1. Of course, the remoteness cannot be too great. If the rural world were fantastic, like the fairylands of romance or the planets as depicted in science fiction, the particular kind of symbolism one finds in pastoral would not be possible. It should be remembered that the remoteness of the pastoral Arcadia is counterbalanced by its closeness to nature and hence to the physical reality underlying all life.

SELECT BIBLIOGRAPHY

Readers are advised to consult the complete books from which extracts have been included in this collection. The following additional studies are recommended.

P. Alpers, 'Empson on Pastoral', *New Literary History*, x, no. 1 (Autumn 1978), pp. 101–23.

P. Alpers, *The Singer of the Eclogues: A Study of Vergilian Pastoral* (Berkeley, Cal., 1979).

G. Boas, *The Cult of the Child* (London, 1966).

R. Bernheimer, *Wild Men in the Middle Ages* (Cambridge, Mass., 1952).

J. E. Congleton, *Theories of Pastoral Poetry in England, 1684–1798* (Gainesville, Fl., 1952).

H. Cooper, *Pastoral: Medieval into Renaissance* (London, 1977).

P. Cullen, *Spenser, Marvell and Renaissance Pastoral* (Cambridge, Mass., and London, 1971).

W. R. Davis, 'Masking in Arden', *Studies in English Literature*, v (1965), pp. 151–63.

E. Dipple, 'Harmony and Pastoral in the *Old Arcadia*', *English Literary History*, xxv (1968), pp. 309–28.

H. N. Fairchild, *The Noble Savage* (New York, 1928).

R. Feingold, *Nature and Society: Late Eighteenth Century Uses of the Pastoral and Georgic* (London, 1978).

N. Frye, *The Return to Eden* (Toronto and London, 1965).

A. Bartlett Giamatti, *The Earthly Paradise and the Renaissance Epic* (Princeton, N.J., 1966).

E. Greenlaw, 'Shakespeare's Pastorals', *Studies in Philology*, xiii (1916), pp. 122–54.

S. K. Heninger, Jnr, 'The Renaissance Perversion of Pastoral', *J. of the History of Ideas*, xxii (1961), pp. 254–61.

T. P. Harrison & H. J. Leon (eds), *The Pastoral Elegy* (Austin, Texas, 1939).

R. F. Jones, 'Eclogue Types in English Poetry of the Eighteenth Century', *J. of English and Germanic Philology*, xxiv (1925), pp. 33–60.

F. Kermode, 'Introduction' to the New Arden edition of *The Tempest* (London, 1954).

A. Lovejoy & B. Boas, *A Documentary History of Primitivism and Related Ideas in Antiquity* (Baltimore, Md, 1935).

M. Mack, *The Garden and the City* (Toronto, 1969; London, 1970).

L. Marx, *The Machine in the Garden* (New York and London, 1967).

E. Panofsky, 'Et in Arcadia Ego', in his *Meaning in the Visual Arts* (New York, 1955).

K. Parkinson & M. Priestman (eds), *Peasants and Countrymen in Literature* (Roehampton, 1982).

C. A. Patrides (ed.), *Milton's 'Lycidas': The Tradition and the Poem* (New York, 1961).

Hallett Smith, *Elizabethan Poetry* (Cambridge. Mass., and London, 1952).

E. W. Tayler, *Nature and Art in Renaissance Literature* (New York and London, 1964).

NOTES ON CONTRIBUTORS TO PART TWO

W. H. AUDEN (1907–73): poet and critic; Professor of Poetry in Oxford, 1956–61.

JOHN BAYLEY: Thomas Warton Professor of English Literature, Oxford; his publications include *Characters of Love: A Study in the Literature of Personality* (1968), *The Romantic Survival: A Study in Poetic Evolution* (1969), *The Uses of Division: Unity and Disharmony in Literature* (1976) and *Shakespeare and Tragedy* (1981).

ROSALIE L. COLIE (1925–75): at the time of her death, Professor of English, University of Toronto; her publications include *Paradoxia Epidemica: The Renaissance Tradition of Paradox* (1966); *'My Ecchoing Song': Andrew Marvell's Poetry of Criticism* (1970) and *Shakespeare's Living Art* (1974).

J. R. EBBATSON: Senior Lecturer in English Literature, Worcester College of Higher Education; his publications include *Lawrence and the Nature Tradition* (1980) and *The Evolutionary Self* (1982).

SIR WILLIAM EMPSON: poet and critic; Professor Emeritus of English, University of Sheffield, and Honorary Fellow, Magdalene College, Cambridge; his publications in literary criticism include *Seven Types of Ambiguity* (1930), *Some Versions of Pastoral* (1935) and *The Structure of Complex Words* (1951).

NORTHROP FRYE: Professor of English, University of Toronto; his publications include *Anatomy of Criticism* (1957), *The Return of Eden* (1965), *Fools of Time* (1967) and *Spiritus Mundi* (1976).

SIR WALTER WILSON GREG (1875–1950): scholar and bibliographer; in addition to *Pastoral Poetry and Pastoral Drama*, he wrote *The Editorial Problems in Shakespeare* (3rd edn, 1954) and edited texts of plays and theatrical documents.

A. C. HAMILTON: Professor of English in Queen's University, Kingston, Ontario; his publications include *The Structure of Allegory in 'The Faerie Queene'* (1961).

FRANK KERMODE: Fellow of King's College, Cambridge, and from 1974 to 1982 King Edward VII Professor of English Literature at Cambridge: his publications include *English Pastoral Poetry* (1952), *Romantic Image* (1957), *The Sense of an Ending* (1967), *Continuities* (1968), *The Genesis of Secrecy* (1979) and the Casebook on *King Lear*.

LAURENCE LERNER: novelist, poet and literary critic; Professor of English, University of Sussex; his publications include *The Truth-Tellers: Jane Austen, George Eliot and D. H. Lawrence* (1967), *The Uses of Nostalgia* (1972) and *An Introduction to English Poetry* (1975).

HARRY LEVIN: Irving Babbit Professor of Comparative Literature, Harvard University; his many publications include studies on Marlowe, Shakespeare, James Joyce, and on comparative literature.

JOHN F. LYNEN: Professor of English Literature, University of Toronto; his publications include *The Pastoral Art of Robert Frost* (1960) and *The Design of the Present* (1969).

PETER V. MARINELLI: Professor of English Literature, University of Toronto; his publications include *Pastoral* in the 'Critical Idiom' series (1971).

RENATO POGGIOLI: at the time of his death in 1963, Curt Hugo Reisinger Professor of Slavic and Comparative Literature, Harvard University; his essays on pastoral were published posthumously in *The Oaten Flute* (1975).

T. G. ROSENMEYER: Professor of Greek and Comparative Literature, University of California; his publications include *The Masks of Tragedy* (1963) and *The Green Cabinet* (1969).

BRUNO SNELL: German classical scholar and authority on comparative culture, Emeritus Professor of the University of Hamburg; among his many publications are *The Discovery of the Mind: The Greek Origins of European Thought* (1953: English translation of the German Original of 1946) and *Poetry and Society* (1961).

MICHAEL SQUIRES: Associate Professor of English Literature, Virginia State University; his publications include *The Pastoral Novel* (1974).

H. E. TOLIVER: Professor of English Literature, University of California; his publications include *Marvell's Ironic Vision* (1965), *Pastoral Forms and Attitudes* (1971) and *Animate Illusions* (1974).

HOYT TROWBRIDGE: Emeritus Professor of English Literature, University of New Mexico; his publications include *From Dryden to Jane Austen* (1977).

JAMES TURNER: Assistant Professor of English Literature, University of Virginia; his publications include *The Politics of Landscape* (1979).

PETER WESTON: Head of the Department of English Literature, Roehampton Institute of Higher Education.

RAYMOND WILLIAMS: Professor of Drama, University of Cambridge; his publications include *Culture and Society* (1958), *The Long Revolution* (1961), *Modern Tragedy* (1966), *The Country and the City* (1973) and *Keywords* (1976).

ACKNOWLEDGEMENTS

The editor is grateful for the benefits of Professor Laurence Lerner's help, as friend and former teacher, in exploring the pastoral terrain.

The editor and publishers wish to thank the following who have given permission for the use of copyright material: W. H. Auden, extract from *Dingley Dell and the Fleet*, 1948, by permission of Faber and Faber Ltd; John Bayley, extract from *Tolstoy and the Novel*, 1966, by permission of Chatto and Windus Ltd; Rosalie L. Colie, extract from *Shakespeare's Living Art*, 1974, by permission of Princeton University Press; Roger Ebbatson, article 'A Darwinian Version of Pastoral: Hardy's Tess' based on chapter 4 in *Lawrence and the Nature Tradition*, 1980, by permission of the author and The Harvester Press Ltd; Sir William Empson, extracts from *Some Versions of Pastoral*, 1950, by permission of Chatto and Windus Ltd; Northrop Frye, article 'Milton's Lycidas', 1958, by permission of the author; A. C. Hamilton, article 'The Argument of Spenser's *The Shepheardes Calender*' in *English Literary History*, xxiii, No. 3, 1956, by permission of Johns Hopkins University Press; Frank Kermode, extract from *English Pastoral Poetry*, 1952, by permission of Harrap Ltd; Laurence Lerner, chapter 'What Pastoral Iris' from *The Uses of Nostalgia: Studies in Pastoral*, 1972, by permission of Chatto and Windus Ltd; H. Levin, extract from *The Myth of the Golden Age in the Renaissance*, 1970, by permission of Faber and Faber Ltd; John F. Lynen, extract from *The Pastoral Art of Robert Frost*, 1960, by permission of Yale University Press; P. V. Marinelli, extract from *Pastoral*, 1971, by permission of Methuen London Ltd; Renato Poggioli, extracts from *The Oaten Flute*, 1975, (c) by the President and Fellows of Harvard College, reproduced by permission of Harvard University Press; T. G. Rosenmeyer, extracts from *The Green Cabinet*, 1969, by permission of the University of California Press; Bruno Snell, extract from *The Discovery of the Mind*, 1960, by permission of Basil Blackwell Publishers Ltd; Michael Squires, extract from *The Pastoral Novel*, 1975, by permission of the University Press of Virginia; H. E. Toliver, extracts from *Pastoral Forms and Attitudes*, 1971, by permission of the University of California Press; Hoyt Trowbridge, extracts from 'Pope, Gay and *The Shepherd's Week*' in *Modern Language Quarterly*, 1944, by permission of the author and the editor; James Turner, extract from *The Politics of Landscape*, 1979, by permission of Basil Blackwell Publishers Ltd; Peter Weston, essay 'Noble Savages', 1981, by permission of the author; Raymond Williams, extracts from *The Country and the City*, 1973, by permission of Chatto and Windus Ltd.

256

INDEX

Page numbers in **bold type** denote essays or excerpts in this Casebook. Entries in SMALL CAPS denote literary characters and mythological figures in a literary context. All literary works cited in the text are listed, either in their alphabetical sequence or under the name of the author.